S. J. Harris's quote, "The whole purpose ~~of~~ ... ~~vs~~,"
serves as an invitation for th   nd
missionary work intersect ii   he
global church to extend its v   re
effectively as it carries out th   le
step towards realizing this as

Rev. Riad Kassis, PhD
International Director, Langham Partnership

Partnering with humility and grace in God's great global mission, this book is an extraordinary collection that provides both dreams and innovative approaches for mission education in the contemporary world. With regional sensitivity and awareness of shifting realities, this text is highly recommended for all those training leaders for global cross-cultural engagement.

Perry Shaw, EdD
Author, *Transforming Theological Education*

The present monograph is filled with outstanding articles and case studies that explore the intricate relationship between education and mission. The seasoned scholars contributing to it have introduced ideas that provoke reevaluation of conventional approaches to mission education within theological institutions. Furthermore, they have delineated methods and resources tailored to meet the needs of individuals currently engaged in missionary work or aspiring to enter the field. This volume is highly recommended for its insightful content.

Frew Tamrat, PhD
Principal, Evangelical Theological College, Addis Ababa, Ethiopia

The Evangelical Missiological Society is a professional organization with more than 400 members comprised of missiologists, mission administrators, reflective mission practitioners, teachers, pastors with strategic missiological interests, and students of missiology. EMS exists to advance the cause of world evangelization. We do this through study and evaluation of mission concepts and strategies from a biblical perspective with a view to commending sound mission theory and practice to churches, mission agencies, and schools of missionary training around the world. We hold an annual national conference and eight regional meetings in the United States and Canada.

Other Books in the EMS Series

Equipping for Global Mission

Theological and Missiological Proposals and Case Studies

Linda P. Saunders, Gregory Mathias, Edward L. Smither,
EDITORS

Evangelical
Missiological
Society
Series

no. **32**

WILLIAM
CAREY
PUBLISHING

William Carey Publishing (WCP) publishes resources to shape and advance the missiological conversation in the world. We publish a broad range of thought-provoking books and do not necessarily endorse all opinions set forth here or in works referenced within this book.

The URLs included in this workbook are provided for personal use only and are current as of the date of publication, but the publisher disclaims any obligation to update them after publication.

Published by William Carey Publishing
10 W. Dry Creek Cir
Littleton, CO 80120 | www.missionbooks.org

William Carey Publishing is a ministry of Frontier Ventures
Pasadena, CA | www.frontierventures.org

Cover and Interior Designer: Mike Riester
The cover photo was taken by Edward L. Smither inside the Cathedral Basilica of St. Augustine (St. Augustine, Florida). The stained glass image depicts St. Augustine of Hippo (354–430) reading his monastic rules (an early way of life and ministry) to the community at Hippo.

ISBNs: 978-1-64508-573-7 (paperback)
        978-1-64508-575-1 (epub)

Printed Worldwide

28 27 26 25 24   1 2 3 4 5   IN

Library of Congress Control Number: 2024940708

Contents

Introduction

Gregory Mathias

In a way, this year's Evangelical Missiological Society (EMS) monograph on *Equipping for Global Mission* may seem superfluous. After all, the stated purpose of the EMS is to facilitate scholarly support of the Great Commission. EMS is a collection of scholarly and educated people who meet regularly to discuss and address areas of education and mission. So, why is there a need for an annual theme and volume dedicated to education and mission?

Education is a maze of models and opinions. From church pastors' conferences conducted each year around the globe to discipleship and leadership-development processes utilized by missions-sending agencies to legacy institutions like seminaries and Bible schools suffering, at times, from outdated and archaic curricula, the maze grows deeper and more complex.

With these models and opinions, one key question comes to the forefront: What are the missiologically responsible, theologically sound, and practically effective best practices in educating for mission today? This is why the theme of this year's monograph is so vital.

The phrase "facilitating scholarly support" in our society's purpose statement helps to answer the question. It emphasizes the multifaceted nature of education while simultaneously pushing back on what some may consider the entire scope of educating for mission—basic Bible literacy and a few discipleship lessons. The Great Commission, people, and the world are too important and complex for a one-dimensional approach to this important topic.

Education, at its base, is about gaining knowledge and acquiring skills to help one interact, navigate, and contribute to the world. Understanding education within the scope of mission allows education to take on a cruciform shape. By this I mean it reflects Christ's sacrifice of status and rights to acquaint himself with people far from God to show them the way back to God. Christ's command to his followers to go and make disciples is built on the assumption of education. Making disciples is contingent upon teaching toward obedience. This command goes beyond a mere transfer of information and positions education as a formative work. Education and mission work together to deepen a love for God that compels one to continually take the posture of a learner for the sake of the gospel.

Education, in addition to being multifaceted, is also a matter of charity and stewardship. Within EMS, we have access to and are exposed to resources of knowledge, research, experience, and study. Should we not seek to share that knowledge and experience with others while being challenged afresh to continue to learn and educate? This volume is an attempt to participate in the Great Commission as a community of humble learners and practitioners.

The title of this volume does point to a weakness. The full scope of educating for mission is far too broad for a single volume to tackle. Any attempt surely needs more completeness and falls short at some level. At best it can only give samples of a richer and deeper conversation. Yet what this volume does is highlight some of what is best in thinking and practice from the classroom, the field, and the church. No matter the context, we agree that as mission changes and adapts so too must the ways we educate.

The hope for this volume is that this selection of essays will enhance the conversation surrounding education and mission by giving a glimpse of the landscape of education and mission with its innovations, challenges, and opportunities.

As with any volume of this kind, choices have to be made. In so doing, there are certainly ideas not discussed. Additionally, and unfortunately, voices go unrepresented. All of this is a salient reminder that this work is a part of wider and ongoing discussions. As making disciples continues, so must our attention and adaption to educating for mission today.

Part 1

Reflections for Educating for Mission

Chapter 1

Applying Ancient Principles to Renew Contemporary Mission Education

Evelyn Hibbert

As I envisage ideal education for and in missions, I see communities of learners who acknowledge they don't have all the answers. All members of these communities respect one another and actively make disciples. They evaluate cognitive knowledge according to real-life experience and the purpose of mission. The Bible is applied as a textbook for life and exemplary Bible teachers live it out in full view of the community. Learning continues as long as each member lives. Whatever is learned is a rich resource received to share freely with others, reproducing learners who perpetually reproduce new learners (Matt 10:8; 2 Tim 2:2). These are the ancient principles: (1) learn in community, (2) learn in everyday life, and (3) reproduce.

Education transforms us, not just through head knowledge but, hopefully, by developing all aspects of our being. Education is something that we do for mission and as missionaries. The specific challenges of cross-cultural ministry make specialized preparation necessary if we are to produce disciples who are not alien to their context. The same applies to education. It should belong to the local context and build up all who participate in it. It should pass on the full depths of the experience of God through whole-of-life exemplars who reproduce themselves in others.

In this chapter, after I introduce myself, I first discuss the nature and role of education in relation to mission. Then I describe the ancient principles, discussing how they can be applied in our current context. I conclude with a plea for renewal.

My Experience in Mission and Education

I became a Christian as a young child. By the age of seven, I knew God wanted me to be a missionary. My mother introduced me to Scripture Union notes and daily quiet times that I diligently practiced throughout my childhood. While studying to become a medical doctor, I also studied Bible and theology through correspondence programs. Throughout my teenage and young adult years, I read just about every available missionary biography. I met my husband at university and together we answered the call to go to the unreached. We completed an obligatory year at a missionary training college and then joined the mission associated with that college.

We went to an unreached creative access nation. There, we were involved in evangelism and pioneer church planting. After this, we moved to Bulgaria. While planting a church in an unreached area, we were immersed in a spontaneous movement of thousands of Muslims to Christ. They refer to themselves as the Millet. We became involved in discipling this movement and developing its leaders. This movement stagnated at the end of its first decade but, as a consequence of the seeding effect of diaspora, has revived and is continuing today (thirty years later), spreading across Europe.

Eventually, we joined the mission's international leadership. Our roles included advising on the mission's strategic development, doing training and consultation across its fields, and evaluating its missionary training colleges across the world.

We pioneered a different way of doing missionary training for missionary candidates because we saw so many missionaries struggling from a lack of appropriate training and poor missiological practice. This training immersed candidates in church planting among unreached people. We also tried to move candidate selection and preparation back into the hands of local churches. This training was developed as a fully accredited program under the Australian government's education system. However, all these innovations were closed down in favor of institution-based training and agency-based selection and preparation. The principles, details, and challenges of this training are outlined in the book *Training Missionaries* (E. Hibbert and R. Hibbert 2016).

Following this, I ended up in a secular university, teaching and researching in education. This university was in a disadvantaged region of Australia. My research focused on the diverse population of that region.

My husband became the director of the Centre for Cross-Cultural Mission at Sydney Missionary and Bible College but remained engaged in cross-cultural outreach to Muslims, insisting on taking students with him. Although I have helped Christian colleges significantly with missiology teaching, research, and program design, as a woman, I remain on the margins of theological education. Realizing that my situation was common for women missionaries and missiologists, and because women-led approaches to research tend to be more collaborative, creative, and flexible, I set up the Angelina Noble Centre. It provides an identity and a supportive research community for women missiologists. We were pushed out of the institution we began in and now function in a marginal, interinstitutional space.

All these things are relevant because they provide you with an understanding of the influences that inform my position on missions education. We cannot deny the effect of what we have experienced on who we are.

Role of Education in Mission

Education is simply a means to fulfill our mandate to disciple the nations. It should not be an end in itself.

Education for mission is necessary as missionaries need specialized, intercultural training. Education in mission (in the context of mission) is inevitable, primarily because discipling and developing leaders are both educational tasks. The same ancient principles apply to both.

As the Brazilian educator Paulo Freire (1970) stressed, education means more than just filling empty vessels with knowledge. Teaching and learning include social connections, feelings, and physical experiences. It is affected by the context of the learning.

Western education has done an outstanding job of separating text-based knowledge from human experience in all its fullness. We have decontextualized knowledge and successfully exported this way of educating around the world. Evangelicals have been among the worst offenders of this approach to education because, often, in emphasizing the written word of God we have neglected the person of the living Word who dwells among us. This "us" refers to the whole community of Christ's body, not just each isolated individual.

I presume that the main reason why we have relegated learning to cognitive tasks in the classroom is that it seems more efficient. A decontextualized knowledge version of Jesus's curriculum could probably have been covered in a six-month lecture series. However, lectures can never have the same impact as the experience of the lesson in context. For example, Peter would no doubt always associate not being afraid with the vivid experience and feelings of being saved from drowning (Matt 14:22–32).

Good education brings transformation by helping us build connections between people, experiences, feelings, cognitive knowledge (represented by written or oral texts), and tacit knowledge (skills performed by bodies). It is holistic. It is embedded and tested in daily life. It is dynamic and, for Christians, life-bringing and reproducing. This type of connected learning has been represented as a circle or spiral (Kolb 1984; Schön 1991), a fence (Ward and Rowen 1972), or railway tracks (Plueddemann 1972). It is lifelong because there is always more to learn.

The need for specialist training for missionaries has been stressed for more than a century (World Missionary Conference 1910). Without specific training, it is normal for missionaries to introduce their own culturally shaped ways of doing things. Consequently, they establish Christianity as an alien presence (Whiteman 1997).

Although missionary-specific training has improved significantly, and many mission agencies offer it, too many missionaries still go into ministry without this training. Sadly, some with this training still practice mission with a seeming disregard for basic missiological principles. And in our churches and theological colleges, Jesus's command to go into *all* the world is too often neglected. That is, the age-old challenge of those without the opportunity to hear about Jesus is still forgotten amid the clamor of the needs of those who are already Christian (e.g., Stetzer 2013). Surprisingly, as the church declines in the West, many seminaries are dropping missiology altogether. We, as missiologists, have failed to effectively communicate missiology's relevance to our own contexts.

If the primary purpose of missiology is to improve the practice of mission, then the primary purpose of teaching mission is therefore to enhance the ministry of missionaries (R. Hibbert and E. Hibbert 2014b).

As the EMS (n.d.) purpose statement outlines: "We exist to advance the cause of world evangelization to fulfill the Church's mandate to disciple the nations." My focus in talking about educating for and in mission is always to see new disciples come into being, who gather into churches, and who then make more disciples, who make more churches.

The Ancient Principles

Throughout the Bible, we see a consistent pattern of teaching and learning. Teachers and learners share life in community, doing ministry in everyday life, reproducing themselves in others as they pass on their life-experienced heritage to ensuing generations of learners.

In Community

We are created as communal, not isolated, individual beings. We need other people. In contrast, when Western individualists read the Bible, they quickly hone in, almost exclusively, on individual people. Examples of biblical learning communities are Jesus and his disciples; Paul and Barnabas, both with their companions; and the Old Testament community of prophets (e.g., 1 Sam 19:20; 1 Kgs 20:35; 2 Kgs 2:1–18; 4:38–44). Even the mentoring pairs in the Bible, such as Moses and Joshua, Elijah and Elisha, and Paul and Timothy, were continuously surrounded by other people.

Co-learners. As a community of Christians, we know that Jesus is among us (Matt 18:20). He alone is our Master Teacher. Learning in community forefronts the equal status of learner and teacher as co-learners under Christ. The focus is on collaboration and building up the body of Christ together. A collaborative orientation highlights the value of what each participant brings to the community. It gives the control of the learning into the hands of the community according to its needs as community members seek to make disciples in their local context.

The biblical learning community is part of the wider community that observes and flexibly joins in the learning. This style of learning is interactive, like an ongoing conversation, as teachers and learners engage with everyday events. Wider community members listen in and interject their questions and challenges.

Including. The principle of community values all participants. It means proactively valuing diverse perspectives. Teachers and learners are together in a dynamic collaboration with Jesus in relation to the issues of the local context. Learning occurs through the community process as well as from other members of the community.

Jesus's way of teaching was inclusive, not competitive. He repeatedly rebuked his disciples for wanting to be better than each other. In contrast, we have successfully exported, developed, and promoted competition as an educative value in theological education.

Competition fosters exclusion rather than inclusion. It creates winners and losers. But we, as missionary teachers and leaders, are commanded to build up Christ's body (Eph 4:12). We are told that *all* believers have gifts that the whole community needs (1 Cor 12; Eph 4:7).

We need each other's perspectives to engage better with the world around us and to construct strong connections between ideas and practice. While there may be scholars in the community, they are not an elite. They are simply learners among other learners (Palmer 1998).

Empowering. Education should enliven and empower, building up rather than crushing God's people. At the time the Millet movement started, they had no Bible to read, and the believers had newly come out of Islam and communism. In keeping with our inherited educative values, we used to test participants on the content we presented in leadership development seminars. Being highly collective, the participants all compared their results. One leader of a growing church did poorly and was laughed at by his peers. He declared he would never again come to a seminar. Education had crushed him and become a barrier to his further learning. I have never set that kind of test again, in any educational context.

In contrast to this Millet leader's experience, education should honor learners' accomplishments. It should value what each learner brings to the community rather than expose deficits. It should draw out learners' positive contributions rather than punishing differences by marginalizing them. We need to hear all learners' insights and learn from their experiences.

Summary. Recognizing that learners are our peers under Christ helps to humble us. This causes us to respect everyone in the community. It encourages us to actively seek out everyday disciple-makers' perspectives and their evaluations of knowledge in relation to all aspects of life and ministry.

To learn together with those we respect means to adopt practices of communicating and learning that learners are familiar with and prefer.

It means meeting them where they are rather than imposing our own approaches. An example of this is being willing to use oral approaches rather than print-based methods, even when people are able to read (Madinger 2015). It certainly means using affordable online tools, tools learners prefer, and meeting at times that suit learners. This might be more demanding for teachers, but it is a basic cross-cultural missionary principle that the missionary should adjust rather than force people into their own mold.

In Everyday Life

Life and ministry together. The community learns as it does life and ministry together. The process of learning and doing ministry, as well as its context, are integral to the learning experience. The community's learning is relevant to real-life challenges and transparent to the surrounding society. Teachers make mistakes, succeed, and fail in full view of the community. When teachers are embedded with learners in community, doing life and ministry together, they become whole-of-life exemplars for learners. Any scholarly knowledge they pass on—text or research based—is only part of the learning. The way of learning, the relationships, and the participants' spontaneous reactions are all part of the whole.

Learning integrated with life. Learning God's word was integrated with Israelite identity and everyday life (Brueggemann 1997). God directed the Israelites to teach their children his commands: "When you sit at home and when you walk along the road, when you lie down and when you get up" (Deut 6:7 NIV). The learning context of Jesus's disciples was daily life. The disciples saw what he did and asked him questions. He taught them object lessons based on what they saw and experienced. He gave them practical tasks based on his personal example in the same context. In the language of institutions, Jesus became a living textbook. In the same way, the Holy Spirit living in us continually teaches and guides us into all truth, transforming us in everyday life. There is no time or place when he is not developing us (John 14:16–17; 1 John 2:27; Gal 5:22).

Grounded in the local context. Being together in a ministry context forces the training to be contextual and oriented to the people in that context (Jeyaraj 2002). Lave and Wenger (1991, 33–34) asserted that if learning is not grounded in a specific situation, it is largely meaningless. Wenger (1998, 79) said that knowledge must be made indigenous so that it is responsive to local conditions.

Not only does everyday life provide a real context for applying what is learned, but it also makes learning flexible and dynamic. The learning community's borders are fluid, allowing people to join in and leave according to the demands of life (e.g., Saul in 1 Sam 10:10 and the composition of Paul's traveling band). The place of learning is not static. The whole group moves around according to the demands of life and ministry.

The transparency and flexibility of the learning community mean that surrounding people can learn themselves and hold learners accountable. That is, there is no secret knowledge or elite group. Jesus's teaching was not exclusive to the disciples either in their own time or since.

Summary. Through doing life and ministry together, participants in the learning community ground their learning in holistic, local experiences. Cognitive knowledge is tested and tempered by what happens, learners' feelings and interactions, and the responses of others in the context.

This approach to education is undoubtedly more chaotic. Teachers are less able to control it. It can threaten teachers as it exposes their weaknesses. They can feel vulnerable because they do not have all the answers. It also leaves much less time for scholars to cloister themselves away from real life. However, it is more easily reproducible in new mission contexts as it is founded simply on people.

Reproducing

The experience of knowing God is a precious heritage to pass down from generation to generation. Reproducing person-to-person is remarkably simple. It simply depends on having people as examples who live the same kind of life and do the same kind of ministry as learners. It uses resources available to the whole community in the context. When co-learners are given control of the learning, when they are able to have a say about how and what they learn, they will happily pass on what they consider relevant and life-giving.

The Apostle Paul told the Corinthians to imitate him as he imitated Christ (1 Cor 4:16; 11:1). He instructed Timothy to be an example in life, not just through what he taught (1 Tim 4:12). Jesus gave three years to his disciples to be with him (Mark 3:13–14). Elisha spent approximately six years traveling with Elijah. Joshua spent forty years watching Moses. In each case, the mentees saw the whole lives and actions of their mentors in both their weaknesses and triumphs. They shared their experiences and emotions. These biblical mentors reproduced themselves in their mentees. As Jesus said, "The student who works hard will become like the teacher" (Luke 6:40 NLT). These biblical mentors did not just model their individual lives, they modeled a way of living in community.

Whole-of-life. Biblical modeling is whole-of-life. Paul confidently stated that Timothy knew everything about him (2 Tim 3:10–11). Models become living references that inform mentees' whole lives into the future (E. Hibbert and R. Hibbert 2018, 2023).

We have a mandate to pass on what we have received. This is not just text-based knowledge but everything we have received. As we have received freely, we are expected to give generously, including ourselves (Matt 10:8; Luke 6:38; 2 Tim 2:2).

Multiplying disciples who multiply disciples. As disciples, we have been created to reproduce. We may be teachers or researchers, but we are disciples first. We have received so much and are commanded to pass it on freely. This passing on should be a self-perpetuating process until Jesus returns.

Fulfilling Jesus's command to make disciples, teaching them to obey everything that he gave to his disciples, is best done by following his example of education for mission. He gathered his disciples into community. This community shared life together and did their ministry learning in everyday contexts. The disciples were able to imitate Jesus because they knew him intimately and could imagine how he would respond in different contexts. His legacy was embodied in people who, although they later produced texts, knew what it meant to follow Jesus in concrete terms because they had been with him.

Summary. We pass on more than what we explicitly teach. As educators, the whole of our lives should be exemplars of disciple-making. In this way, we pass on a perpetuating heritage that will multiply itself until Jesus comes again.

Andrew Walls (1996) emphasized that the missionary role is transient and catalytic. However, global theological education has created institutions that have depended on missionaries for decades and even, occasionally, centuries. One reason for this has been a focus on the institution rather than the purpose of creating disciple-makers. Let's review our educative values and materials to ensure that what we are reproducing is in line with Jesus's expectations.

The Challenge of Institutional Theological Education

The assumption that the institution-based theological education model is essential is being increasingly concretized beyond redemption. For centuries, much research and scholarly writing has pointed out the inadequacy of this model (ICETE 1983; Farley 1983; Banks 1999; Ott 2001; Jeyaraj 2002; Mwangi and de Klerk 2011; Ball 2012; R. Hibbert and E. Hibbert 2014a). I will not outline the arguments here. Most people reading this chapter are committed to formal theological education and will no doubt defend it strenuously. Yet, that model is associated with a major decline in Christianity in the West (from where this model has been so strongly propagated, especially through missions). It has failed to protect many of its graduates from burnout and moral failure. It has also systematically excluded women, minorities, and everyday people from recognition in Christian contexts. Alarmingly, we continue to promote this model despite its tendency to marginalize mission (Taylor 2006, x).

Scholars are not intrinsically special. Too often, people seem to think that because they can read and write at an advanced level, have read a large number of books and papers, and can argue ideas thoroughly, they are somehow better than others. Of course, Christians would never say this. However, they think it and act it. For most scholars, it means that they had access to money to pay for a lot of institutional education. They probably benefited from an upbringing, including schooling, in which they were coached to think and write in a way that brought success in Western and Western-style institutions (Heath 1983). Someone, probably their spouse and/or parents, also gave them time out from other things to read, write, and research. They have simply gained a skill that others could also acquire if given the same opportunity. People don't have to go to university to learn critical thinking. They don't have to go to Bible college to learn the Bible. They don't have to get a doctorate to do missions research.

So how can we do things better? What if the primary qualification for teaching was ongoing effectiveness in ministry? What if the qualification for learning was passion in ministry? And what if we had more time in ministry than learning in classrooms? What if the assessments for qualifications were based on ministry effectiveness rather than writing essays? What if we valued the DMin more than the PhD? Ward (1996, 45) lamented that as long as "practical experience" is treated as a poor cousin of intellectual learning, as long as "Christian service assignments" are weekend outings divorced from "academic learnings," and as long as theological education is only considered preparatory for ministry, education will weakly affect church development.

I accept that one of the reasons for the development of institutions is the problem of scale. It seems much easier to pass on scholarly knowledge through lectures to large groups than to invest our lives into the few people that we can engage with in this way. It takes time, effort, and cost to be immersed in the messy situations of everyday life.

But that is where learning comes to life and makes a difference. If missiological scholarship does not result in the growth of Christ's kingdom on earth, especially through the salvation of new and unreached people, what is the point of it? What account will we give to our Lord who commanded us, "Go and make disciples ... teaching them to *obey* everything I have commanded you" (Matt 28:19–20)?

How Can We Apply These Ancient Principles in Our Current Setting?

Some concrete steps that institutions and mission agencies could take to bridge the gap between contemporary missiological education and a more ideal approach are to create communities of practice, facilitate scholars staying in practice, honor everyday practitioners, and evaluate programs according to the purpose of mission.

Developing *missiological communities of practice* among missionaries who want to improve their ministry is one simple way to practice these principles. "Communities of practice" is a phrase that was coined to describe groups of people who intentionally gather to learn how to do a specific practice better (Wenger 1998). Peers learn together by trying out new practices and sharing what they learn with one another. As missionaries walk side-by-side in ministry, they can commit to reflecting on what they are learning from external sources in the light of their continuing experience (R. Hibbert and E. Hibbert 2014b). Seminary professors and independent or mission agency missiologists could be resource members and mentors for these groups. Scholarship and any other expertise are simply a resource for the whole group. This means the group should determine how that resource should be used rather than scholars controlling the conversation.

Let's facilitate *scholars staying in ministry*. Graduates could be welcomed as an extension of seminaries, forming a network of peer mentors. There is already a casualization of higher education faculty. But adjuncts tend to be an exploited resource rather than engaged with as valued members of institutional learning communities. This is a more organic way to conceive of the scholarly community. It requires a mindset shift away from the physical institution. This would take teaching and learning out into the field, not by foray (where a lecturer visits for seminars) but by ongoing practice. It would also foster its replication through modeling. Scholar-practitioners not only model practice, but they also model how to keep on learning and passing on that learning amid the demands of ministry (R. Hibbert and E. Hibbert 2014b).

We should intentionally *honor everyday disciple-makers* in our teaching processes. The church has consistently grown through lay movements and especially through women. Similarly, the initial evangelical missionary movements were also lay led. We dishonor the leaders of those movements when we say or imply they are not enough.

We often imply these leaders need the knowledge that we have gained, frequently without relevant experience, to make them better Christians. There is something wrong here, especially if they are more effectively introducing people to Jesus than we are. If we want to see the earth filled with the knowledge of the Lord but we crush the very people who are likely to make it happen, we have subverted our purpose. We need to listen to and learn how to include these people in our learning communities.

The main ways we currently *evaluate* our programs are by student numbers, institutional funding (including its research), academic publications, and whether current students and recent graduates like our teaching. None of these things measure up *according to the goal of mission*. If we are serious about our missions training programs, the bottom line is whether graduates are making disciples across cultures and gathering them into churches that multiply. This is a long-term evaluation project. It has very different evaluative indicators.

Accreditation is often used as an excuse for not pursuing mission purpose. Accreditors are seen as the enemy rather than learning partners who can help us do a better job. Accreditation usually does not prevent us from being innovative, but resistance to change certainly does. Accreditation simply requires that we justify what we do in terms of predefined learning outcomes.

With a spirit of generosity and blurring the boundary between institutions and the world of ministry, the application of these ancient principles may bring some renewal into theological education. Like the EMS is already doing by including practitioners in the scholarly community, if we extend the community out into mission contexts, we may be able to achieve our primary purpose of making disciples who make disciples.

Conclusion

Missiology is marginalized in theological institutions. This is the case even in those that were established by missionaries for missions. But this marginalization gives us an opportunity to be a renewing influence from the edges. The edges often have more freedom to experiment as the center tends to be more tightly controlled. Not only can we do education for missions differently, having the opportunity to set up new education systems or influence existing ones, but we can model a different way. This way brings people together in community rather than pushing them apart through competition and exclusion. It grounds the Bible and theology in everyday life. It freely passes on the resources of research and learning for the glory of Jesus and the multiplication of his disciples.

As a missiological society that welcomes members from outside the academy, we could do more to foster missiological learning communities across the world. One simple way we could make the community more accessible is by shifting our mindset beyond North American institutions. This would affect the timing and location of learning community interactions, as well as making the most of technology to foster collaboration and include currently excluded voices.

As scholars, we need to learn to honor everyday Christians, recognizing we have much to learn from them. At the very least, we could include them as resource people in classroom teaching. This means having an attitude of honor rather than critique. Having a PhD does not make us better people. Having a Bible college degree does not make us better Christians. We are all one in Christ, no one better than any other. Any knowledge we do have is not our own. It is given to us to pass on freely to others.

I know all these things raise huge issues, such as the funding of institutions. Yet, somehow, God still brings people to himself, largely through people who haven't been to Bible college, who spread the gospel to others and plant churches. If we are to educate them, we need to do it humbly and in ways that do not stop them from multiplying churches. Let's take the knowledge we do have to offer and walk alongside them in ministry. Let them test what we bring in real life and ministry. Let's learn together from their evaluations. Let us proactively empower them to pass on what they learn to others.

"Missions has always been an on-the-edge endeavor. Missionaries step into places that the rest of the church does not go. They take risks for the sake of the gospel that are unthinkable for many. Perhaps it is time for missiologists to lead in a new paradigm of theological education" (R. Hibbert and E. Hibbert 2014b, 15). It is as we work and learn together in everyday life that we will fulfill our purpose of seeing the earth filled with the knowledge of God (Hab 2:14) and people from every nation worshiping around the throne (Rev 7:9).

References

Ball, Les. 2012. *Transforming Theology: Student Experience and Transformative Learning in Undergraduate Theological Education*. Preston, Victoria: Mosaic.

Banks, Robert J. 1999. *Reenvisioning Theological Education: Exploring a Missional Alternative to Current Models*. Grand Rapids: Eerdmans.

Brueggemann, Walter. 1997. *Theology of the Old Testament: Testimony, Dispute, Advocacy*. Minneapolis: Fortress.

EMS. n.d. "Who is the Evangelical Missiological Society?" Accessed August 19, 2023. https://www.emsweb.org/about/who-is-ems/.

Farley, Edward. 1983. *Theologia: The Fragmentation and Unity of Theological Education*. Philadelphia: Fortress.

Freire, Paulo. 1970. *Pedagogy of the Oppressed*, translated by Myra Bergman Ramos. New York: Herder and Herder.

Heath, Shirley Brice. 1983. *Ways with Words: Language, Life, and Work in Communities and Classrooms*. Cambridge: Cambridge University Press.

Hibbert, Evelyn, and Richard Hibbert. 2016. *Training Missionaries: Principles and Possibilities*. Pasadena, CA: William Carey Library.

Hibbert, Evelyn, and Richard Hibbert. 2018. *Walking Together on the Jesus Road: Discipling in Intercultural Contexts.* Littleton, CO: William Carey Publishing.

Hibbert, Evelyn, and Richard Hibbert. 2023. *Multiplying Leaders in Intercultural Contexts: Recognizing and Developing Grassroots Potential.* Littleton, CO: William Carey Publishing.

Hibbert, Richard, and Evelyn Hibbert. 2014a. "Assessing the Need for Better Integration in Theological Education: Proposals, Progress, and Possibilities from the Medical Education Model." In *Learning and Teaching Theology: Some Ways Ahead,* edited by Les Ball and James R. Harrison. Sydney: Morning Star Publications.

Hibbert, Richard, and Evelyn Hibbert. 2014b. "Nurturing Missionary Learning Communities." Association of Professors of Mission, University of Northwestern, Saint Paul, MN, June 2014. http://place.asburyseminary.edu/firstfruitspapers/33/.

ICETE. 1983. "ICETE Manifesto on the Renewal of Evangelical Theological Education." Accessed October 3, 2023. https://icete.info/resources/the-icete-manifesto/.

Jeyaraj, Jesudason Baskar. 2002. *Christian Ministry: Models of Ministry and Training.* Bangalore: Theological Book Trust.

Kolb, David A. 1984. *Experiential Learning: Experience as the Source of Learning and Development.* Englewood Cliffs, NJ: Prentice Hall.

Lave, Jean, and Etienne Wenger. 1991. *Situated Learning: Legitimate Peripheral Participation.* Learning in Doing. Cambridge: Cambridge University Press.

Madinger, Charles. 2015. "Will Our Message 'Stick?' Assessing a Dominant Preference for Orality for Education and Training." In *Beyond Literate Western Contexts: Honor and Shame and Assessment of Orality Preference,* edited by Samuel E. Chiang and Grant Lovejoy, 125–34. Hong Kong: International Orality Network.

Mwangi, James K., and Ben J. de Klerk. 2011. "An Integrated Competency-Based Training Model for Theological Training." *HTS Theological Studies* 67, no. 2 (January): 1–10. http://www.scielo.org.za/scielo.php?script=sci_arttext&pid=S0259-94222011000200016&lng=en&nrm=iso&tlng=en.

Ott, Bernhard. 2001. *Beyond Fragmentation: Integrating Mission and Theological Education: A Critical Assessment of Some Recent Developments in Evangelical Theological Education.* Regnum Studies in Mission. Oxford: Regnum.

Palmer, Parker J. 1998. *The Courage to Teach: Exploring the Inner Landscape of a Teacher's Life.* San Francisco: Jossey-Bass.

Plueddemann, Jim. 1972. "The Real Disease of Sunday School." *Evangelical Missions Quarterly* 9, no. 2: 88–92.

Schön, Donald A. 1991. *The Reflective Practitioner: How Professionals Think in Action*. Aldershot: Arena.

Stetzer, Ed. 2013. "Missions vs. Missional? We Really Need Both." *Christianity Today*, September 9, 2013.

Taylor, William. 2006. "Foreword." In *Integral Ministry Training: Design and Evaluation*, edited by Robert Brynjolfson and Jonathan Lewis, vii–xiv. Pasadena, CA: William Carey Library.

Walls, Andrew F. 1996. *The Missionary Movement in Christian History: Studies in the Transmission of Faith*. Maryknoll, NY: Orbis Books.

Ward, Ted W. 1996. "Evaluating Metaphors of Education." In *With an Eye on the Future: Development and Mission in the 21st Century: Essays in Honor of Ted W. Ward*, edited by Duane Elmer and Lois McKinney, 43–54. Monrovia, CA: MARC.

Ward, Ted W., and Samuel F. Rowen. 1972. "The Significance of the Extension Seminary." *Evangelical Missions Quarterly* 9, no. 1: 17–27. https://missionexus.org/the-significance-of-the-extension-seminary/.

Wenger, Etienne. 1998. *Communities of Practice: Learning, Meaning, and Identity*. Learning in Doing. Cambridge: Cambridge University Press.

Whiteman, Darrell L. 1997. "Contextualization: The Theory, the Gap, the Challenge." *International Bulletin of Missionary Research* 21, no. 1 (January): 2–7. https://doi.org/10.1177/239693939702100101.

World Missionary Conference. 1910. *Report of Commission V*. Edinburgh: Oliphant, Anderson & Ferrier.

Chapter 2

Rescuing the Mind from Academics

A South Asian Perspective on *Missio Dei* and the *Telos* of Theological Education

Paul Cornelius

Last year, at a gathering of theological educators in India, in my final words to the group, I expressed with some passion my disillusionment with theological education in general. This disillusionment was occasioned by a defining conversation with leaders of two seminaries after a horrific rape crime some years ago. Right-thinking citizens in the city of Bangalore were out on the streets in protest. I remember, vividly, asking these leaders how they felt about suspending classes for a day or two and having their educational communities participate in what was becoming a call for serious incarnational engagement in the life of a nation. With disbelief writ large on their faces, they voiced their concern at the loss of class time and the impact it would have on the completion of curriculum and coursework. It was inconceivable that I would, in my role with the Asia Theological Association, have the audacity to suggest something as outlandish as reducing the time that would be better spent in the great pursuit of theological knowledge and academics, training women and men for ministry and mission.

A second conversation was equally instructive. On an evaluation visit to a seminary in South India, I raised the troubling issue of the lack of clarity on how exam questions were crafted. The design in question was one typically used in an educational system that emphasized recall and/or framing an appropriate response. The difficulty for the students was that the questions were so vague that they could have invited any response. Upon asking how the students would know what was expected of them as they formulated their response, the faculty member in question said, "Well, they should know what I am thinking in my mind!"

These two examples, among many others, offer us a glimpse into some of the basic assumptions that undergird training in most theological institutions and possibly other institutions of Christian higher education in South Asia. First, as we will soon note, is the focus on the intellectual and cognitive aspects of theological education. Second is the underlying assumption that a degree-oriented education is more than sufficient for meaningful engagement in the lived realities of the people. Little emphasis is laid on the ability to *do* meaningful theology in context. In this chapter, I will focus on Christian education as it pertains to seminary and Bible college training in South Asia and India in particular. At times comparisons or reflections from the Western context will help clarify that what is discussed here is not merely a problem in South Asia but one that is more widespread.

A case in point is a study by Elizabeth Lynn Wheeler and Barbara Wheeler (1999) that arrived at the disturbing conclusion that theological schools were virtually unknown in public society and therefore exerted little influence on it. The survey, conducted in four major North American cities, concluded that seminaries were viewed neither as civic assets nor as educational assets. Their lack of visibility and involvement in the public arena raises the potentially alarming issue of their continued relevance and vitality, not only in North America but also around the globe. The problem then is that seminaries have failed to produce the desired product—skilled leaders for the community. Further, the purpose of theological education is not understood, and therefore theological curriculum is in disarray. There is a general sense that theological education "is ineffectual if all that is produced is knowledge of a set of propositions, polished skills, or a well-stocked mind" (Cannell 2006, 43).

The Question of Emphasis

Theological education in its earliest forms was simply the recounting of the disciples' experience of Christ and his life. Subsequently, as Christianity began its expansion across the Roman world, leaders and teachers viewed their task in terms of sifting through and filtering the growing corpus of records to determine what was authentic and what was not (Jackson 1997). Further, the increasing challenge posed by Greco-Roman thinkers as they examined the new faith compelled the church fathers to redefine their faith in intellectually acceptable categories. The result was that "Christianity came to be recognized as possessing a collection of beliefs whose subtleties of language as well as actual differences led to the invention of different dogmatic systems among believers" (504). These developments led to two traditions not only running parallel to each other but also at times complementing or suppressing the other. These are referred to as the "experiential" and "cognitive" traditions (507).

Theological education in the experiential tradition places a high priority on the ethical and relational aspects of the Christian faith. It is based on events of personal experience and "is the result of an individual, personal encounter of a person with the living Christ, an event transforming the new believer by a 'spiritual re-birth' and initiating him/her as a convert into membership of the church" (505). It is knowledge born out of experience. In the cognitive tradition, "Revelational 'Truth,' the truth of God, is the prized object of spiritual pursuit" (506). The diligent discipline of the mind and ongoing, godly study of the Scriptures are the focus. Importance is placed on "intellectual understanding, correct thinking, and rational commitment to 'revealed Truth'" (507), which could be verified by reasoned judgments of its authenticity. Arguably, the second is the more dominant, even in current approaches to theological education in South Asia.

The emphasis on the cognitive often results in a wide gap between what is expected as the outcome and what is actually delivered, creating a void that desperately needs to be filled. Reflecting on this, Ralph Enlow (2006) raises the question, "Could we not benefit from a form of theological education that exchanges (or at least moderates) competitive and detached intellectual discourse for communal engagement that forms the person for ministry?" It seems then that theological education not animated by and oriented to the transformational mission of the church is in danger of remaining irrelevant and obsolete.

Drawing upon Andrew Walls, Enlow (2006) further notes that Western theological education in particular struggles with the inability to penetrate and push the boundaries of Christianity into its own culture and context. This insightful comment is affirmed by the magnitude of articles and books that have emerged out of the Western context. Building on this argument, one must take issue with non-Western theological institutions that import some, if not all, of the theological curriculum from the West. On what grounds is it justifiable to borrow from a model that is struggling to come to terms with its effectiveness in its own culture and context? Again, drawing upon Walls, Enlow (2006) calls for "an awakening of theological schools to the true task of theology, namely, to bring the whole of Scripture to bear upon the questions and choices with which ordinary believers are confronted in their calling to live out the Gospel in their native context." The true task of theological education, accordingly, is to form women and men in such a manner as to ensure that the gospel is lived and practiced meaningfully within specific communities, cultures, and contexts.

Formation and Education for Mission

Formation, with respect to theological training, is not new. Most often it is used to address the matter of spiritual formation as opposed to an academic and knowledge-based focus. However, formation attends to the whole person, including being formed into the "mind of Christ" (1 Cor 2:16). If our approach to academics does not serve the higher purpose of forming individuals and communities into the mind of Christ, then theological education has failed. In a blog post, Chuck DeGroat (2017) writes, "'Putting on the mind of Christ' was like checking the theological boxes of Calvinistic, Reformed theology. ... [It was] akin to plugging into the timeless, absolute, propositional truths in the mind of God." He continues, "The 'truths,' in the end, usually looked less like the messy, winding, and multiperspectival narratives of scripture and more like propositions ready for mental deposit."

The theological education enterprise is beset by a fundamental conundrum of a missional nature. Countless vision and mission statements bear witness to this problem. While some statements evidence theological and/or missiological intent, others are clichéd, grandiose declarations, saying much but meaning or achieving little. For a vast number of seminaries, the lack of theological and missiological reflection regarding the goal of their endeavor results in significant gaps—between context and curriculum, church and academia, and isolation and engagement, to name a few. These are symptoms of a lack of purpose. The problem, it seems, stems from a narrow definition of mission. The fallout is that an impoverished view of missional purpose leads to an impoverished approach to all that happens in a theological institution. Bosch (2006, 494) articulates this clearly when he says, "We are tempted to incarcerate the *missio Dei* in the narrow confines of our own predilections, thereby of necessity reverting to one-sidedness and reductionism. We should be aware of any attempt at delineating mission too sharply."

Decades earlier, in the International Missionary Council's 1938 meeting in Tambaram, India, the council observed that theological education was the weakest link in mission (Esterline 2010). The council formed a theological education fund as a step toward mitigating this problem. Problems continued to abound, as subsequent reflections and writings from across the continents indicate. In 2010, the Cape Town Commitment made this unequivocal statement: "Our mission is wholly derived from God's mission, addresses the whole of God's creation, and is grounded at its centre in the redeeming victory of the cross." It went on to assert that the mission of theological education is to "strengthen and accompany the mission of the Church." This chapter notes these assertions in an attempt to bring specificity and clarity to the relationship between the *missio Dei* and the purpose of theological education.

Surprisingly, despite a significant amount of reflection and writing on the *missio Dei*, it appears that a clear understanding of the mission of God does not find a place in overall institutional thinking and practice. If we were to put it in educational terms, unclear outcomes lead to unclear processes. The question is, How does one arrive at a cogent and coherent goal? Is an overarching *telos* possible, which institutions can draw upon to help articulate their missional purpose? This chapter makes the case that a clearer understanding and appropriation of the *missio Dei* as forming people and leading them toward social engagement is necessary for theological educational institutions as they seek to frame the purpose of their existence and mission.

Missio Dei

Views and approaches to mission have varied, but a significant shift has taken place in the past fifty years. The term *mission* was used in different ways. Typically, it referred to the act of evangelizing an individual, thereby saving that person from hell. For the Christian West, it meant moving toward unreached peoples with the gospel or referred to strategies and deadlines of global outreach (Bosch 2006). As early as 1932, Karl Barth conceptualized mission as the activity of God himself. His thinking led to serious theological and missiological reflection and shaping of the concept of the *missio Dei*. Mission now began to be defined anew with a clear distinction between missions in the plural, as it referred to church activities including sending missionaries to faraway geographical locations, and mission in the singular, that which emanates from God and his action toward all of his creation through the church.

In this schema, the *missio Dei* was seen to be grounded in the character of God; God's very nature is missionary. Therefore, mission is not an activity of the church but an "attribute of God" (Bosch 2006, xxx). This can be described in two ways. First, contrary to popular perception, a nuanced understanding is that the *missio Dei* is first about *being* and then about *doing*. God acts because of who he is. The fact that he is holy, righteous, loving, just, and merciful causes him to act to bring about the righteous kingdom he desires. Therefore, one can talk about the missionary character of God. Second, God is not only a God of action, but he is also a sending God. The Father, Son, and Spirit work together within the church to bring her to maturity and to send her to fulfill the *missio Dei* in the world.

The *Missio Dei* Involves Forming the People of God

Scripture, from its earliest pages, vividly captures God's redemptive and restorative acts. That God initiates and makes the first move reflects the missionary nature of the divine. God's involvement in the affairs of the world predates the formation of the people of God in the Old Testament and the creation of the church in the New Testament. So, it is important to recognize that mission does not begin with the church. Referring to this aspect of the *missio Dei*, Timothy Tennent (2010, 55) states, "A new model of mission was proposed that clearly articulated that God's redemptive action in the world precedes the church, meaning the church should not perceive itself as the starting point for mission activity in the world." In the Old Testament, as much as the focus is on the liberation aspects of the Exodus, the primary purpose was to form the people of Israel into a "treasured possession ... a kingdom of priests and a holy nation" (Exod 19:1–6 ESV). Israel's calling was to be the people of God and establish a community that reflected the divine character. Numerous passages address this fundamental element of God's mission. In truth, God's call and formation of a people was the first step in his mission of establishing his rule and reign over all creation. Both redemptive and restorative acts are evident in the forming and shaping of the life, values, and witness of this community. Christopher Wright (2006) sees the Exodus as Yahweh's redemptive act and the practice of the Jubilee as the restorative act. The people of Israel were the primary beneficiaries as they were formed into a living witness based on their salvation and healing as a community.

God's redemptive and restorative acts are embodied fully and finally in Christ's incarnation and are to be manifest in the life and witness of the church. This is amply borne out by the Gospels and other New Testament writings. In Mark 3:14 (ESV) we read that Jesus "appointed twelve ... so that they might be with him, and he might send them out." The emphasis is first on being with Christ, to be shaped and formed into his likeness, before the doing. Jesus's mission, as the Gospels affirm, is the formation of a new covenant community, sending them out to bear witness to him through proclamation and kingdom living (Matt 5, 11; John 17). The New Testament writers' primary audience was the church in its varied contexts— encouraging her toward Christlike maturity as well as proclamatory and embodied witness.

The *Missio Dei* Involves Establishing the Kingdom of God

We must refresh our thinking on the biblical, theological, and missiological insights into what the kingdom of God is and entails. While the kingdom of God is most explicitly used in the New Testament, it is implied in many passages in the Old Testament. Scot McKnight (2014) suggests five key aspects that clarify what the kingdom of God is—the reality of a king; the rule of this king demonstrated in his redemptive and governing acts; a redeemed people; the will, law, and ethics of the king; and the spaces that his people inhabit (from the land in the Old Testament to the incarnational living spaces of the church in the New Testament).

I would like to focus on the last characteristic—the witness of the people of God in their contexts. Both the Old and New Testaments provide key markers to flesh out the characteristics of the kingdom of God. First, it is characterized by community, beginning with the formation of the people of God. Second, it establishes a credible witness and ushers in the reality of the kingdom of God incarnationally. Third, it is the prophetic voice as God's people speak to and engage with the fragmented, decayed, inhuman, broken systems of culture and society in such a manner that kingdom values of shalom, justice, upliftment, equality, integrity, and hope are engendered and fostered. It is clear that God's intentions in the *missio Dei* are that his people engage in redemptive and restorative acts as signs that the kingdom of God is present among us. Holistically speaking, the kingdom of God seeks to address and redress the whole human predicament (Wright 2006). This is the scope of God's intent and action.

The *Missio Dei* Gives Purpose to Theological Education

Two points of clarification are needed here. First, the intent of this reflection is not to argue for the place of missiology in the overall curriculum or to make a case for the importance of missiological education. This has been done most admirably by others. Second, as much as theological education is generally used to denote ministry training universally, it is easy to miss the particular and local component in this expression and the significant role it plays in its formulation and delivery. It is important to guard against talking about theological education so generally as to make it an abstract construct. Theological education takes place in concrete settings—formally, nonformally, and informally—in and through specific institutions, defined by specific contexts and established with specific visions. Institutions and churches are on the ground, addressing needs through either formal programs or church-based trainings. There can be no escape from the fact that these institutions must engage in continuous self-reflection about the identity and purpose of theological education. Rozko (n.d., 7) put it well when he says, "As God's missionary nature finds expression in his movement toward and for the good of the world, we do well to understand the purpose of theological reflection as contributing towards that same aim." If God is characterized by being a missionary God, then theological education and reflection must have a missionary and missional purpose. The foregoing discussion suggests two major areas of alignment that in turn will sharpen the missional purpose of institutions engaged in theological education. These two areas of alignment are foundational to the mission of any training, whether in a formal or nonformal approach. They are intrinsically bound to the life and witness of the church in its particular and universal expressions. Ironically, many theological education programs have unknowingly (or knowingly) marginalized these areas of alignment and centralized a knowledge-based purpose, even if these are their stated goals. However, the margin must become the center. This has clear implications for how curriculum is designed and formational processes are developed.

First, drawing from this brief study of the *missio Dei*, theological education in both its broader and specific contexts must emphasize and include the formation of God's people into kingdom communities. Irrespective of the different vocations that students are being trained for, the institution must focus on forming its immediate community as kingdom citizens and influencers and not merely on knowledge gain. In most cases, character formation is relegated to the margin. Looking at it from the vantage point of the *missio Dei*, formation must be holistic and integrated. Second, the *missio Dei* anticipates that the people of God will participate in establishing the kingdom of God and his reign on earth. For theological education, this is a prophetic engagement that takes on two dimensions. First is prophetic engagement toward the church, speaking God's truth into and addressing life issues in building up God's people into maturity. This is a sacred responsibility and cannot be neglected in its overall purpose. Second is prophetic engagement with the church, bringing the work of the kingdom to fruition in the spaces that the church occupies. Again, theological education is both proclamatory and participatory, incarnational and kerygmatic.

Conclusion

The mind can be rescued from a mere academic and degree orientation. It requires theological education to emphasize doing theology in context— engaging with the mind, heart, and hands of Christ and the lived realities of the people and communities in which we live. Impactful mission and engagement cannot happen unless our own deeply embedded worldviews are challenged and changed by the gospel. Training and education in this manner are beyond intellectualism. Here are some implications for training that focuses on formation:

1. Curriculum becomes dynamic, addressing the needs of the learners as they seek to be equipped for meaningful engagement.

2. Methodology focuses on learning and not teaching, integration and not fragmentation, and reflective engagement and not mere accumulation of knowledge.

3. Faculty become facilitators of learning and transformation, mentoring and modeling by being and doing.

4. Students actively participate in their own learning and formation.

5. Theology that engages where individuals and communities experience and are transformed by the inbreaking of the kingdom of God.

This reflection is about moving the *missio Dei* from the margins to the center of theological education. Alignment to the *missio Dei* in its formation and engagement purposes will move theological education a step closer to fulfilling its rightful role in the kingdom of God.

References

Bosch, David. 2006. *Transforming Mission: Paradigm Shifts in the Theology of Mission*. Indian Edition. Bangalore: Centre for Contemporary Christianity.

Cannell, Linda. 2006. *Theological Education Matters: Leadership Education for the Church*. Newburgh, IN: EDCOT Press.

DeGroat, Chuck. 2017. Putting on the Mind of Christ. *Reformed Journal* (blog). June 5, 2017. https://blog.reformedjournal.com/2017/06/05/putting-on-the-mind-of-christ/.

Dyrness, William. 2004. "A Holistic Curriculum for Theological Education: With Special Reference to Africa." Paper presented at Colloquium on Education and Mission, International Council on Higher Education, Calcutta, India, February 2004.

Enlow, Ralph E. 2006. "Global Christianity and the Role of Theological Education: Wrapping Up and Going Forward." Paper presented at the International Council for Evangelical Theological Education, Chiang Mai, Thailand, August 2006.

Esterline, David. 2010. "From Western Church to World Christianity: Developments in Theological Education in the Ecumenical Movement." In *Handbook of Theological Education in World Christianity: Theological Perspectives, Regional Surveys, Ecumenical Trends*, edited by Dietrich Werner, David Esterline, Namsoon Kang, and Joshva Raja, 13–22. Regnum Studies in Global Christianity. Oxford: Regnum.

Jackson, Walter C. 1997. "A Brief History of Theological Education including a Description of the Contribution of Wayne E. Oates." *Review and Expositor* 94, no. 4: 503–20.

Lausanne Committee for World Evangelization. 2011. *The Cape Town Commitment: A Confession of Faith and a Call to Action*. South Hamilton, MA: Lausanne Movement.

McKnight, Scot. 2014. "Kingdom: A Proposal." *Jesus Creed* (blog), *Patheos*. November 19, 2014. https://www.patheos.comblogs/jesuscreed/2014/11/19/kingdom-a-proposal/.

Rozko, JR. n.d. "Towards a Mission-Shaped Vision of Theological Formation: Implications of the *Missio Dei* for Theological Education." Accessed September 1, 2023. https://www.academia.edu/4148062/Toward_a_Mission-Shaped_Vision_of_Theological_Formation_Implications_of_the_Missio_Dei_for_Theological_Education.

Tennent, Timothy C. 2010. *Invitation to World Missions: A Trinitarian Missiology for the Twenty-First Century*. Grand Rapids: Kregel.

Wheeler, Elizabeth Lynn, and Barbara G. Wheeler. 1999. *Missing Connections: Public Perception of Theological Education and Religious Leadership*. New York: Auburn Theological Seminary.

Wright, Christopher J. H. 2006. *The Mission of God: Unlocking the Bible's Grand Narrative*. Downers Grove, IL: IVP Academic.

Chapter 3

Missionary Education and Effective Great Commission Participation

Does Missionary Education Work?

Kenneth Nehrbass, David R. Dunaetz, and Joyce Jow

While enrollment in missions-related degrees has been declining in the USA, the proliferation of these formal missiological degrees seems to indicate that many mission-oriented students believe that they will receive a level of training that will prepare them well for cross-cultural service. Of the 150 institutions that belong to the Coalition of Christian Colleges and Universities (CCCU), thirty institutions offer bachelor degrees in intercultural studies, and twenty-three others offer missions-related undergraduate or graduate degrees with similar monikers such as "missional ministries" (Bethel University), "cross-cultural studies" (Messiah University), "intercultural ministry" (Northwest Nazarene), "urban and intercultural ministry" (Redeemer University), and "global service" (Abilene Christian University). A few other universities offer specialized missions-related degrees like "agricultural missions" (Dordt University) and "missionary aviation" (Cornerstone University). Additionally, many seminaries offer graduate degrees in missions, such as Fuller Theological Seminary and Trinity Evangelical Divinity School. A great many more institutions allow students to minor in a missions-related degree or to receive a Christian ministries degree with an emphasis on missions. However, many missionaries enter the field having attained undergraduate or graduate degrees in other relevant (or at times even seemingly irrelevant) fields such as international business, education, public health, and even chemistry or dance. To what degree do these various forms of education contribute to missionary effectiveness?

Some descriptive research has been carried out to understand trends in the North American missionary force (Newell 2017). Lin's (2023) qualitative study revealed missionaries' perceptions of their formal missions education: They perceived that their Bible and contextualization courses provided a good foundation (129), and they experienced spiritual growth as a result of their education (130); yet they found that much of their coursework was difficult to put into practice.

Beyond these descriptive studies, little quantitative research has been done to understand the levels of formal education attained by the missionary force. Few studies have established a relationship between formal missiological education and missionary activities. Do courses in contextualization impact the way someone shares the gospel across cultures? Does formal linguistics and language training increase one's engagement in another culture? Do those with advanced missiological degrees reach out more, or less, to their host communities? Does the modality of delivery affect the relationship between education and missionary activities?

This study examines the relationship between various aspects of higher education and the recent ministry activities of 198 missionaries in evangelical mission organizations. Specifically, we will examine how educational variables are correlated with behaviors related to the Great Commission such as sharing the gospel, baptizing, teaching the Bible, and training others to teach.

Definitions

The concept of *formal missions education* (that is, the education of missions at the university level) must be kept distinct from *education in missions* and *missionary training*. Each will be described briefly here.

Education in Missions

A great deal has been written on "education in missions," which is a missionary strategy that involves establishing primary and secondary schools in missionary fields (Seton 2013; Holmes 1967; Plueddemann 2018) or carrying out theological training in a host culture (Dunaetz 2018; Grant 1999; Kim 2004).

Missionary Training

This type of training is carried out by mission agencies and tends to be more practical than theoretical. The curriculum involves strategies for evangelism and discipleship, establishing rapport across cultures, and dealing with culture shock. This training may supplement or replace formal missions education, according to the norms of the mission agency.

Formal Missions Education

This refers to the curriculum at universities designed to contribute to the expansion of Christianity across cultures. Courses include the history of missions, theology of missions, anthropology, intercultural studies, and intercultural education, among other topics (Nehrbass 2016). Majors related to formal missions education go by names such as "intercultural studies," "global studies," or "missions," and they can be associated with a host of degrees (BA, MA, MDiv, DMin, etc.).

Some may take issue with the notion that a degree in intercultural studies from a Christian university is primarily about the education of missionaries. However, 83 percent of the forty-six websites for degrees in intercultural studies (or similar degrees) at CCCU schools indicate that their degree program can contribute to missionary preparation in some way:

- To prepare "students to enact positive social change by addressing global issues in multicultural societies" (Biola University)

- "For students who feel called to advance the mission of God and use their compassion and skills to disciple others" (Bethel University)

- To "prepare you to engage with God's redemptive mission in the world and reflect critically and productively on the church's kingdom activity" (Taylor University)

- To "deepen your biblical understanding, strengthen your intercultural ministry skills and elevate your intercultural communication skills" (Trinity Evangelical Divinity School)

Other CCCU programs use broader terms such as "appropriate interaction," "transformational work," or "expand your view of the world."

The research presented here focuses specifically on formal missions education. We want to know if formal missions education is a good predictor of missionary activities. The section below summarizes research that has delineated the parameters of formal missions education. In addition, we provide a summary of previous studies that connect formal missions education to missionary activity.

The Curriculum of Formal Missions Education

The body of literature used to educate missionaries and missiologists is so extensive that it can seem impossible to create a manageable set of themes covered. Fortunately, several works form a sort of *implicit* canon for missions education. Moreau's (2008) "Bibliography for Missionary Training" contains about seventy-five entries, many of which fit into this "canon." Often, missiologists have conceived of this implicit curriculum as having three major categories: the history of missions, theology of missions, and anthropology (Nehrbass 2016). However, this tripartite model has been strongly challenged as numerous other fields (such as language studies and pastoral counseling) are also leveraged by missiologists (Nehrbass 2021).

Delineating the Objectives and Content of Missions Education

Some missiological works have examined earlier efforts to train missionaries. For example, Chambers's (2016) autopsy of the Basel Missionary Training Institute during the nineteenth century argues that the Europeans' emphasis on piety led to a sort of legalism that undermined missionary efforts in Ghana. Henderson (1993) noted that before the 1930s, Church of Christ missionaries only received training in theology. But by the mid-twentieth century, missiologists within the movement began teaching language and history courses as well as courses on evangelism. By the 1970s, the Churches of Christ had caught up with other evangelical movements in offering robust missiological training. Elsewhere, Ma (2014) gave a brief history of the key players who established the missionary training institute at Asia Pacific Theological Seminary (APTS). The article contains data on enrollment trends and the missionary fields and careers of its graduates; but it does not examine the missionary activities of those graduates, let alone make a connection between the graduates' perceptions of their training at APTS and their subsequent ministry activities.

As far as the content of missions education goes, David Lee (2008, 116) provided a history of the Global Missionary Training Center in Asia, noting that the curriculum included aspects of spiritual maturity, stable family life, resilience, relationship-building skills, not to mention basics in theology and missiology. Others would certainly tack on additional competencies for missionary training. For example, when examining what post–World War II missionary training would involve, Weddell (1944) suggested that missionaries would need to know how to teach literacy and public health. In a more recent example, Cheng (2001) suggested that missions education should include a component on "inner-healing" to help missionaries deal with trauma. And Hibbert and Hibbert (2016) stressed that missionaries must be trained to experience God, to use the Bible, to engage with cultures, and to relate to others.

Note, though, that while these conceptual pieces provide a perspective on the development of thought related to missionary training, none endeavored to use empirical research to understand the impact of those training efforts on their students.

Literature on the Impact of Missions Education

A small number of studies have examined the impact of missions education. Nehrbass (2020) carried out a qualitative study on the long-term impact of missions-related doctorates ($n = 18$). While the study could not establish a statistically significant relationship between formal missiological education and an increase in missionary activities, the participants did perceive that advanced missiological study improved their work:

> A missions-related doctoral program is an experience of reflection, resulting in a deeper understanding of students' own cross-cultural experiences. This deeper understanding has a personal and interpersonal impact: Graduates use their broader perspectives to develop contextually appropriate approaches in their own work; and many transfer this understanding to others through consulting work, publishing, and training. (41)

Nehrbass ended the study with a call for quantitative studies that can help clarify the relationship between mission studies and missionary activities. One example is Paul Lee's (2019) use of a pretest-posttest control group design ($n = 45$) to determine the effect of a certain missionary candidate training program on intercultural readiness. The results showed that those who received the training were statistically more "ready" for the field than those who did not, in the domains of interpersonal relationships, cultural adaptation, family relationships, and assessment of previous learning experiences (257).

Conclusions from the Literature Review

Missiological education is wider than just missionary training. As Yeh (2016, 32) pointed out, the purposes of missiology are contested, ranging from "evangelizing every people group," to mobilizing Christians for social action, to simply discussing "a fascinating subject that deserves much study." However, universities within the evangelical tradition indicate that their missions-related degrees are intended to improve missionary practice. To date, little is known about the education levels of the missionary force, and less is known about the impact that this education has on missionary activities.

Methods

The purpose of this survey-based study is to better understand how missionary preparation and education are related to missionary effectiveness, defined as activities that are closely associated with the Great Commission (Matt 28:18–20).

Participants

For this study, the authors contacted their personal network of leaders within evangelical mission organizations, including WorldVenture, Wycliffe Bible Translators, YWAM, Frontier Ventures, IMB, Cru, and Christar. These leaders were asked to distribute an anonymous survey to members, focusing on those who had an overseas ministry. During the fall of 2022, 198 responses, all of which were usable, were collected. Table 1 presents the demographics of the participants.

Table 1. Demographics of the Participants

Characteristic	Value
Average length of ministry in country of service	16.5 years
Average age	50.6 years
Fraction female	39%
Ethnicity	
Asian or Pacific Islander	11%
Latino or Hispanic	2%
White	88%
Native American/First Nation	3%
Black	0%

Note. N = 198. Participants were allowed to choose more than one ethnicity.

Measures

Participants were asked a series of questions about their educational background, various activities associated with the Great Commission, and the nature of their ministry.

Educational background. Participants responded to a series of questions about the undergraduate school(s) that they attended, the first school from which they received a bachelor's degree (if they had graduated), and their graduate education. Missionaries most often attended (and usually graduated) from an evangelical university. The majority of missionaries had at least one master's degree. A summary of their educational background is found in Table 2.

Table 2. Educational Background

Characteristic	Value
Undergraduate Education	
Undergraduate school(s) attended	
Public	43%
Private (secular)	10%
Private (evangelical)	57%
Private (other Christian)	4%
Attended only secular undergraduate school(s)	38%
Attended only Christian undergraduate school(s)	46%
Undergraduate school where degree granted	
Public	33%
Private (secular)	9%
Private (evangelical)	51%
Private (other Christian)	2%
Total graduated with a bachelor's degree	95%
Graduate Education	
Any seminary degree	49%
MDiv degree	18%
ThM degree	7%
Any master's degree	54%
Non-PhD doctorate (DMin, DEd, MD, etc.)	10%
PhD	5%
Any doctorate	13%
Overall Education	
Average total number of degrees (bachelor's and above)	1.78
Fraction of participants having any degree in the sciences	32%

Note. N = 198.

Data was also collected about the missions classes that the participants have taken and their education since entering into missionary service. This section included questions about the subject of their missions classes, cross-cultural internships, language school, percentage of missions classes taken online (or by distance education), and percentage of missions courses taken since arriving on their foreign field of service. This data is summarized in Table 3.

Table 3. Missions Courses and Education on Foreign Field of Service

Characteristic	Value
Mission Courses	
Average number of mission courses	
All types of missions courses (total)	6.02
Contextualization courses	1.58
Evangelism and church-planting courses	1.58
Language and cross-cultural courses	1.67
Participation in a cross-cultural internship	31%
Fraction of missions courses taken online	18%
Fraction of missions courses taken since arriving on field	24%
Language Study	
Fraction having at least started language school	70%
Fraction having completed language school	65%
Fraction not needing language school	27%
Fraction who learned a new language but training was not available	6%

Note: $N = 198$.

Type of ministry. One item in the survey asked participants to indicate the primary nature of their ministry. Their responses were classified into one of five categories: evangelism and church planting, administration, service, leadership development, theological education, or other. The last category included missionaries who indicated that they were on home assignment and not currently involved in their main ministry. Details are provided in Table 4. This question was not included in the first version of the survey, but it was added once its absence was noticed, yielding data from 150 participants.

Table 4. Types of Ministry

Type of Ministry	Examples	Distribution
Evangelism and Church Planting	Evangelism	32%
	Church planting	
Administration	Organizational leadership	24%
	Mobilization	
	Member care	
	Administration	
	Fundraising	
	Short-term missions coordination	
Service	Medical ministry	23%
	Relief and aid	
	Community development	
	Bible translation	
	Teaching English	
	Ministry to children or teens	
	Media	
	Christian camps	
Leadership Development	Leadership development	7%
Theological Education	Theological education	10%
Other	Language school	4%
	Retired educator	
	Business as mission	
	Home assignment	

Note. N = 150.

Great Commission activities. To measure a missionary's contribution to fulfilling the Great Commission, a missionary effectiveness scale was developed. Such a measure is undoubtedly imperfect, only partially measuring the work missionaries do to contribute to fulfilling the Great Commission. Based on the verbs in Matthew 28:19–20 (and assuming that as missionaries, all had accomplished the "go" of the Great Commission), this scale asked how many times the participant shared the gospel, baptized a person, had been involved in organizing a baptism (an activity somewhat broader than baptizing a person but still necessary for the baptism to occur), taught the Bible, taught others how to evangelize, trained others to study the Bible, and trained others to teach the Bible. For each Great Commission activity, the frequency was measured for three types of audiences: individuals, small groups, and large groups.

The prompt for the items measuring Great Commission activities was "Please indicate how true the following statements are for your ministry. Some or all of the following may not be relevant to your ministry. In that case, simply choose 'Not true' for these items." In the section labeled "Sharing the Gospel," the first statement was "I have shared the gospel with an individual (one-on-one) in the last month." The second statement was "I have shared the gospel with a small group of non-Christians in the last month." A third statement asked about sharing with a large group. The choices for the responses included Not true (= 1), Unsure (= 2), Definitely true, once (= 3), Definitely true, 2 or 3 times (= 4), and Definitely true, 4 or more times (= 5). Similar sections were labeled "Baptisms," "Teaching the Bible and Evangelism Training," and "Training Ministries." The choice "Unsure" was included because many activities associated with the Great Commission are not binary in nature (e.g., sharing the gospel). For example, sometimes we might share a bit of the gospel but not enough for the person to decide if they want to follow Christ or not. Certainly, this contributes more to the Great Commission than not sharing any of the gospel. But it also likely contributes less than a complete gospel presentation.

Participants were asked to report their Great Commission activities during the last month for several reasons. First, by October of 2022, when we started collecting data, most of the pandemic restrictions around the world (with China as a notable exception) had been lifted for over a month; asking for descriptions of missionary activity over a longer period would have covered atypical periods of restriction. Second, accuracy in describing one's activities over the past month is more accurate than descriptions over longer periods. Third, the law of large numbers (Hsu and Robbins 1947) states that a large sample size will produce an accurate average of whatever we are measuring, even when using a relatively narrow slice of time.

In total, participants responded to twenty-one items concerning their Great Commission activities. The average score over twenty-one items was

1.72. Scores were computed for various dimensions as shown in Table 5 by averaging the responses to the questions relevant to that dimension. Evangelism and teaching the Bible were the two most common activities done by missionaries. Baptism activities (baptizing and organizing baptisms) were the least common, followed by training people how to teach the Bible. Missionaries minister to individuals and small groups more frequently than they do to large groups.

Table 5. Descriptive Statistics of Great Commission Activities

Great Commission Activity	Number of Items	Mean	Standard Deviation	Range	Coefficient of Reliability
Category					
Evangelism	3	2.16	1.04	1.00–5.00	.69
Baptism	6	1.10	0.30	1.00–3.00	.75
Total Teaching	6	1.92	0.64	1.00–4.00	.82
Teaching Bible	3	2.73	1.17	1.00–5.00	.67
Teaching Evangelism	3	1.60	0.96	1.00–5.00	.82
Total Training	6	1.66	1.01	1.00–4.00	.91
Training in Bible Study	3	1.86	1.16	1.00–5.00	.82
Training in Bible Teaching	3	1.47	0.98	1.00–5.00	.91
Target Audience					
Individuals	7	1.80	0.78	1.00–4.00	.81
Small Groups	7	1.83	0.74	1.00–4.00	.77
Large Groups	7	1.52	0.48	1.00–3.86	.77
Total Great Commission Activities	21	1.72	0.65	1.00–2.95	.90

Note. N = 198.

Several other observations can be made from Table 5. In addition to being the least common Great Commission activities, baptizing and organizing baptisms had the narrowest range of responses. No missionaries reported baptizing a large group or helping to organize a baptism for a large group. This lack of baptismal activity challenges some dramatic claims about mass conversions being the norm in many mission fields. None of the missionaries in this study seemed to be working with churches where this was happening, or at least they were not providing leadership concerning baptisms. In fact, only 4.5 percent of the missionaries in this study reported baptizing an individual or a small group of believers, and 13 percent participated in organizing a baptism for individuals or a small group of believers.

The coefficients of reliability are reported in Table 5. These describe the degree to which the set of survey items measures a single phenomenon by combining the scores (Cronbach 1951). Values greater than .70 are satisfactory and greater than .80 are considered good indicators that a single phenomenon is being measured (Nunnally and Bernstein 1994). As could be expected, the coefficient of reliability for baptism is low since no large group baptisms were recorded and appear to be rare. Moreover, evangelism (three items) and teaching the Bible (three items) also had low coefficients of reliability. This most likely indicates that sharing the gospel with individuals, small groups, and large groups requires different skill sets and that people who do much of one type do not correspondingly do as much of the other types. The same is true for teaching the Bible. The activities with low coefficients of reliability can be understood as being indices, combining different activities rather than scales measuring an activity common to all of its items.

Results and Discussion

To better understand how education is related to Great Commission activities, Pearson correlation coefficients (*rs*) were calculated to show the degree to which each variable was related to the others. The Pearson correlation coefficient (*r*) can vary from -1 to 1. The greater the absolute value, the stronger the relationship between the two variables. A positive *r* indicates that as one variable goes up, the other variable goes up as well. For example, if missionary education is positively correlated with Great Commission activities (as it generally is; see below), this means that missionaries with higher levels of education perform more Great Commission activities than missionaries with lower levels of education. A negative *r* indicates that as one variable goes up, the other goes down.

In the discussion that follows, statistically significant correlations between education and Great Commission variables will be noted and analyzed. Those that are significant at $p < .05$ are marked *, $p < .01$ are marked **, and $p < .001$ are marked ***. A *p*-value, such as $p < .05$, means that the correlation measured in the sample collected from missionaries in this study is so strong that there is less than a 5 percent chance of getting this value if a correlation in the observed direction did not exist in the broader community of North American missionaries, assuming that the missionaries who participated in this study are representative of North American missionaries.

Since this was an exploratory study, all p values in this study are two-tailed. This means that, since we did not know before this study if missionary education was going to be positively or negatively related to Great Commission activities, we tested the relationships in both the positive and negative direction to make sure we did not miss any.

An r can also be used to indicate the difference between two groups concerning the outcome variable that we are interested in (by treating the grouping variable as dichotomous with values of 0 and 1). For example, missionaries who have an MDiv degree perform significantly more Great Commission activities than those who do not have an MDiv, $r = .20^{**}$ (see details below). By using r to measure the effect size, direct comparisons can be made between relationships between continuous variables and differences between groups (Rosenthal, Rosnow, and Rubin 2000).

In a cross-sectional correlational study such as this, causation cannot be demonstrated but only association. For example, to demonstrate that mission education causes missionaries to perform more Great Commission activities, we would need to do a true experiment, with random assignment to the conditions. We could randomly choose some missionaries to receive a year of graduate education in missiology and afterward measure whether their Great Commission activities changed, both relative to before the training and to missionaries who did not do an additional year of graduate education. However, such a study is not feasible. A correlational study such as this one simply indicates that two phenomena are associated, for example, missions education and Great Commission activities. We cannot determine the direction of causation. Perhaps education causes people to share the gospel more. Perhaps sharing the gospel more makes people want to get more education. Perhaps a passion for evangelism causes people both to share the gospel and to get more education. It is possible, and perhaps even likely, that causation, to some degree, happens in multiple directions.

The following are some of the most important relationships discovered in this study, all of which are consistent with the idea that the more education missionaries have, especially theological education, the more Great Commission activities they perform.

What Type of Undergraduate Education Best Predicts Great Commission Activities?

We asked several questions about what type of undergraduate universities (including colleges) the participating missionaries attended (a state school, a private secular school, a private evangelical Christian school, or a private non-evangelical Christian school). Missionaries who attended an evangelical Christian university for at least part of their undergraduate education perform more Great Commission activities than those who did not attend one, $r = .19^{**}$. Those who attended only secular universities performed the least, $r = -.23^{**}$.

Similarly, we asked about the undergraduate university from which the mission workers graduated. Those who graduated from a private, evangelical university performed the most Great Commission activities, $r = .17^{**}$, while those who graduated from a public university performed the fewest, $r = -.17^{**}$.

These results point to the importance of an evangelical Christian undergraduate education. The most productive missionaries, in terms of Great Commission activities, tend to have attended and graduated from such schools. A possible reason for this phenomenon may be that evangelical universities instill the values and provide training experiences that contribute to effective Great Commission activities, as well as provide knowledge that is useful for fruitful ministry. It is also possible that students who are the most interested in the Great Commission tend to choose to attend evangelical universities. Additional studies should be conducted to better understand this relationship.

Is Graduate Education Associated with More Great Commission Activities?

Several items in the survey collected information concerning the participants' graduate education, including whether they had a seminary degree and the names of their degrees. Variables calculated included the total number of degrees earned beyond the bachelor's degree and whether the participant had specific degrees (MDiv, ThM, PhD, or non-PhD doctorate). The best predictor of Great Commission activities was the total number of degrees held by the participant, $r = .25^{***}$. Of all the educational, demographic, and ministry-related variables measured in this study, no other variable had a stronger relationship with Great Commission activities. A possible reason for this is that additional graduate education provides the knowledge, skills, and attitudes necessary to maximize opportunities for sharing the gospel, helping people become disciples of Jesus, teaching them the Bible, and training them to do the same with others. However, it is also possible that the personal characteristics needed to complete graduate education are also the personal characteristics needed for effective, long-term missionary service (e.g., perseverance and intelligence).

The MDiv is the specific degree that best predicts Great Commission activities, $r = .20**$. However, having any seminary degree (vs. not having a seminary degree) was also a good predictor of Great Commission activities, $r = .19**$. The ThM, PhD, and any other non-PhD doctorate (e.g., DMin or EdD) were also good predictors of Great Commission activities, each with $r = .15*$. This again suggests that graduate education makes a valuable contribution to a missionary's ability to contribute to fulfilling the Great Commission. The MDiv degree may be the most important because it is a long degree (two or more years of full-time study) that covers more ministry-related content than other seminary degrees. As a professional degree, it focuses on developing not only the knowledge necessary for full-time Christian service but also the skills and habits needed to be an effective minister of the gospel.

Are Missions Courses and Cross-Cultural Internships Associated with Great Commission Activities?

Participants indicated the total number of mission courses they had taken, specifically, the number of courses in contextualization, language and cross-cultural ministry, and evangelism and church planting. They also indicated whether they had participated in a cross-cultural internship. The total number of missions courses was positively correlated with their Great Commission activities, $r = .15*$. The number of contextualization courses and the number of language and cross-cultural ministry courses were positively and weakly associated with Great Commission activities, but the correlation was not significant. Only the number of evangelism and church planting courses was significantly related to Great Commission activities, $r = .23***$. It is possible that evangelism and church-planting courses focus more on learning skills, strategies, and models that can be used directly in Great Commission activities, whereas contextualization, language, and cross-cultural ministry courses may be more theoretical and less practical.

Missionaries who had participated in cross-cultural internships also participated in more Great Commission activities, $r = .14*$. It is possible that a cross-cultural internship during their seminary years provided the context necessary to make their mission courses more relevant, motivating them to exert additional effort to master the material and link it to their cross-cultural experiences.

Are Online Mission Courses and Mission Courses Taken after Arriving on the Field Effective?

Participants provided information about the percentage of their mission courses that they had taken online and the percentage that they had taken since arriving on their field of service. As mentioned above, the total number of mission courses taken was one of the best predictors of Great Commission activities. Online courses were just as effective as traditional on-the-ground courses; there was no significant difference between them in terms of being associated with more frequent Great Commission activities.

Similarly, there was no difference between courses that were part of one's education before going overseas and the courses taken since arriving on the field. All were equally associated with an increase in Great Commission activities.

Because online courses are logistically simpler and less expensive than on-the-ground courses, these results indicate that mission organizations should not shy away from, and perhaps even promote, online theological education, both pre-field and on-the-field.

Are Language School–Related Variables Associated with Great Commission Activities?

Several variables related to language learning were measured, including the number of months spent in language school. However, no significant correlation with Great Commission activities was found. The frequency of Great Commission activities did not depend on the time spent in language school. In addition, no differences in Great Commission activities were found between missionaries in an English-speaking setting compared to those in a foreign language ministry setting. Similarly, there were no differences found in native English speakers (vs. non-native English speakers), those currently enrolled in language school (vs. those who have finished language school), those who needed language school (vs. those who did not need language school), and, among those who needed to learn a new language, those who went to language school (vs. those who were not able to).

In summary, no variable associated with language learning was correlated with Great Commission behaviors. This contrasts with other forms of education (specifically attending a Christian undergraduate university, graduating from seminary, the number of graduate degrees, and the number of missions courses taken), which were clearly associated with more Great Commission activities. The reason for this is not clear. It is possible that language courses have less of an influence on the attitudes, values, and beliefs that influence missionary behavior than theological and ministry-focused courses.

What Ministries Are Associated with More Great Commission Activities?

Although not a measure of missionary education, the participants provided information about their ministries, which were classified into several groups (see Table 4). Only the missionaries involved in evangelism and church planting (compared to missionaries not involved in evangelism and church planting) performed more Great Commission activities, $r = .28***$. Two groups (compared to those not in each of those groups) participated in fewer Great Commission activities: administration, $r = -.19*$, and service (including social services), $r = -.23**$. The missionaries in the other two groups, leadership development and theological education, did not significantly differ from those not in leadership development and those not in theological education, respectively.

In terms of education, missionaries in theological education (compared to those not in theological education) had more degrees, $r = .40***$, while those in evangelism and church planting, $r = -.18*$, and in service, $r = -.20*$, had fewer degrees. Those in evangelism and church planting had relatively fewer doctorate degrees. Those in service had relatively few MDivs and doctorate degrees, but they had relatively more "other" seminary degrees (i.e., not an MDiv, ThM, or doctorate). Similarly, missionaries in service ministries had taken significantly fewer mission courses compared to other missionaries, $r = -.29***$. It appears that missionaries' education corresponds to their interests and ministries.

Is Participation in Great Commission Activities Related to Demographics?

This study also measured age, sex, and ethnicity. No relationship was found between age and Great Commission activities; older and younger missionaries were equally active. However, Latinos performed more Great Commission activities than non-Latinos, $r = .17**$. No other relationships between ethnicity and Great Commission activities were found.

Men performed more Great Commission activities than women, $r = .23^{***}$. This relationship was still significant even when controlling for a total number of degrees ($\beta = .17^*$, where β is an effect size that is comparable to r). This may be due, in part, to the fact that women in this study held fewer degrees, on average, than men, but other factors may include women's child-rearing responsibilities.

In terms of education, age and total number of degrees were correlated, $r = .28^{***}$, perhaps because many graduate degrees are earned after on-field ministry has begun, enabling older missionaries to have earned more degrees than the younger ones. Males (compared to females) had more degrees, $r = .27^{***}$, as did Whites (compared to non-Whites), $r = .17^{**}$.

In terms of ministry type, Latinos (none of whom were serving in their country of origin) were more involved in evangelism and church-planting ministries compared to other ethnicities, $r = .16^*$. When controlling for the total number of degrees, Latino ethnicity was an even stronger predictor ($\beta = .17^*$) of being a church planter. This perhaps indicates a cultural preference for church planting that is not strongly related to education. There were no other significant differences in ministry related to ethnicity.

Conclusion

This study examined the relationship between education and missionary involvement in Great Commission activities. In general, evangelical undergraduate education and seminary training were good predictors of increased participation in evangelism, church planting, baptizing, leading Bible studies, teaching others to share their faith, and training others to study and teach the Bible. The number of missions courses that missionaries had taken, especially evangelism and church-planting courses, was also a good predictor of increased participation in Great Commission activities. Those with ministries in North American Christian universities and seminaries can rest assured that their ministry of training future overseas missionaries is bearing fruit and is contributing to the accomplishment of the Great Commission.

Acknowledgment

The authors thank Greg Parsons of Frontier Ventures for his contacts in distributing the survey for this study.

References

Chambers, Carl. 2019. Review of *Pitfalls of Trained Incapacity: The Unintended Effects of Integral Missionary Training in the Basel Mission on Its Early Work in Ghana (1828-1840)*, by Birgit Herppich. *Churchman* 133, no. 3: 274–76.

Cheng, Maynor Clara. 2001. "Integrating Inner-Healing into Missions Education." *Mission Studies* 18, no. 2: 126–45.

Cronbach, Lee J. 1951. "Coefficient Alpha and the Internal Structure of Tests." *Psychometrika* 16, no. 3: 297–334.

Dunaetz, David R. 2018. "Cognitive Science and Theological Education in Technologically Developing Countries." *International Journal of Frontier Missiology* 35, no. 3: 135–43.

Grant, A. E. 1999. "Theological Education in India: Leadership Development for the Indian or Western Church?" Unpublished doctoral dissertation, Biola University.

Henderson, Alan. 1993. "A Historical Review of Missions and Missionary Training in the Churches of Christ." *Restoration Quarterly* 35, no. 4: 203–17.

Hibbert, Evelyn, and Richard Hibbert. 2016. *Training Missionaries: Principles and Possibilities*. Pasadena, CA: William Carey Library.

Holmes, Brian, ed. 1967. *Educational Policy and the Mission Schools: Case Studies from the British Empire*. London: Routledge & Kegan Paul.

Hsu, P. L., and Herbert Robbins. 1947. "Complete Convergence and the Law of Large Numbers." *Proceedings of the National Academy of Sciences* 33, no. 2: 25–31.

Kim, S. Y. 2004. "Theological Education among Dominican Republic Pastors in Corona, New York: A Study of Motivational Factors and Barriers That Influence Their Participation." Unpublished doctoral dissertation, Biola University.

Lee, David Tai-Woong. 2008. "Training Cross-Cultural Missionaries from the Asian Context: Lessons Learned from the Global Missionary Training Center." *Missiology* 36, no. 1: 111–30.

Lee, Paul Sung-Ro. 2019. "Impact of Missionary Training on Intercultural Readiness." *Mission Studies* 36, no. 2: 247–61.

Lin, Arthur. 2023. "The Role of Theological Institutions in Missionary Training." *Journal of the Evangelical Missiological Society* 3, no. 1: 128–43.

Ma, Julie C. 2014. "The Significant Role of the Asia Pacific Theological Seminary and Missionary Training Institute for Equipping the Asian Church for Missions." *Asian Journal of Pentecostal Studies* 17, no. 1: 55–72.

Moreau, Scott. 2008. "Bibliography for Missionary Training." *Missiology* 36, no. 1: 131.

Nehrbass, Kenneth. 2016. "Does Missiology Have Three Legs to Stand On? The Upsurge of Interdisciplinarity." *Missiology* 44, no. 1: 50–65.

Nehrbass, Kenneth. 2020. "Reflecting to Improve Practice: The Long-Term Impact of Missiological Doctoral Programs at Protestant Graduate Schools." Unpublished master's thesis, Biola University.

Nehrbass, Kenneth. 2021. *Advanced Missiology: How to Study Missions in Credible and Useful Ways.* Eugene, OR: Cascade.

Newell, Peggy E., ed. 2017. *North American Mission Handbook: US and Canadian Protestant Ministries Overseas 2017–2019.* 22nd ed. Pasadena, CA: William Carey Library.

Nunnally, Jum C., and Ira H. Bernstein. 1994. *Psychometric Theory.* 3rd ed. New York: McGraw-Hill.

Plueddemann, James E. 2018. *Teaching across Cultures: Contextualizing Education for Global Mission.* Downers Grove, IL: InterVarsity Press.

Rosenthal, Robert, Ralph L. Rosnow, and Donald B. Rubin. 2000. *Contrasts and Effect Sizes in Behavioral Research: A Correlational Approach.* New York: Cambridge University Press.

Seton, Rosemary. 2013. *Western Daughters in Eastern Lands: British Missionary Women in Asia.* Santa Barbara, CA: Praeger.

Weddell, Sue. 1944. "Missionary Training in North America." *International Review of Mission* 33, no. 4: 368–75.

Yeh, Allen. 2016. *Polycentric Missiology: Twenty-First Century Mission from Everyone to Everywhere.* Downers Grove, IL: IVP Academic.

Chapter 4

Future Missionary Training
In Light of Current Developments and Challenges

Craig Ott and Minwoo Heo

The world has been experiencing dramatic and accelerating change in recent years due to the global pandemic, rising inflation, soaring university tuition, worsening mental health issues, increasing xenophobia and nationalism, enhanced AI technology, and international crises. What does this mean for the future of missionary training? These events put enormous pressure on international mission work and demand that mission training adapts to the new global realities. Missionary mobilizers and trainers cannot continue with "business as usual" in light of these present and emerging challenges. This project seeks to identify these issues so that mission leaders and agencies can adequately prepare and support cross-cultural workers for today's and tomorrow's world.

Anticipating the turn of the millennium, nearly twenty-five years ago, literature was being produced looking to the future of missionary training (e.g., Woodberry, Van Engen, and Elliston 1996; Elmer and McKinney 1996; Elliston 1999; Ott 1998). But the world has experienced a quantum leap since 2000. Various helpful titles have since appeared related to missionary preparation (e.g., Brynjolfson and Lewis 2006; Hibbert and Hibbert 2016; Wan and Hedinger 2017). These, however, for the most part, address familiar and important topics that have been on the missionary training agenda for decades. But we asked, more specifically, what are the more current and future challenges of which missionary educators may be less aware but should be?

To identify the emerging challenges, we conducted a qualitative, convenience sample survey of thirty mission leaders from five continents, including a mix of academic missiologists, missionary trainers, and mission agency leaders. They were asked to name the five most pressing and emerging issues facing the future of mission training. These findings were compared with global trends and emerging missiological issues. The six most prominent emerging challenges for missionary training were identified. These were then presented at the International Council for Evangelical Theological Education (ICETE) consultation in Izmir, Turkey, in November 2022, where discussion groups with thirty participants were formed to further explore these needs. The findings of the ICETE discussion groups yielded a more complete picture of the challenges and opportunities for future mission training. These findings were further elaborated through a review of the relevant missiological and social science literature. Our aim in this chapter is not to provide practical solutions but rather to identify the emerging challenges as a starting point for collaboratively producing creative solutions that will strengthen mission training.

The six pressing and emerging issues we identified are:

1. Addressing mental health and personal development issues
2. Adapting the training to face the complexity of the modern world
3. Maximizing digital learning and remote ministry possibilities
4. Raising awareness of the need for missionary training
5. Strengthening biblical understanding
6. Developing alternative funding, sending, and support models

We have only identified those training issues related to emerging trends and have not included longstanding and ongoing training needs such as spiritual formation, intercultural competency, and language acquisition skills. Missionary training is understood here to include not only pre-field preparation but also lifelong learning for the ongoing development of cross-cultural missionaries.

Addressing Mental Health and Personal Development Issues

Numerous mission agency leaders and trainers responded that mental health is one of the most serious and fastest-growing issues they are facing among candidates and staff. Those respondents remarked that mental health challenges had been gradually increasing but were aggravated by the global pandemic, the overuse of technology, and social media. One respondent also said, "These days it seems every person is traumatized by something.

I don't want to question the experiences that lead to traumatization, but we need to train Christian workers to overcome these traumatic experiences." Another respondent notified us that "trainers now must be keenly aware of the generational problem of mental health issues among the Millennials and Gen Z and provide adequate care."

A similar concern was reflected in responses in a Missio Nexus survey of 230 mission leaders in which 22 percent see stress and fear as top risk factors for missionaries (Missio Nexus 2022). A 2006 study of missionaries found that 80 percent of missionaries have experienced some form of traumatic stress:

- Forty-five percent were related to failure in personal relationships
- Twenty-eight percent were related to a personal crisis
- Forty-eight percent experienced acute onset (sudden or unexpected)
- Younger missionaries were more vulnerable (Irvine, Armentrout, and Miner 2006)

A 2015 study of 393 career healthcare missionaries found 47.9 percent of female and 42.1 percent of male missionaries experiencing anxiety, and 32.5 percent of female and 27.5 percent of male missionaries experiencing depression (Strand et al. 2015). David Dunaetz (2023) examined the seriousness of mental health issues among Generation Z (those born between 1990 and the early 2010s). He identified the most critical issues as malaise from social media, online game addiction, pornography, and fragility from overprotection. These issues were not experienced at the same level by previous generations. For example, social media particularly affects teenage girls because they are bombarded with unrealistic images of women, which leads to dissatisfaction with their body image and hence reduced self-esteem and self-worth. Male members of Generation Z are affected more by video games and pornography. Dunaetz argues that the pandemic-induced social isolation aggravated the problem of addiction. Fragility from overprotection is another issue due to overly protective parenting techniques that have reduced Generation Z's resilience in navigating challenges and adapting to new situations (see Wallace 2023; LeMoyne and Buchanan 2011). This could impact future missionary attrition.

Mental health concerns are not unique to missionaries or Westerners. According to the World Health Organization, mental health problems have been increasing globally at an alarming rate. For example, there has been a 13 percent rise worldwide in mental health illnesses in the decade ending in 2017. Suicide has become the second leading cause of death among fifteen-to-twenty-nine-year-olds (World Health Organization n.d.). United Nations Sustainable Development Goals (n.d.) also recognized the need to address the growing mental health problem and included it as one of its global project goals. Despite these figures, the global median of government health expenditure allocated to mental health is still less than 2 percent (World Health Organization n.d.). Also, the gap between those who need mental health care and those with access to mental health care is still vast and growing.

Within the growing problem of mental health issues, we identified two sets of emerging needs that missionary trainers must address. First, training should prepare missionaries to monitor and maintain their own mental health. Dunaetz (2023, 59) proposes that mission organizations provide "greater social support and accountability through missionary teams … and provide the appropriate structure for developing a healthy missionary community." Second, missionaries should be equipped to identify mental health issues among those to whom they minister and be able to advise them on where to receive care. Edmund Ng (2023) in an article published by the Lausanne Movement underscores the urgency of mental health literacy for missionaries by examining data on mental health in Southeast Asia, where the challenge is significantly worse than in the rest of the world. For example, according to the World Health Organization's "Mental Health Atlas" (2021a), the number of mental health workers per 100,000 people in Southeast Asia is 2.8 compared to the global median of 13.0 and the European median of 44.8. Southeast Asia, which occupies nearly 25 percent of the world population, accounts for 39 percent of 700,000 suicides globally (World Health Organization 2021b). Ng (2023) asks, "Will the Asian church be missing out on this big window of opportunity to minister to the needs of others? Will we be missing out on bringing the good news to the lost in Asia through this huge avenue of entry?"

Thankfully, some mission trainers have noticed the increasing mental health challenge and have been responding. For example, one trainer said that he would focus on "careful screening for potential psychological issues or the ability to work together effectively with others. This has always been a huge issue, but I think that especially coming out of the trauma of COVID and the many social problems associated with the growing dominance of technology and assorted media in our lives this is significant." Another respondent commented that mission agencies should consider working with professional psychologists in examining and evaluating the mental health conditions of missionaries and candidates because mission trainers are not always equipped with psychological expertise. Another respondent pointed to the brighter side that counseling sessions and regular check-ins have become more accessible and inexpensive due to online technology. Therefore, although mental health has become one of the most serious challenges, mission agencies are not without help or solutions. In *Missionaries, Mental Health, and Accountability* (Bonk et al. 2019), various authors seek to understand mental health illness among Korean missionaries in a comprehensive way with case studies, surveys, and personal reflections, helpfully categorizing types of mental illnesses. They then provided insights into how mission agencies can deal with the issue.

Adapting Training to Face the Complexity of the Modern World

The world is changing faster and becoming more complex than ever before. Multiple factors add to the complexity: globalization, counter-globalization, counter-modernization, technological advancement, environmental issues, demographic changes, increasing political polarization, war, economic inequality, and growth of nationalist and xenophobic movements.

In particular, the growth of nationalist and xenophobic movements demands that mission training quickly adapts to the new emerging global reality. The Pew Research Center (2018) suggests that 83 percent of the world's population now lives in regions with a high or very high level of restrictions on religion. Government restrictions on religion are at the highest levels they have been since 2007. Our interviews and other research suggest that mission leaders are aware of such changes. For example, according to Missio Nexus's (2022) survey of 230 mission leaders, 48 percent viewed security as the largest risk (COVID-19 being the second risk with 23 percent). One respondent told us, "Missionary training should now include data surveillance, tracking, and security, as the digital surveillance of governments can regulate individuals more effectively than before." Another respondent added, "Once authorities find that one person in the field, an entire network is now exposed. Security training needs to be taught sooner than later."

The issue of security risks is only one factor that adds to the complexity of missionary training. Other complex global issues are at hand, such as the increase in human migration and diaspora. Today 281 million people, 3.6 percent of the world population, live outside their country of origin (United Nations Human Rights Office of the High Commissioner n.d.; UNHCR n.d.). One mission leader commented, "People are migrating at an alarming rate globally, and missionaries should be trained to handle the global diaspora issues." Another respondent was concerned with missionaries' simplistic understanding of the complex world: "Missionaries might interpret a complicated national event or political movement from a simplistic and naive point of view without comprehensive training."

How then do these mission leaders assess the current adaptability of mission training to the rapid changes in the world? One group's discussion from the ICETE consultation starkly portrayed the current reality: "Society changes so much faster than we adapt. We do not innovate enough in education. It is easy to stay in what we do. The program of missionary training is the same as it was fifteen years ago—it hasn't changed. Innovation and design are needed. It is disruptive to the norm so there is fear of change." One respondent suggested that mission training must be transformed at a fundamental level, from a simple and traditional one to a comprehensive one so that missionaries and candidates can critically engage with the complexity of the world.

Maximizing Digital Learning and Remote Ministry Possibilities

Although the global pandemic caused immense human suffering, it also brought an unexpected gift: the advancement of remote, online learning and video conferencing technologies. Individuals and organizations were forced to adopt online technology virtually overnight for remote work, classes, meetings, and training. However, online technology offers not only new opportunities but new challenges. Therefore, discerning how best to utilize and hybridize digital training for the maximum outcome has become an emerging issue.

In our interviews, most respondents were positive about adopting digital technology for missionary training. The reasons they gave are as follows: First, digital education makes lifelong learning possible without missionaries leaving the mission field. Second, one respondent said it is now easier "to form online learning communities," which help missionaries be more collaborative and polycentric. Third, another respondent noted, "We no longer have to retain the traditional division between pre-field and on-field training. Both types of mission training can happen simultaneously. Getting pre-field training on-site can be more effective." Another way of describing this is "just in time" training versus "just in case" training, that is to say, training can be delivered close to the time it is needed, not months or years in advance. Another respondent concurred, "I found that many missionaries could not fully understand the pre-field training without prior cross-cultural experience, and they forget what they learned after arriving in the field, especially when they are struggling with cultural stress." Remote digital training can minimize these problems, and learning in the context of application increases relevance and effectiveness. Fourth, after paying the high initial cost and effort of producing the online content, subsequent online training is low cost. However, one respondent cautioned that online content needs to be regularly reviewed and updated to reflect the rapidly changing global reality. Fifth, digital training fits a recent trend expressed by one respondent that "fewer and fewer mission candidates are seeking to be full-time missionaries ... [and they] do not have time to dedicate themselves exclusively to studying or training. For these candidates, digital training can be particularly effective." Another respondent said, "Gen Zs prefer online training over in-person training." Sixth, digital learning is a valuable tool, especially for people who face persecution and cannot meet face-to-face.

However, mission trainers should consider some potentially negative aspects of digital training, such as increased digital distraction, increased screen time, increased isolation and loneliness, and thus increased mental health risk, reduced attention span, and decreased time spent with the local people. Therefore, a great opportunity comes with a potentially great cost. Therefore, discerning what can be done online and what should stay offline has become an essential and emerging task in designing missionary training. A thoughtful integration will maximize remote learning for missionary training.

Raising Awareness of the Need for Missionary Training

Many respondents expressed the need to raise awareness of the necessity of missionary training. They reported that recently it has become increasingly difficult to motivate missionaries and candidates to receive training, especially in the areas of cross-cultural training and language learning. Respondents gave multiple reasons for this. One person said that access to the internet fosters a false sense of overconfidence and naivety that they have become culturally competent and skillful in navigating the challenges of cross-cultural ministry. Another respondent concurred that missionaries are ironically becoming less and less equipped to handle cross-cultural conflicts. Not only is there a need for intercultural competence, but regarding cultural understanding another respondent commented, "This concept of contextualization has been important for a very long time, and I don't see that decreasing." Contextually appropriate ministry requires preparation in both cultural insight and theological competence. This issue seems to be particular to Western-sent missionaries. Ironically, missionaries in many emerging Majority World mission movements have a great desire for more missionary training, which is harder for them to find.

One respondent attributed declining interest in missionary training to people's changed concept of missions from being a calling to a career option. He said, "Nowadays, most missionary candidates do not view missionary careers as long-term commitments but as short-term commitments of five to ten years of service on the field. As a result, they do not see the need for comprehensive or dedicated mission training" (see also Donovan and Myors 1997). Another person in a theological seminary observed a similar pattern: "The formal academic education (MA) focused on the global mission seems less relevant due to the career pattern change." One reason why traditional mission training has decreased is the importance of secular vocational education: "to serve in restricted access countries, secular degrees are more valuable than the missionary courses."

Language acquisition skill is another area that deserves raised awareness. Language learning is difficult and a lifelong process. Missionaries are less motivated to take up the heavy task of learning the local language if they see missionary service as a vocational option that may change after a few years. Furthermore, in many parts of the world, one can get by with English, so the importance of learning the heart language of local people is underestimated. One respondent told us that due to the rising use of English, especially in meetings conducted on Zoom, "American missionaries are less and less inclined to learn other languages." In the words of another respondent, "Ease of travel and communication is causing the language and cultural acquisition to fade in importance." Because we can now "drop in" to global locations and engage in some type of ministry work, or coach remotely via Zoom, many are less inclined to follow Jesus's example and do the hard work of "taking on (human) local skin and moving into the neighborhood (John 1:14)."

The seeming unimportance of language learning is further reinforced through the availability of modern technologies such as AI-generated translation and transcription, Google Translate, Otter, Zoom, and more recently ChatGPT, which have been vastly improving in quality.

Based on our interviews, several respondents suggested helpful ways to motivate candidates to receive training. First, provide a clear vision for the training. The goals of many mission trainings are often vague and therefore do not motivate people to receive training. However, explaining the specific purpose and clear objective of the mission training aligned with the mission organization's vision can better motivate and persuade people to receive mission training. Second, mission training curriculum should be flexible in providing various training platforms, such as in-person as well as remote online training, and fixed classes as well as self-paced learning, to accommodate a wide range of missionaries and candidates.

Strengthening Biblical Understanding

Not a few respondents voiced concern that many missionary candidates today come with weaker biblical-theological foundations than candidates in earlier generations, and many respondents proposed restoring standards of strong biblical and theological preparation. One respondent told us, "Biblical literacy is now a new challenge. We are finding that candidates come to us with less biblical literacy than they have had in the past." Another mission trainer told us that many new Western missionaries do not believe in the infallibility of the Bible. But "they arrive in countries and work among national Christians that still believe in the Bible as it was written and are appalled if they discover that the missionary doesn't."

There are multiple possible reasons for the decrease in biblical and theological knowledge. First, according to one professor in intercultural studies, "Pluralism and universalism lead us to think that mission and mission training are not that necessary because there are many other paths to Jesus apart from Christianity." Second, as previously discussed, many candidates' view of missionary calling has shifted from long term to short term and from general to specialized. Therefore, they tend to prefer getting practical training that helps them to reap results immediately while they are on the field. As a result, the biblical-theological foundation is neglected. Because many are entering missionary service later in life, the prospect of attending seminary or taking time to acquire deeper theological knowledge is too daunting and appears too costly in terms of time and money.

One missionary in the field told us, "We often include evangelism, discipleship, church planting, and other tools within our missionary training, but do we need to increase training in Bible and theology? Yes." Fewer missionaries are doing pioneer evangelism, and more are involved in teaching and leadership development (Esler, Newell, and VanHuis 2017, 58–59). But what will they teach? One respondent said that a strong biblical foundation is paramount because missionaries must think biblically and theologically to be able to address the complexity of contextualization, globalization, new ecclesial forms, and religious pluralism.

Then what do the respondents suggest in terms of the solutions? Interestingly, three people responded that mission training should emphasize the theology of suffering. Also, "missionaries are in pain because they have failed to forgive." Another respondent said that missionaries should contemplate the theology of risk or suffering more thoroughly because it will make them more resilient.

In the end, a strong biblical foundation is the basis of missions. One respondent desperately said, "Get to the roots of why more missionaries from the West have a weak understanding of the Bible. How are they being taught the basics of the gospel, their relationship with Christ, and ministry issues? If they have not been discipled, how do they intend to disciple others?"

Developing Alternative Funding, Sending, and Support Models

Missionary funding has always been one of the most hotly debated issues and, strictly speaking, is not an emerging trend or challenge. Still, many respondents informed us that funding has resurfaced as one of the critical issues in mission training. Some 40 percent of North American mission executives see innovation in financial models as a priority (Newell 2017, 27). This is because of recent changes such as global economic challenges, a dramatic rise in inflation, automation-led job displacement, fluctuating exchange rates, the volatility of the job market, and generational changes. The cost of sending a missionary has increased, and the length of time needed to raise individual support is typically eighteen months or more. To this can be added the increasing burden of student debt among potential missionary candidates. One leader in a mission organization told us that steeply rising university tuition and student loans put a heavy financial burden on students after graduation. "They are understandably concerned about how to pay these off," making it increasingly challenging to consider additional mission training after graduating from university.

Furthermore, the new generation is largely unfamiliar with the traditional way of raising money, such as raising pledges from friends, family, and churches. One mission trainer told us, "Many of my students are very uncomfortable with existing support models." Another respondent similarly testified, "Students are unfamiliar with and uncomfortable with the traditional method of raising money." Although some denominations and agencies still have centralized pools of mission funding, some of these have had to move to the more common individual support system whereby a missionary candidate must find individuals or churches that will pledge individual financial support. Potential missionaries find this approach not only strange but also off-putting.

As a solution, one respondent mentioned that mission training should introduce step-by-step training as to how to raise funds. He stated that the current need is "for 'scaffolding' that helps and supports young people make the eventual move to long-term mission work." He said, "The idea of becoming a long-term missionary feels, for many of the young persons I know, like an overwhelming prospect. Where do they start, and are there organizations that walk alongside them over a period of time to help move in that direction? I know of some, but more is needed."

The funding challenge is particularly acute for emerging Majority World missionary sending. This was highlighted in a recent article in *Lausanne Global Analysis* in which Krist Rievan describes the limitations of the individual support approach so common in Western missionary sending. However, he presses further, "I propose that financial sustainability for international mission organisations involves more than just changing the individual support system. Changes are needed in *thinking, structures, and practices*" (Rievan 2023).

What alternative funding models do we have? Many respondents mentioned business as mission (BAM) and tentmaking as sustainable alternative solutions for raising mission funds. This is an especially compelling model for younger missionaries. According to the *North American Mission Handbook* (Newell 2017, 51), the number of BAM/tentmaking missionaries has increased from 1,476 in 1996 to 4,137 in 2016. However, this approach comes with both great opportunities and great challenges. BAM and tentmaking missionaries can build relationships and share the gospel with the local people in an authentic, natural, and relevant way within the context of their work. Also, the work can provide sustainable funding in the long term without having to rely on external support. BAM workers can create job opportunities and support the local economy, which is an effective way to do a holistic mission.

However, the respondents also cautioned us about the real challenges of BAM and tentmaking that they have observed. Maintaining a healthy balance between the demands of work and ministry proves to be extremely difficult. Since missionaries are to divide their attention, they are likely to be more ineffective in both fields than those who focus on only one. Especially challenging are cultural differences and thorny ethical dilemmas, such as labor laws, bribery, and environmental sustainability. To this can be added the fact that most missionaries are not skilled businesspeople who know how to run a profit-making business in their own culture, much less in a foreign culture. For the funding of Majority World missions, Rievan (2023) recommends the localization of mission leadership and training organizational leaders. More specifically, he suggests alternatives such as project-oriented fundraising that would include support of staff, better church engagement, monetizing assets (such as renting property), allowing staff to earn supplemental income, and entrepreneurial innovation. Some organizations have created local profit-making agricultural or commercial businesses that become sources of mission funding. Such efforts are, however, vulnerable to market forces and in worst-case scenarios can drain funds to avoid bankruptcy. In 2023 Tim Welch published *New Funding Models for Global Mission: Learning from the Majority World* in which he reassesses the pros and cons of traditional missionary funding. He suggests adding innovative ways that are more suitable for the younger generation, such as crowdfunding and endowment funds. Welch encourages others to also look for innovative ways because the economy constantly changes.

As we can see, securing mission funding has once again resurfaced as an emerging issue because of the changing global realities and generational differences. Mission agencies and training programs should provide step-by-step instructions and guidance on fundraising approaches with which younger candidates are more familiar and comfortable.

How Should Mission Training Change?

So how should future missionary training change in light of all these challenges? Some specific possibilities have already been described. More generally, almost all respondents welcomed changes in current missionary training practices. Their responses can be summarized in three points.

Understand Missionary Training as a Lifelong Process

First, mission training should go beyond pre-field training and be reshaped to become a lifelong learning process. One missiologist explains, "Because the mission fields are becoming increasingly complicated, missionaries should form the habit and culture of lifelong learning. Missionaries should not assume they have learned everything they need to know once their pre-field training is finished." The lifelong learning process is not without difficulty, as we previously discussed, but it is not impossible, especially considering the new possibilities of online and remote learning as a supplement to in-person training. Mission agencies now must think deeply about how to promote lifelong learning more intentionally as part of a comprehensive training program.

Reconceive Missionary Training as Dynamic and Comprehensive

Second, missionary training can no longer remain simple and traditional but must be dynamic and comprehensive. We have long recognized the importance of missionary preparation that addresses the classic three dimensions of head (knowledge), heart (character), and hand (skills). However, not only does the content of training need to address the challenges identified in this study but also the forms of delivery and pedagogy of missionary training must be updated. In their book *Relational*

Missionary Training (2017), Enoch Wan and Mark Hedinger offer just one example of a fresh, more holistic approach to missionary training.

Of course, no training program can address every potential challenge, reach the depth of formal theological education, or unravel the complexities of ministry in the modern world. Nevertheless, missionary training must model the integration of theological understanding and cultural insight. More important than offering answers and ministry methods is providing missionaries with the tools for *how* to find answers and develop methods, *how* to understand the complexity of their world, *how* to maintain personal health, *how* to solve problems, and *how* to develop contextually appropriate strategies.

One respondent proposed a partnership between seminaries and mission agencies for missionary training, saying, "Is it possible to integrate them? Should seminaries and mission organizations collaborate to train missionaries? Actually, there are already some seminaries that partner with other mission agencies to make the cross-cultural internship more meaningfully integrating knowledge and practice. They require a one-year cross-cultural internship under the supervision of a mission agency and, during that year, some online or intensive courses with school faculty for reflection and deeper application."

Introduce Changes in Missionary Training but Do So with Care

Third, changes in missionary training should take place with wisdom and care. A leader of a mission agency said innovation in mission training should be introduced in a "winsome" and "nonthreatening" way because these changes "will bring risk to traditional agencies." Mission agencies tend to be traditional and resistant to change. Senior missionaries, who are often responsible for training, can be tempted to idealize the "good old days" of mission life and the rigor of earlier missionary training programs. Innovation may be seen as compromise and the younger generation can be viewed negatively. Such attitudes will not serve the next generation of missionaries well. Training programs must adapt to the current realities of the modern world and of the younger generation. But such change needs to be introduced in a manner that is neither haphazard, just for the sake of change, nor disrespectful of generations past. Make wisdom and innovation partners, not enemies.

Conclusion

The sad reality is that much mission training has not kept up with the changes of modern society and has remained stagnant. However, to train faithful workers of the gospel we must actively identify emerging challenges and turn them into opportunities. This chapter has aimed to raise that awareness and offer a starting point for mission agencies and trainers to renew their training programs. While some aspects of this study appear specific to Western missionary training, it would be a mistake to think that non-Western missionaries are not facing the same challenges. Six emerging issues were identified based on the input of mission leaders from around the world and the findings of current research. Our hope is that mission trainers and leaders everywhere will be stimulated to develop more effective and relevant training so that missionaries will be better prepared to participate in God's mission.

References

Bonk, Jonathan J., J. Nelson Jennings, Jinbong Kim, and Jae Hoon Lee, eds. 2019. *Missionaries, Mental Health, and Accountability: Support Systems in Churches and Agencies*. Littleton, CO: William Carey Publishing.

Brynjolfson, Robert, and Jonathan Lewis, eds. 2006. *Integral Ministry Training: Design and Evaluation*. Pasadena, CA: William Carey Library.

Donovan, Kath, and Ruth Myors. 1997. "Reflections on Attrition in Career Missionaries: A Generational Perspective into the Future." In *Too Valuable to Lose: Exploring the Causes and Cures of Missionary Attrition*, ed. William D. Taylor, 41–73. Pasadena, CA: William Carey Library.

Dunaetz, David R. 2023. "The Struggles of Generation Z and the Future of North American Mission Organizations." *Global Missiology* 20, no. 1: 53–63.

Elliston, Edgar J., ed. 1999. *Teaching Them Obedience in All Things: Equipping for the 21st Century*. Pasadena, CA: William Carey Library.

Elmer, Duane, and Lois McKinney, eds. 1996. *With an Eye on the Future: Development and Mission in the 21st Century*. Monrovia, CA: MARC.

Esler, J. Ted, Marvi J. Newell, and Michael VanHuis. 2017. "Mission Handbook Survey: Perspective and Dynamics." In *North American Mission Handbook: US and Canadian Protestant Ministries Overseas 2017–2019*, edited by Peggy E. Newell, 43–93. 22nd ed. Pasadena, CA: William Carey Library.

Hibbert, Evelyn, and Richard Hibbert. 2016. *Training Missionaries: Principles and Possibilities*. Pasadena, CA: William Carey Library.

Irvine, Julie, David P. Armentrout, and Linda A. Miner. 2006. "Traumatic Stress in a Missionary Population: Dimensions and Impact." *Journal of Psychology and Theology* 34, no. 4 (October): 327–36.

LeMoyne, Terri, and Tom Buchanan. 2011. "Does 'Hovering' Matter? Helicopter Parenting and Its Effect on Well-being." *Sociological Spectrum* 31, no. 4: 399–418.

Missio Nexus. 2022. "Global Missions and Risk." Accessed March 22, 2023. https://missionexus.org/global-missions-and-risk/.

Newell, Peggy E. 2017. "Mission CEO Survey Summary." In *North American Mission Handbook: US and Canadian Protestant Ministries Overseas 2017–2019*, edited by Peggy E. Newell, 19–29. 22nd ed. Pasadena, CA: William Carey Library.

Ng, Edmund. 2023. "Mental Health Literacy as a Ministry Skill: Basic Ways to Equip Church Leaders in Asia and Beyond." *Lausanne Movement* (blog). January 24, 2023. https://lausanne.org/about/blog/mental-health-literacy-as-a-ministry-skill.

Ott, Craig. 1998. "Die Ausbildung von Missionaren für das 21. Jahrhundert" [The Education of Missionaries for the 21st Century]. In *Theologie, Mission, Verkündigung: Festschrift zum 60. Geburtstag von Helmuth Egelkraut*, edited by Jürgen Steinbach and Klaus W. Müller, 75–83. Bonn: Verlag für Kultur und Wissenschaft.

Pew Research Center. 2018. "Global Uptick in Government Restrictions on Religion in 2016." June 21, 2018. https://www.pewresearch.org/religion/2018/06/21/global-uptick-in-government-restrictions-on-religion-in-2016/.

Rievan, Kirst. 2023. "Beyond Self-Support: Fundraising for Missions: Thinking, Structures, and Practices for Majority World Missionaries." *Lausanne Global Analysis* 12, no. 5 (September). https://lausanne.org/content/lga/2023-09/beyond-self-support-fundraising-for-missions?utm_source=Lausanne+Movement+List&utm_campaign=7e4a7208ad-Lausanne_Global_Analysis-Sept2023&utm_medium=email&utm_term=0_602c1cb67d-7e4a7208ad-91687201.

Strand, Mark A., Alice Chen, Jarrett W. Richardson, and Lauren M. Pinkston. 2015. "Mental Health of Cross-Cultural Healthcare Missionaries." *Journal of Psychology and Theology* 43, no. 4: 283–93.

UNHCR. n.d. "Key Facts and Figures." The UN Refugee Agency. Accessed January 7, 2024. https://www.unhcr.org/us/?gclid=Cj0KCQjwjt-oBhDKARIsABVRB0yOBytqOP8ObDN9O-hZSTqs3T5VJ9zAcdo7TH2dr7iIR8qm2Isw-hYaAvIvEALw_wcB.

United Nations Human Rights Office of the High Commissioner. n.d. "OHCHR and Migration." United Nations. Accessed January 7, 2024. https://www.ohchr.org/en/migration?gclid=Cj0KCQjwjt-oBhDKARIsABVRB0wjMq-3eaZzYiTRCsD4yA_1_u65YY5F2rSsVhyOpEyvnJOghtfe2moaAhfiEALw_wcB.

United Nations Sustainable Development Goals. n.d. "Good Health and Well-Being." United Nations. Accessed October 2, 2023. https://www.un.org/sustainabledevelopment/health/.

Wallace, Stephen Gray. 2023. "Young People Navigating the American Mental Health Landscape." *Psychology Today* (blog). February 2, 2023. https://www.psychologytoday.com/intl/blog/decisions-teens-make/202302/young-people-navigating-the-american-mental-health-landscape.

Wan, Enoch, and Mark Hedinger. 2017. *Relational Missionary Training: Theology, Theory and Practice.* Skyforest: Urban Loft.

Welch, Tim. 2023. *New Funding Models for Global Mission: Learning from the Majority World.* Littleton, CO: William Carey Publishing.

Woodberry, J. Dudley, Charles Van Engen, and Edgar J. Elliston, eds. 1996. *Missiological Education for the 21st Century: The Book, the Circle, and the Sandals.* American Society of Missiology 23. Maryknoll, NY: Orbis Books.

World Health Organization. n.d. "Mental Health." World Health Organization. Accessed October 2, 2023. https://www.who.int/health-topics/mental-health#tab=tab_2.

World Health Organization. 2021a. "Mental Health Atlas 2020." Geneva: World Health Organization. https://www.who.int/publications/i/item/9789240036703.

World Health Organization. 2021b. "Strengthen Mental Health Services: WHO." World Health Organization. October 9, 2021. https://www.who.int/southeastasia/news/detail/09-10-2021-strengthen-mental-health-services-who.

Part
11

Proposals for Educating for Mission

Chapter 5

Allowing a Theology of Mission to Shape Theological Education in the Majority World

Will Brooks

The field of missiology is a broad discipline that includes aspects of biblical studies, theology, history, and cultural anthropology. In some schools, though, it is simply designated as "practical theology" and relegated to strategies for evangelism or church planting. Despite this narrowing of the discipline to solely practical strategies, missiology in fact has much to offer other theological fields of study. As one possible stream of how missiological insight can aid other fields, in this chapter I want to explore how a theology of mission should shape and inform theological education in the Majority World.

The reason it will be helpful to explore this connection is because of a couple of common issues in theological education in the Majority World. The development of more informal training programs for those with low education levels is helpful, but many of those programs simply translate content written in the West with little thought to contextualization. Additionally, they often use a content transfer approach, which gives students little time for internalization of the material. Second, when it comes to formal programs, more missionary theological educators are Western trained in fields like New Testament, Old Testament, and systematic theology. Again, this is helpful in one sense, but their lack of understanding of key aspects of mission theology leads them—perhaps unknowingly—to teach in Western ways, neglecting cultural forms of learning or key issues in that context. It is my hope that a brief exploration of a theology of mission will alleviate these challenges.

Before examining these topics, let me first define a couple of terms or at least narrow the scope of this chapter. Since theology of mission is a massive field that I couldn't possibly cover in any depth in this chapter, my intention here is to take a biblical theological approach and attempt to briefly sketch the arc of salvation history with two questions in view: (1) What is God's view of the nations throughout biblical history (and subsequently how that affects our attitude toward partnership), and (2) What must happen theologically as the gospel spreads into new cultural contexts?

In terms of theological education, I envision degree (formal) or certificate level (informal) theological education in the Majority World. This is not an attempt to devalue other types of pastoral training approaches but is simply a means of narrowing the focus. One of the reasons for narrowing in this way is the increasing interest in theological education in those parts of the world where Christianity is growing, that is, the former missionary-receiving nations.

Theology of Mission

When considering a theology of mission, we are envisioning the grand scope of God's salvation plan from creation to future reign. Specifically, a theology of mission focuses on how God accomplishes that plan of saving people from "every tribe and tongue and people and nation" (Rev 5:9 NIV) and unites them to himself. As Christopher Wright (2006, 22–23) says, "Our mission flows from and participates in the mission of God."

A biblical theology that sees the Bible as one interconnected story helps us here since even in the Old Testament we see God deeply concerned for the fate of the gentiles (Callaham 2019, 11; Sun 2019, 67). His calling of Abraham had the nations in view (Gen 12:1–3; 22:18). The covenant with Israel at Sinai had the nations in view (Exod 19:4–6). The covenant with David mentioned the one who would sit on David's throne forever and rule over the nations (2 Sam 7:12–13), and David's response recognized the implications for all nations (2 Sam 7:19). Even as the Old Testament points to the new covenant that would be established, it has the promised blessing of the nations in view (e.g., Isa 55:3–5) (Sun 2019, 95).

In the Gospels and Acts, we see these promises fulfilled through the faithful covenant-keeping work of Christ. In this part of the story, it becomes clear that Christ is the promised seed who ushers in God's end-time promises and accomplishes salvation for all the peoples of the earth. This promised blessing is extended to the nations through Christ's sending of the church. Through sending the Spirit, Christ empowers the church to proclaim his goodness and faithfulness among the nations.

Thus, this idea of sending is important in the New Testament. Christ commands the church to make disciples of all nations, and while all believers are commanded to be a witness to the nations around them, some have the unique calling of being sent *to* the nations. These "sent ones" make it their aim to intentionally cross geographic, linguistic, and cultural borders for the sake of proclaiming the good news and replicating their own experiences of Christ—namely by planting churches where others can experience Christ in worship.

Here, John Piper's (2022, 3) words are helpful: "Missions exists because worship doesn't." As the church experiences Christ in worship, it simultaneously recognizes that in other parts of the world, countless multitudes are not worshiping him due to never having heard the gospel nor having been convinced of their need for it. Thus, churches should consistently be burdened to send members to these people and these locations as emissaries of Christ and witnesses of the greatness of God.

Returning to the New Testament and the rest of the biblical story, we see that in Acts and the Epistles, as the early church was sent out and proclaimed the gospel to the nations, they needed to wrestle with *how* to bring the gentiles into the people of God. What emerges from Peter's vision in Acts 10, the Jerusalem council in Acts 15, and Paul's missionary efforts is a balanced view that both respects people and their cultural identities while also ensuring the gospel message remains pure and unchanged.

This process continues in the Pauline Epistles, where Paul wrote letters to individual churches and addressed the issues they were facing. In many cases, the theological issues that Paul discussed arose from their specific cultural context, and Paul helped these new believers see how the gospel confronted or transformed their worldview. Important for our purposes is the recognition that as the gospel goes out and is planted in new cultural contexts, believers must consider how to live out their faith in their cultural contexts. They must think through how the gospel shapes and informs, or even contradicts, their traditional ways of thinking, and they must determine how to continue to live in that cultural context while maintaining the gospel tradition passed down to them.

What we see in the Epistles are new discussions. This is not just because the events surrounding Jesus's life, death, resurrection, and the coming of the Spirit were recent ones historically, but they were also new conversations because the gospel was penetrating new areas. From those new contexts arose new questions and issues. Though difficult at times, these discussions of contextualization helped both the church in that time and churches throughout history better understand and reflect on the core elements of the gospel.

One final aspect of the biblical story that is important for us is the concept of missionary exit (International Mission Board 2018, 17; Pearce 2022). In his missionary identity, Paul saw his role as one who would bring the gospel to new areas. He saw himself as one who would lay the foundation (1 Cor 3:10–15) but not one who would stay and lead the church in that area long term. Instead, he would plant a church, raise up leaders, and then entrust them to God (Acts 20:32) as he sought to take the gospel to even more areas. This nature of "sent ones" who spearhead new efforts but do not build on the foundations laid by others should not be seen as an attempt to work quickly and then abandon the new believers. Instead, it is a way of valuing these new believers as partners and co-laborers who are worthy and able to lead this newly planted church.

Thus, in answering the two questions we posed at the outset, this brief survey of the biblical story shows that God has always valued the nations as people created in the image of God, and he has been working to bring them to salvation. Such a statement should impact how we see them as potential partners and contributors to the global theological discussion. As the gospel spreads into new areas today, just as it did in the New Testament period, the church must wrestle theologically with the critical issues of that cultural context from a biblical perspective.

Theological Education

With this brief survey of the biblical story in mind, we now can consider some implications for theological education in missionary contexts.

Theological Education (TE) Is Needed and Valuable

The global church needs missionaries to provide theological education. At times, missionaries are so concerned about the spread of the gospel into new areas that they forget that once the gospel takes root in those areas, these newly planted churches still need support (Brooks, 2017). Missionaries should not abandon them and hope that everything works itself out. Instead, like Paul, they should help lay a solid foundation so that these churches may persevere for many generations.

A key aspect of this task is training pastors for these new churches. We'll say more about how missionaries should go about this task below, but for now, we simply want to recognize the importance of this training as part of the missionary task. As we already saw, when Paul planted churches in the New Testament period, those churches had to wrestle with how to live out the gospel in their contexts. By his own admission, Paul invested a considerable amount of time to teach them and help them mature. Even after he left, he sent others to teach them and wrote letters to help them think theologically.

This training may take on a variety of shapes and forms. In those places or among these people where missionaries have only recently planted the gospel, training will likely be informal since no institutions exist in that context yet. For example, some coworkers in South Asia utilize an approach where they ask church leaders, "What are common misunderstandings people in your context have about Christ?" or "What are the most frequently asked questions about Christ in your context?" Then the leaders come together, study those questions from a biblical perspective, and together write a statement that addresses those misunderstandings (Lawless 2022). This informal TE is necessary and helpful in the way it addresses theological error.

To make such a statement, though, does not in any way lessen the value of formal theological education. Formal, degree-granting approaches to TE are extremely valuable in the Majority World since in many of these contexts, Asia for example, people highly value formal education. Additionally, by providing such education, missionaries could train and equip local theologians who not only have the ability to provide high-quality theological education to the next generation in their context but can also contribute to the global networks of scholars.

Theological Educators Should Value All People as Contributors

Theological educators in the Majority World should value all believers as contributors to the global theological discussion. In our brief survey of a theology of mission, we saw that God's heart has always been set on saving the nations and bringing them into the people of God. All people are created in the image of God and thus worthy of honor. Certainly, these truths influence the church's desire to get the gospel to all people, but once the gospel gets there, it should also influence how the church sees them as partners and collaborators in the theological task.

When we consider the missionary task, one potential danger (which happened so often during the colonial days and still happens in some areas today) is that the recipients of the gospel elevate the missionary, the missionary's culture, or even the missionary's theology to an exalted status. Because the missionary is often sent from a place where the church has existed for a longer time, the church in that location will have had longer to train pastors, develop seminaries, and write theologically oriented books. The easiest path for the missionary to train pastors in these situations is to say, "Here is what we have decided is correct theology."

Is not teaching in this way okay, though? In some sense, yes. From a positive perspective, missionary theological educators who do so are simply passing on what the historic church has affirmed to be orthodox theology. This helps church leaders in this new context to understand and relate to the legacy entrusted to them by a "previous" generation. At the same time, though, a danger exists where teachers set the standard for this new generation of church leaders that this is the only appropriate way to think. This danger exists for both informal programs that may be content heavy and formal programs that are more academic and primarily build upon Western material.

This danger may be especially real in places where missionaries are providing theological education at formal institutions. A greater power distance exists in such locations where students accord respect to teachers in such a manner that they are rarely questioned. Similarly, in an honor-shame culture, students will likewise not ask questions since doing so would cause the teacher to lose face. It is as if the student is saying, "I need to ask this question since you didn't explain the content clearly enough."

As a result, teachers must take additional steps to ensure that classrooms are safe spaces for students to ask questions, dialogue, and explore questions that are interesting to them. Missionary theological educators must see church leaders—even if they are students—as partners and potential contributors to the global theological discussion. Instead of seeking to have them memorize or distribute the missionary's preprepared materials, the missionary's goal is to help them develop in such a way that they can contribute to important theological discussions.

A helpful analogy is James Plueddemann's (2018, ch. 1) pilgrim-teacher analogy. Teachers and students are pilgrims on a journey together, though as it relates to the course content, teachers are a bit further down the road. In this model, instead of seeing themselves as the experts who convey all of the knowledge students need, teachers are fellow sojourners. Additionally, even though students may not be as far along in the journey, they still have something to contribute. This is also true in the seminary classroom, especially when the missionary is the teacher, since students likely have greater knowledge of their context and the needs of their local church. Wise teachers will listen to students and adjust their teaching accordingly since they recognize that students are on a similar pilgrimage and can contribute to the overall journey.

A critical aspect of this "journey" is the relationship between student and teacher, but developing this relationship takes time. At the beginning of a course, students may be skeptical of teachers who value others as contributors. They may wonder or even ask, "Why don't you just tell us all the answers?" or "Can't you give us a PowerPoint with all the notes on it?" Teachers must be intentional to communicate in culturally appropriate ways about the pilgrim analogy and how it influences their philosophy of teaching. They ask questions, initiate conversation, and guide evaluative processes not because they don't know their subject area but because they desire their students to develop the ability to contribute to the global conversation.

One way we have sought to implement this value in Southeast Asia is by starting a yearly theological society meeting, where students have the opportunity to present their research to others. While many academic society meetings are geared toward scholars and experts in their fields, this one is organized around students and is conducted in multiple languages. This meeting allows us to select quality papers from students and then work with them to edit and revise the paper before the meeting, thus providing another cycle of the learning process, from which they can improve their research and writing abilities.

A second way is similar in that we developed an academic journal that, again, is not driven by finding the most academic papers from experts, but one that is driven by the desire to give students the opportunity to publish. With this journal, we look for quality student papers and then support them through the learning process as they edit, revise, and prepare their papers for publication. This desire to help students learn in a nonthreatening way that does not affect their grades is one of the things that Bain (2004, ch. 3) found that good college teachers do, for example, when they ask, "How will I create a safe environment in which students can try, fail, receive feedback, and try again?" Doing so both values them as contributors and develops in them a curiosity and excitement about continuing to learn.

Theological Educators Should Aim to Equip People with Skills to Do Theology

The goal of theological education should be to equip people with the skills to do theology in their contexts. This point follows the previous one in that when missionaries see all people as made in the image of God and as potential contributors to the global theological discussion, they should seek to equip them with the skills to do so. Such a statement is a shift in the way many institutions operate since knowledge transfer is the go-to approach in theological education.

Many people teach others using the methods with which they were taught (Coley 2023, 114). One problem is that the lecture remains the dominant approach to teaching in Western theological institutions (Coley 2019). In the Western context, though, a greater emphasis is placed on critical thinking, even in primary-aged education. Thus, when students reach the master's level, they have typically developed a greater ability to listen and then unpack the content of the lecture, or to listen and consider possible applications to their ministry context.

In the Majority World, though, most educational systems follow a method of rote memorization and test preparation. In class, the instructor teaches the correct answers for the test, the students memorize those answers, and then they eventually take and pass the test. Such an approach, while having some benefits, does not prepare students well for ministry.

Instead, instructors should use a head, heart, and hands approach that teaches students the content they don't know (head) in a way that leads them to love God more (heart) and equips them with skills for future ministry (hands). In that sense, the goal is to teach in a way that students internalize the content, can recall it, and can use it to teach others.

One problem from a missiological perspective, especially when it comes to nonformal certificate programs, is the idea of reproducibility (Barnes and Brooks 2023). While a helpful principle, reproducibility taken to an extreme means "how *quickly* can the local believers pass on the content of the missionary?" The missionary prepares all the content, decides what questions need to be answered, and then teaches. In certificate-oriented pastoral training, this approach is "reproducible" when the missionaries give the students their notes, and then the students use those notes to teach others.

If missionaries value local believers as partners in the task of theology, the goal in the classroom is not for these believers to memorize the missionary's answers as quickly as possible. Such an approach does not allow the students time to internalize the material, nor does it actually equip them with skills for ministry. The goal in the classroom is for genuine learning to place and for instructors to help students learn the processes for doing theology. Clark Sundin makes a similar point when he explains the approach they took in the classroom:

> What we needed was not to teach as much knowledge as possible, but to train students to read and interpret Scripture, theologize within their contexts, and apply their newly gained practical skills to their ministries. In other words, our focus shifted from content to process. Thus, we stopped giving all the answers and started teaching students how to answer the questions. (Sundin 2022)

I need to make clear here that this type of approach should be used not only in the missiology classroom, but as this article has tried to explain, these missiological insights should influence *every seminary classroom*. Whether hermeneutics, New Testament, Old Testament, systematic theology, counseling, or preaching, the goal of the instructor is not simply to raise up content distributors but content creators. In other words, the goal is to equip the students with the necessary skills to do theology *on their own* (in community).

Let me give a few examples of how theological educators can accomplish this aim. When teaching hermeneutics, the instructor must certainly address important content like who determines the meaning of a text or what principles guide believers in studying different genres of Scripture. At the same time, though, the instructor must give opportunities for the students to practice those principles with specific texts. Given that many students in the Majority World don't enter seminary with good critical thinking skills and for cultural reasons tend not to question those in authority, teachers can't assume that students will apply or implement these principles on their own. Teachers should use classroom time to guide them in practicing interpretation.

For example, I teach a class on 1 Peter. While one objective of the course is to help students better understand the content of the epistle, a broader and more far-reaching aim is to equip them with the skills to interpret any New Testament letter. My hope is that as they learn the process for interpreting 1 Peter in this course, they will learn it well enough to apply that process when they study other New Testament books. Thus, instead of starting with "This is what this text means," I need to first ask them what it means, which often leads to a question like "And how do you know it means that?" This points students to the text and forces them to wrestle with how they would explain what it means and what grammatical or syntactical details in the text support those conclusions.

Similarly, in a practical course like preaching or counseling, it is even easier to raise specific scenarios or case studies from that cultural context that students are sure to face. These practical exercises force students to learn to *do theology* as they wrestle with how they would respond. Many places in the Majority World are collectivistic, and thus, it makes sense to utilize group assignments or discussions in the classroom space. Proposing a specific scenario and then having students work together to say how they would apply specific passages of Scripture to that issue helps to equip them with specific skills and to learn the process of doing theology as opposed to just providing them with content or telling them the "correct" answers.

Theological Educators Should Aim to Raise Up Local Theologians

For theological educators in missionary contexts, the goal is to raise up local theologians. In our brief theology of mission section above, we saw that missionaries are sent out from the local church to intentionally cross cultural boundaries for a season. All missionaries will eventually exit from their fields of service, and when it comes to training church leaders, their goal is not to provide all of the content or answers but to raise up local theologians who have the exegetical skill to do theology in that context.

Additionally, we considered the New Testament Epistles which, on some level, each display some level of contextualization. What I mean by that is that the authors of the Epistles helped believers think through how the gospel shaped, informed, confronted, or corrected issues in their contexts. Paul Hiebert's (1994, 88–92) critical contextualization is helpful here as believers work through a process of evaluating various cultural norms or other aspects of their worldview through a biblical lens. To do so, though, they need the necessary exegetical and theological acumen to study Scripture and apply it to their context.

The ability to perform such theological evaluation is even more important after the missionary leaves. At this point, new issues will likely emerge that the missionary never addressed. If the training for church leaders only focused on providing them with answers that the professors thought they needed to know, then these church leaders would be ill-equipped to answer new questions. Unless they have the ability to go to the word and study it for themselves, they will not be able to guide their churches through these challenges. The same can be said when new forms of heresy or false doctrine arise in their context.

On a different level, when missionaries raise up local theologians it benefits the global church. Because of their unique cultural outlook, these theologians look at Scripture or theology from a different perspective. They sometimes see themes in Scripture that those in other cultures have overlooked, or they sometimes have the ability to nuance certain theological debates in a helpful, more balanced way (Brooks 2022).

We may ask, though, what about theological educators who are teaching in multicultural classrooms? How can they possibly raise up indigenous theologians, teach in culturally appropriate ways, or walk alongside their students to address key issues in their contexts when they have students from a variety of cultural backgrounds? This is an important question since megacities are increasingly becoming multicultural hubs with numerous immigrant groups, and more and more schools have the opportunity to reach people from a variety of backgrounds with their online programs.

For students from backgrounds that have a large power distance or have little emphasis on critical thinking, it is not enough to simply give them the building blocks and expect them to do contextualization on their own later. Instructors must walk with them further down the road of contextual theology so that students both understand the process and know they have the ability to apply Scripture to the pressing issues of their contexts. To do so, though, requires instructors to invest even more time in intentionally learning about their students.

Again, let me give a few examples of how educators might accomplish this aim. In a Christian theology or systematic theology course, the teacher needs to present a certain amount of content—and this content relates to both biblical teaching on certain doctrines and how the church throughout history has wrestled with those doctrines. At the same time, the teacher must give space for students themselves to wrestle with how Scripture speaks to the doctrine in question. One coworker of mine used a debate approach, where students evaluated specific positions and then argued about which one best explained the relevant texts.

Similarly, lecturers—especially cross-cultural missionary educators—need to learn from their students about the specific challenges churches are facing in those contexts. In the theology classroom, as the class studies issues like Christology, soteriology, or even theories of the atonement, an opportunity exists for educators to walk with students through a process of evaluating how those doctrines should shape the contemporary church's response to those challenges. Alternatively, professors can allow students to reflect on how key doctrines speak to pressing concerns in their context. For example, ancestor worship is not normally addressed in a Western theology course, but in Asian contexts, it should be. Doing so can start the process of raising up local theologians who can speak to the pressing issues in their contexts.

To give an example from a discipline other than theology or biblical studies, we can consider church history. This course is typically taught in a way that leans heavily on Western church history. But to develop local theologians, seminaries must also educate students on the history of the church *in their contexts*. Many places in the Majority World have a rich history of Christianity, a history of which historians trained in the West may be unaware. Missiologists can help in this area since, in many of these locations, the history of the church is intricately connected to the history of missions.

Conclusion

Though it is often relegated to simply practical methods for evangelism and church planting, the discipline of missiology has much to offer a vision for theological education, especially theological education in the Majority World. Applying missiological insight to the task of teaching theology helps us to focus on the process of doing theology rather than just providing the correct answers. It enables us to see local believers as partners and potential contributors to the global theological conversation. A theology of mission points us to the goal of raising up local theologians, which benefits the global church and keeps the local church healthy for future generations.

References

Bain, Ken. 2004. *What the Best College Teachers Do*. Cambridge: Harvard University Press. Perlego.

Barnes, Phil, and Will Brooks. 2023. "Rethinking Reproducibility: An Equipping Model for Missionary Theological Educators." *Global Missiology* 20, no. 2 (April): 31–38. http://ojs.globalmissiology.org/index.php/english/article/view/2731/6904.

Brooks, Will. 2017. "Hermeneutics for Healthy Churches." *Evangelical Missions Quarterly* 53, no. 1 (January). 35–40.

Brooks, Will. 2022. *Interpreting Scripture across Cultures: An Introduction to Cross-Cultural Hermeneutics*. Eugene, OR: Wipf & Stock.

Callaham, Scott N. 2019. "Old Testament Theology and World Mission." In *World Mission: Theology, Strategy, and Current Issues*, edited by Scott N. Callaham and Will Brooks, 3–32. Bellingham, WA: Lexham.

Coley, Ken. 2019. "Educational Methodology." In *Christian Education: A Guide to the Foundations of Ministry*, edited by Freddy Cardoza, 119–31. Grand Rapids: Baker Academic.

Coley, Ken. 2023. "The Perspective of Mind, Brain, and Education Research." In *Transformational Teaching: Instructional Design for Christian Educators*, edited by Kenneth S. Coley, Deborah L. MacCullough, and Martha E. MacCullough, 103–25. Nashville: B&H Academic.

Hiebert, Paul G. 1994. *Anthropological Reflections on Missiological Issues*. Grand Rapids: Baker Books.

International Mission Board. 2018. *IMB Foundations*. Richmond, VA: IMB.

Lawless, Chuck. 2022. "Urgency and Healthy Church Planting." *Great Commission Baptist Journal of Missions* 1, no. 1.

Pearce, Preston. 2022. "Exit: Training and Trusting." *Great Commission Baptist Journal of Missions* 1, no. 1.

Piper, John. 2022. *Let the Nations Be Glad! The Supremacy of God in Missions*. 30th-anniversary ed. Grand Rapids: Baker Academic.

Plueddemann, James E. 2018. *Teaching across Cultures: Contextualizing Education for Global Mission*. Downers Grove, IL: InterVarsity Press. Perlego.

Sun, Wendel. 2019. "Biblical Theology and World Mission." In *World Mission: Theology, Strategy, and Current Issues*, edited by Scott N. Callaham and Will Brooks, 33–66. Bellingham, WA: Lexham.

Sundin, Clark. 2022. "Why We're in Crete: Leadership Development as Preparation for the Unexpected." *Great Commission Baptist Journal of Missions* 1, no. 2.

Wright, Christopher J. H. 2006. *The Mission of God: Unlocking the Bible's Grand Narrative*. Downers Grove, IL: IVP Academic.

Chapter 6

The Local Church as Mission Academy

Phil Wagler

What do Aretha Franklin, Katy Perry, Justin Timberlake, John Legend, Whitney Houston, and Allen Stone have in common? Besides being famous musical artists, they all learned to sing in church. While far from a scientific survey, simply watching reality music shows reveals a high percentage of aspiring singers who say something like, "I learned to sing in church." It should not surprise even the most ardent secularist that excellent musicians and singers are trained in local churches, where praise with tambourines and dancing as well as psalms, hymns, and spiritual songs is a central practice. If the local church can train singers, will it also train missionaries?

In *The Spirit of the Disciplines,* Dallas Willard (1988, 247) implored the local fellowship to "become an academy where people throng from the surrounding community to learn how to live." His main point is that every neighborhood Christian community should be a place where people learn how to become flourishing human beings as they are formed as apprentices of Jesus's character and likeness. This is the nature of discipleship—the imitation of Christ and being yoked to him (Matt 11:29–30). Every church, Willard dreamed, "will be a school of life … where all aspects of that life seen in the New Testament record are practiced and mastered under those who have themselves mastered them through practice. Only by taking this as our immediate goal can we intend to carry out the Great Commission" (247). Elsewhere, Willard (2002, 250) contended that the local church will explicitly do two things: *expect* disciples to do the various things that Jesus taught and *announce* that the church aims to teach people to do what Jesus said to do.

Every local church, large or small, of every denomination, ethnicity, or geography, believes it is doing what Willard highlighted. However, a 2017 Evangelical Fellowship of Canada (EFC) study revealed that when it comes to challenging their people with personal responsibility for the Great Commission, "Half of pastors (49%) said their congregations did so at least a few times a month, and another quarter (25%) said monthly" (Hiemstra 2017, 17). This was the case, despite the same survey revealing that "the majority of pastors (85%) and lay respondents (63%) agreed that the local church holds the primary responsibility for the Great Commission" (4). When the study asked about the training long-term mission workers need to be successful, the areas most identified were understanding culture, language training, training in the majority religion of the country, Bible college or seminary, professional or trade accreditation, community development training, training in English or French as second language, and university studies (33). All these areas are valuable for anyone considering service in another culture. What is striking, however, is that the local church is not even named as a necessary training ground for Great Commission workers, despite a majority of Christians believing that responsibility for the Great Commission rests with the local church.

What emerges is a disconnect between church, discipleship, and mission. These terms have become dichotomized; however, the biblical worldview presents a more holistic vision. The church Jesus will build that hell will not overcome (Matt 16:18) is ecclesia, those "called out of the world to become light for the world, accepting responsibility for the world and transforming the world into a place according to the teaching of Jesus on the Kingdom of God" (Reimer 2017, 48). The fulfillment of the Great Commission is inseparable from forming the type of people who will go to all peoples. This is precisely the missionary training Jesus was doing with his followers. Every faithful disciple, not just those sent *over there*, is a missionary; a "sent one" (John 20:21). Jesus's Great Commission is about making disciples among all peoples, "where all aspects of that life seen in the New Testament record are practiced and mastered under those who have themselves mastered them through practice" (Willard 1988, 247). The local church is central to this holy enterprise. What Miroslav Volf (2019, 10) says of the theologian is no less the task for the pastor of a local church: "fostering the kind of social agents capable of envisioning and creating just, truthful, and peaceful societies, and on shaping a cultural climate in which such agents will thrive." Who are these social agents if not the variety of gifted disciples entrusted to a local church—all of whom enter each new day on the front line advancing the kingdom of God as missionaries?

In what cultural climate will these agents thrive except for a cross-defined, Christlike, and shalom-centered local Christian fellowship where transformative discipleship and mission training are the expectation and announcement? The local church is a mission academy. The local church, in its faithful teaching, life, and practice, ought to focus on the formation of transformative social agents—only a small percentage of whom will be called to another country. This, as I have written elsewhere, will produce a cultural climate where "the greatest witnesses of the coming Kingdom are seen in any community on the planet where people of incredible variety are committed to living life together under the Lordship of Jesus" (Wagler 2009, 129). This local church as mission academy will not only produce musical artists who are social agents of the kingdom but also educators, health care workers, business leaders, athletes, coaches, plumbers, retirees, and even preachers and theologians who expect to be formed into the likeness of Christ and be sent as he was sent.

How Can the Local Church Be Faithful to This Mandate as a Mission Academy?

I propose four community practices that can form the local church as a mission academy. These thoughts emerge from three decades of learnings and yearnings as a disciple who has served as a pastor, Bible college educator, mission agency worker, and now liaison with the EFC and director of the World Evangelical Alliance's Peace and Reconciliation Network. These neighborhood, denominational, countrywide, and global experiences have deepened my conviction that the local church is uniquely designed by God to be the first training academy of mission for every believer. These experiences, including my own failures and lack of courage at times, have led me to lament how the local church has neglected this greater responsibility for the lesser aim of building a great church or becoming mere dispensers of spiritual services for religious consumers.

To reclaim its crucial role as a mission academy the local church must grasp two key elements, one theological and one practical. First, the church requires *an integral understanding of church, discipleship, and mission*. These are not dichotomized things, but they are one vision of God revealed in Christ for the salvation, redemption, and restoration of his world through the new humanity who is the dwelling place of God (Eph 2:14–22). Metaphorically, it is helpful to think of this as one family composed of a household, covenant, and vocation. A household (church) is a people who share life under one roof (though the house, hut, or yurt is only a container for household identity). A covenant (discipleship) is confirmed by marriage (though a marriage relationship recognizes a deeper covenant and fidelity). Finally, a vocation (mission) is the members of the covenant-keeping household serving in their local context using talents or entrepreneurship that intersect with need and opportunity. A more holistic approach would be to consider the weight of household, covenant, and vocation in our theological understandings to disentangle ourselves from the dichotomized and programmatic conceptions that have overtaken our understanding of church, discipleship, and mission. This will then reposition the local fellowship to be an academy for the mission vocation of the covenant household of God. Cross-cultural mission is ultimately local, wherever it is expressed.

Second, church leaders expect this integral way of being to shape the missionary vocational reality of their people, and they announce that this is what the congregation is about. The church as a mission academy requires humble yet clear congregational leadership that will speak, model, and form it. Church leaders who know that the way of Jesus is an upside-down kingdom (Kraybill 2011, 9) must resist the temptation to build comfortable, religious organizations. Instead, the gifts given to the church—apostle, prophet, evangelist, pastor-shepherd, and teacher (Eph 4:11–13)—must be used to shape diverse, unified, mature, ministering, missionary disciples who are a "constant disturbance in human society … [refusing] to allow things as they are to remain set in concrete" (de Gruchy 2002, 211). In each new generation, the hope of God's kingdom, manifested to the world through the *ekklēsia* (Eph 3:10), must be renewed. Therefore, leaders of the local, contextualized body of Christ—even the smallest Christian fellowship—must expect and declare that their church is always training its members to be ready, responsive, and obedient to the Holy Spirit as witnesses in their context. With these elements in view, we now turn to four community practices that shape the local church as a mission academy.

Commit to Calling

The first call is not to a ministry role or vocation but to a relationship with Jesus and submission to him as Lord. "'Come, follow me,' Jesus said, 'and I will send you out to fish for people'" (Matt 4:19 NIV). The local church as a mission academy will be committed to helping those who have not yet heard this call to hear it. The church must be committed to helping people hear Jesus's call, "The kingdom of God has come near. Repent and believe the good news!" (Mark 1:14–15 NIV). Since Jesus is the sender, it is his voice—not denominational or theological distinctives or the local church's vision—that must be obeyed. This "calling and election," of which the local church is convinced, is of primary importance. From this first call, the holy qualities of Christlike character and fruitfulness emerge (2 Pet 1:3–10). This requires calling disciples to be formed by Scripture and to know and live by God's revealed wisdom (1 Cor 2:7–10) lest, as John Stackhouse (2022, 116) writes, the Bible becomes "less a window into a divinely ordained reality to which one [has] to submit than a mirror of one's own perceptions and preferences ... thus rendering evangelicals liberals in all but name."

Second, the local church as a mission academy is committed to calling disciples to know their gifts and use them to build up the church. The church is not just another place where one might volunteer time and energy. To follow Jesus as Lord is to be part of the body of which he is head, a body in which every member has its place and role (1 Cor 12). Numerous New Testament passages emphasize that being part of the church means that disciples exercise their spiritual gifts (Acts 6:1–7; Rom 12:4–8; 1 Cor 12:1–11). Paul did not present positions in terms of volunteers but as gifts of the Spirit given to covenanted disciples, which demand activation to build up the household of faith for its shared vocation in the world (1 Cor 14; Eph 4:11–16; 2 Tim 1:6). In the calling out and exercising of the variety of gifts, the disciple becomes seen and known, can be exhorted and encouraged, and can discover more fully their unique contribution in the harvest fields. The local church as a mission academy will not simply prioritize volunteer roles to fulfill an organizational vision, but it will build a culture where disciples are called to "fish" (Matt 4:19), "wait on tables" (Acts 6:1–7), or lead because they share responsibility for the common missional vocation God has given the church.

Third, the local church as a mission academy is committed to calling disciples to fervent prayer. This was the practice of the first Christians in Jerusalem when persecution arose, and the fruit of this prayer erupted into an effective mission despite opposition (Acts 4:23–31). This practice was directly connected to what the disciples saw in Jesus and knew of the history of the Hebrew people. A commitment to prayer as a disciplined practice of missionary preparation and sending was what Jesus did in choosing the Twelve and instructing them: "The harvest is plentiful, but the workers are few. Ask the Lord of the harvest, therefore, to send out workers into his harvest field" (Luke 10:2 NIV). This call to prayer was what Paul insisted upon so that mission might be spiritually focused and effective (Eph 6:10–20).

Embrace Reconciliation

I once served as a transitional pastor in a church recovering from deep conflict. During the first congregational meeting, a person pointedly stated that broken relationships and fractured trust existed in the fellowship. The next speaker appealed for the church to get more involved in the neighborhood, which was filled with traumatized and broken families. A missional collision was apparent. What was needed? To heal internal conflict until we were fit for neighborhood mission or to prioritize the need of neighborhood mission above internal conflict? The answer was to embrace both.

The local fellowship can be tempted to fear, ignore, or even escalate conflict. This usually means the conflict metastasizes, becoming contagious as festering offenses shape congregational culture. Sometimes this can be passed on to other churches when hurt members move to new congregations. More positively, conflict can be addressed but often at the expense of mission. "We will get to mission when we've healed" becomes the sentiment. But sometimes this never happens, and the church, having experienced God's healing, settles into an internally focused posture to keep "that loving feeling." After all, newcomers may not like what they learn about the "real" us, or they may bring new issues that disturb the hard-earned peace. As Miroslav Volf (2019, 332) writes: "The insistence on perfect reconciliation and embrace will result in no embrace at all. As I see it, the practice of embrace requires 'courage to imperfection'—and hope for the final embrace ... in the coming world of love."

Addressing conflict in order to embrace learning God's reconciliation, even imperfect reconciliation, is a crucial course in the local church's mission academy curriculum. Conflict is human, and every culture and community can erupt with conflict quickly. Consider what the COVID-19 pandemic did to families, communities, and churches as "they fought over toilet paper" as one Canadian denominational leader put it. Church conflict should be expected, just as it is in increasingly pluralistic societies. Localized conflict is the laboratory of God's reconciliation and way of shalom, and this is the missional vocation of the covenanted household of faith (2 Cor 5:18). The gospel of Jesus breaks down dividing walls of hostility (Eph 2:14), and the church becomes a place of new humanity where enemies of God and one another are adopted into a family fellowship.

The local church is the missional school of reconciliation. In his formation of the Twelve, a group of political and theological rivals, Jesus modeled such an academy of reconciliation. The group lived together in peace amid the ripples of conflict. They strived to practice long-suffering, forgiveness, humility, washing one another's feet, and putting others first (Rom 12:9–21). If a church calls its people to worship at the altar but not to pursue reconciliation (Matt 5:23–24), then it will not produce missionaries able to solve conflicts in their neighborhoods or around the world where the issues of fighting—"sword" and "spear"—remain (Isa 2:1–5; Mic 4:1–5).

As a mission academy, the local church will also receive requests from outside the church to help solve world conflicts. When the United Nations made such a request of faith communities, the World Evangelical Alliance's Peace and Reconciliation Network was founded. Canada's Truth and Reconciliation Commission (2015, Action 49) made a similar request: "We call upon all religious denominations and faith groups who have not already done so to repudiate concepts used to justify European sovereignty over Indigenous lands and peoples, such as the Doctrine of Discovery and terra nullius." The opportunity to embrace the ministry of reconciliation has become a necessary part of the church's mission.

A commitment to reconciliation will often be costly and uncomfortable. No longer seeing others as we once did (2 Cor 5:16), the body of Christ must see conflict transformation "more than a set of specific techniques; ... [but as] a way of looking as well as seeing" (Lederach 2003, 9). This way of seeing will elevate reconciliation as a metric of congregational faithfulness to God's shalom vision for the world. The church can do so in confidence knowing that Jesus is the Great Reconciler. When he is lifted up, people will be drawn to him (John 12:32). The church will humbly take this practice into their neighborhoods and to the nations. Reconciliation work requires biblical teaching, skill development, and modeling from church leaders who demonstrate the values of peacemaking (Matt 5:9; Prov 12:20).

Engage Socially

The idea of the socially engaged church is fraught with controversy and complexities. The idea can conjure up images of political right-wing Trumpist evangelicalism, progressive identity politics, or social justice stances. Some local fellowships dive headlong into the realities of their social context. They partner with non-faith-based organizations like food banks or building projects, while others, wary of being "yoked to unbelievers" live more separately, delivering valuable ministries of mercy and compassion. Regardless, the need for the local church as a mission academy to be engaged socially is nonnegotiable. An awareness of, awakening to, and participation in the needs of the context is critical for both the church's missional vocation as well as the training of transformative social agents. This engagement with the *polis* (city) is necessary for the local fellowship to truly be ecclesia as Bonhoeffer describes: "In what way are we the Ecclesia, 'those who are called forth'; not conceiving of ourselves religiously as specially favoured, but as wholly belonging to the world. Then Christ is no longer an object of religion, but something quite different, indeed and in truth the Lord of the World?" (1963, 92).

As a mission academy, the local church cannot remain focused on privatized spirituality, the success of its identity as a religious institution, nor simply be pleased with its members' occasional volunteering efforts that, while noble, can often be done for the church's own sake and be disconnected from the mission of the church. "If faith," wrote Miroslav Volf (2011, 16), "*only* heals and energizes, then it is merely a crutch to use at will, not a way of life. But the Christian faith, as a prophetic religion, is either a way of life or a parody of itself." Given the world's increasing pluralism and the clash of civilizations (Huntington 1996), the local church must not be separatist but instead be socially engaged. It must recognize with humility that it must become "more comfortable with being just one of many players so that from whatever place they find themselves—on the margins, at the center, or anywhere in between—they can promote human flourishing and the common good" (Volf 2011, 79).

As a mission academy, the local church must see social engagement as exercising a living and active faith that seeks the shalom of its context (Jer 29:4–9). It must teach community engagement and development— involvement, context analysis, theological reflection, spirituality, and collaborative plans for action (Reimer 2017, 87). Our prayer for the kingdom to come on earth as it is in heaven must be accompanied by steps of obedient, risk-taking activity where the local church trains, takes, and commissions its membership to engage with the complex issues facing a city or county. Beyond volunteering, they should purposefully build relationships and cultivate a presence that leads to influence for the common good, including realizing more just systems and structures.

This posture and engagement will train covenanted disciples to see and engage the world as God does. When Jesus sought to open his disciple's eyes to the harvest in Samaria (John 4:35), he implored them to awaken to the political, religious, and cultural realities that had shaped Jewish-Samaritan social relations and to join expectantly with God's activity to bring transformation and shalom. In the same way, the local church must take its social context seriously, regard community engagement as a way to train disciples, and see this as a metric of faithfulness. The church must not exist merely for its own good but for the common good. Bonhoeffer (1963, 166) wrote: "The Church is her true self only when she exists for humanity. … She must take her place in the social life of the world, not lording it over men, but helping and serving them. She must tell men, whatever their calling, what it means to live in Christ, to exist for others." This "telling" must be rooted in the local church as a mission academy.

Prioritize Interdependence

Interdependence means acknowledging one's need and others' strengths to meet that need and recognizing the opportunity to accomplish more together by learning from and leaning on one another. It is necessary for human and social flourishing. The local church as a mission academy has a unique responsibility to train social agents through prioritizing interdependence in three areas: intergenerational, intercultural, and interinstitutional.

Intergenerational. In Western societies, outside of family, few places remain where people across generations intersect for mutual encouragement, respect, and hospitality (Lev 19:32; Ps 145:4; Mark 9:36; Matt 19:14; 1 Tim 4:12; Tit 2:2–8). As a mission academy, the church must maximize its unique relational and training opportunities not only to mentor but also to combat generational "siloing" and isolation. The church must train its members of all ages and genders to interact with and impact society. Prioritizing intergenerational interdependence is one of the greatest gifts the local church possesses. The generational diversity of local churches should not be seen as opportunities for homogenous groups in ministry programs but as opportunities for training that leverages the wisdom and experience of the mature with the enthusiasm and vision of the young. For example, small discipleship groups can be intergenerational and focused on Scripture, prayer, character development, and missional activity.

Intercultural. In John's apocalyptic vision, people from every nation, tribe, people, and language are gathered around the throne (Rev 7:9). The church is a multicultural organism. Jesus's prayer for unity (John 17) is not about absorbing or colonizing cultures within the church into monotone sameness but about mimicking the communion enjoyed by the Father, Son, and Holy Spirit. Before God's throne, ethnic and cultural diversity is celebrated. In the same way, the church as a mission academy will prioritize interdependence with this intercultural fellowship.

Jesus's warning that the Spirit would move the church beyond the comforts of monocultural kingdom building in Jerusalem to the ends of the earth (Acts 1:8) serves as a signpost for how the Spirit moves in every context. Training for global intercultural ministry ought to begin in the multicultural context of the local church's immediate community. Led by the Holy Spirit, church leaders must lead their congregations in local intercultural ministry. If not, people will follow the general trend to huddle with those who are like them (Matt 5:46–47). Congregational leaders must call for this intercultural vocation for the church's own vitality and for its members to become agents of transformation.

In one Canadian church, a discussion among Caucasian women about the choice of music for a special event revealed a lamentable surprise. Asked to propose a song, one woman chose one from her native South Africa. Her peers were shocked to learn that she loved this style of music and that she had sacrificed her preferences for years to be part of this Canadian church. They also realized that they had been robbed of being a more global church in their worship styles. This experience led to a special Sunday morning service where Scripture was read in the eight different languages spoken in the small fellowship of fifty believers. This small act of intercultural prioritization awakened a new sense of who the congregation was and who it might be for the world.

Interinstitutional. When the local church heeds the Apostle Paul's instruction to guard the unity of the Spirit and the bond of peace (Eph 4:3), it also practices Jesus's prayer for unity (John 17). Only a few decades after the resurrection, a prophetic voice was needed to call the church to interdependence as it became increasingly multicultural. Paul's insistence that the gentile fellowship care for Hebrew Christians in their suffering in Jerusalem should be seen, at least partially, through this lens (Rom 15:26–27).

No local church, denomination, or parachurch ministry can do everything. With the vast majority of Canadian churches numbering less than 150 people (Hiemstra and Callaway 2023, 20) and 90 percent of American churches averaging less than 250 in weekly attendance (Thumma 2021, 5), the church's institutional strata that support its identity and mandate must foster strong interdependence. Congregational leaders should ask: To whom can we send our disciples to grow, learn, and contribute? What fellowships in our community can train our people in an area of gifting and expertise that we do not have? What resources and personnel can we share with the wider church in our area? What interdenominational or organizational relationships, including those with social and governmental agencies, do we need to build? How can we not sow seeds of competition or foster divisions in the disciples we are making?

One Canadian church that was experiencing conflict and division saw more than one hundred people leave to join another growing church plant. The church plant outgrew its meeting space and was struggling to find a new space. Since the church in conflict was shrinking, its space was now too large and too expensive. The two pastors met and the declining church offered to give up its space to the growing church plant. This act of humility and interdependence deflated resentment, built trust, and fostered collaboration and mutual generosity in the years that followed. This interdependence also trained the members of each church in what the shared mission of the body of Christ could look like.

Conclusion

The local church is a mission academy of first importance. It is the community within which the vast majority of Christians around the world will have their only opportunity to be equipped as transformative social agents and missionaries. As such, the Christian community must intentionally practice a commitment to calling, embracing reconciliation, engaging socially, and prioritizing interdependence. National, denominational, and congregational leadership should maintain this expectation and announce this vision. In this way, they follow Jesus's way with his disciples and the practice of the early church.

References

Bonhoeffer, Dietrich. 1963. *Letters and Papers from Prison*. London: SCM.

de Gruchy, John W. 2002. *Reconciliation: Restoring Justice*. London: SCM.

Hiemstra, Rick. 2017. *Canadian Evangelicals and Long-Term, Career Missions: Calling, Sending and Training*. Toronto: Faith Today.

Hiemstra, Rick, and Lindsay Callaway. 2023. *Significant Church: Understanding the Value of the Small Evangelical Church in Canada*. Toronto: Faith Today.

Huntington, Samuel P. 1996. *The Clash of Civilizations and Remaking of World Order*. New York: Simon & Schuster.

Kraybill, Donald B. 2011. *The Upside-Down Kingdom*. 5th ed. Harrisonburg, VA: Herald Press.

Lederach, John Paul. 2003. *The Little Book of Conflict Transformation: Clear Articulation of the Guiding Principles by a Pioneer in the Field*. New York: Good Books.

Reimer, Johannes. 2017. *Missio Politica: The Mission of the Church and Politics*. Carlisle, UK: Langham.

Stackhouse, John G., Jr. 2022. *Evangelicalism: A Very Short Introduction*. New York: Oxford University Press.

Thumma, Scott. 2021. *Twenty Years of Congregational Change: The 2020 Faith Communities Today Overview*. Hartford, CT: Hartford Institute for Religion Research.

Truth and Reconciliation Commission of Canada. 2015. *Truth and Reconciliation Commission of Canada: Calls to Action*. Ottawa: Truth and Reconciliation Commission of Canada.

Volf, Miroslav. 2011. *A Public Faith: How Followers of Christ Should Serve the Common Good*. Grand Rapids: Brazos.

Volf, Miroslav. 2019. *Exclusion and Embrace: A Theological Exploration of Identity, Otherness, and Reconciliation*. Nashville: Abingdon.

Wagler, Phil M. 2009. *Kingdom Culture: Growing the Missional Church*. Winnipeg: Word Alive.

Willard, Dallas. 1988. *The Spirit of the Disciplines: Understanding How God Changes Lives*. San Francisco: Harper & Row.

Willard, Dallas. 2002. *Renovation of the Heart: Putting on the Character of Christ*. Colorado Springs: NavPress.

Chapter 7

Competency-Based Missiological Education

Its Time Has Come!

Larry W. Caldwell

A new model for educating for mission is competency-based theological education (CBTE). CBTE is gaining increasing popularity among theological institutions, accrediting associations, and mission organizations worldwide. CBTE is quickly developing into a global theological education phenomenon. Since CBTE is especially adaptable to missiological education, I propose in this chapter that we take the conversation further and consider competency-based missiological education (CBME).

This chapter consists of three parts. Part one will examine the question, Why CBTE? Here I discuss the roots of competency-based theological education, survey the strategy, and consider its advantages for theological education. In part two, I address the possibility of CBTE for missiological education—competency-based *missiological* education (CBME)—arguing that teaching missions is especially suited for this method. Finally, in part three, I conclude with two practical examples: first, a mission organization that is already using CBME, and second, an example of a veteran Global South missionary who recently received a missiological degree through CBME.

Why Competency-Based Theological Education?

Origins

CBTE grew out of the formal and nonformal competency-based education (CBE) systems that began in the 1960s and 1970s in North America (Nodine 2016, 5–11). CBE soon found its way throughout the world in both the Global North and Global South (Anderson-Levitt and Gardinier 2021). CBE focuses on the competencies necessary to do a specific job or task (the outcome). What do you need to *know* (content) and *do* (craft) to succeed in your work? In other words, what is the outcome (integrated learning goal) that is ultimately desired, and what are the competencies necessary to successfully fulfill that outcome? CBE emphasizes outcomes and competencies rather than courses and credit hours. CBE is now found in more than five hundred institutions of higher learning throughout North America (LeBlanc 2021, 31–32).

CBTE

What then is competency-based *theological* education? CBTE was first pioneered a decade ago in the United States by Kairos University (formerly Sioux Falls Seminary). Through their innovative Kairos Project, Kairos University added the T to CBE: the crucial theological character component of being. Thus, CBTE focuses on outcomes and competencies in the areas of content (*know*), character (*be*), and craft (*do*). By working with a three-member mentor team (faculty, vocational/ministry, personal), each student demonstrates competency in traditional subject areas like spiritual formation, biblical literacy and interpretation, theology, culture, and church history with outcomes specifically developed for each subject area. CBTE begins with the end in mind. In other words, what outcomes and competencies does the student need to demonstrate in terms of content, character, and craft so that the student is best able to do ministry in their unique vocational/ministry context? As the student progresses through their CBTE discipleship journey in Kairos, they will know they have completed the particular outcome when they and their mentor team have determined—through a formal master assessment—that competency has been achieved in terms of content, character, and craft related to the particular outcome.

In CBTE, the student is in the driver's seat, so to speak, guided by the wisdom of their mentor team. Furthermore, students progress at their own pace; there are no course or assignment deadlines (LeBlanc 2021, 26–27). Together the student and their mentor team work out a unique development pathway for each of the outcomes, based on perceived competencies that the student may already have in the outcome area, as well as on what other competencies the student and mentor team believe will be necessary for them to be competent in their specific vocational/ministry context. Put another way, the development pathway helps guide the student and mentor team to a combination of content, character, and craft coursework and assignments that will cover the general area of the outcome in light of the specific competency needs of the student in their ministry context. The student's ministry context is integrated into the educational process and their pathway; their ministry context is the classroom.

How does all of this work out in practice? Let's look at examples of two outcomes from Kairos University's Master of Divinity (MDiv) program. We will look first at the outcome related to the Bible and its interpretation entitled Skillful Biblical Exegesis, followed by an examination of the outcome related to church history entitled Christian Tradition. For each example, we will examine both the language used to describe each outcome as well as components that will typically be incorporated into the development pathway for each outcome, including the areas related to content, character, and craft.

Skillful Biblical Exegesis. The outcome language for Skillful Biblical Exegesis implies that the student will know they have completed this outcome when they and their mentor team have determined that the student can "demonstrate skillful exegesis through in-depth biblical study and awareness of methodological frameworks." As the student and their mentor team work on the development path for this outcome, they will make certain that the student:

- Becomes conversant with the stories, characters, contexts, and literature of both the Old and New Testaments;
- Develops familiarity with the cultural and historical contexts of the biblical world;
- Cultivates best practices for studying and interpreting the Bible;
- Discerns the impact of their community of faith and their theological commitments on the way they read and interpret the Bible;
- Reflects upon their strengths and weaknesses in the task of interpreting the Bible and ways in which other interpretations can inform and transform their life;
- Identifies ways the Bible can inform and transform their life;
- Discovers ways to put the Bible into practice appropriately in their cultural and vocational context.

In relationship to the three areas of content, character, and craft, for this Skillful Biblical Exegesis outcome, the student will typically focus on:

- Content related to the way their context/tradition understands the content of the whole of Scripture. Often students discover new vocabulary and frameworks concerning confessional traditions and intellectual processes that inform interpretation;

- Character related to what it means to exemplify this outcome based on how their tradition/context understands Scripture's normative and formative impact on life and faith;

- Craft related to demonstrating the skills and practices of their interpretive work in their vocational context.

Again, the development path as well as the content, character, and craft aspects of the student's journey of discipleship related to the Skillful Biblical Exegesis outcome will be heavily influenced by the current (or future) vocational/ministry context of the student. A student whose future vocational context will involve teaching the Bible at the seminary level, for example, will need to demonstrate competency at a far higher level of content and craft, such as in the original languages, than will a Filipino missionary who plants underground churches in Saudi Arabia. However, both students will need to develop their character in alignment with the study of Skillful Biblical Exegesis and its impact on their lives and faith. Such character formation will involve both formal and nonformal interactions with peers as well as other communal interactions both inside and outside the academy.

Christian Tradition. The outcome language for Christian Tradition implies that the student will know they have completed this outcome when they and their mentor team have determined that the student can "demonstrate appreciative and critical awareness of their own and other Christian traditions as implemented in strategies for ministry." As the student and their mentor team work on the development path for this Christian Tradition outcome, they will typically make certain that the student:

- Explores the development of their ecclesial tradition;

- Identifies how their tradition is situated in the history of Christianity;

- Identifies and engages with significant people, events, and resources important to their theological tradition;
- Discovers historical resources and deals with them in a credible way to consider how they might help address current issues;
- Discerns critical appreciation for those different from them;
- Discovers specific ways their tradition impacts their vocational context.

In relationship to the three areas of content, character, and craft, for this Christian Tradition outcome, the student will typically focus on:

- Content related to the historical development of the church's faith and practice, particularly as it relates to their tradition. Often students discover new vocabulary and frameworks concerning confessional traditions and intellectual processes that inform theological reflection and practice;
- Character related to how they incorporate the insights gained in this outcome into their life, faith, and engagement with others;
- Craft related to demonstrating the skills and practices related to thinking historically and working with groups involving theological differences in their vocational context.

Like the Skillful Biblical Exegesis, the Christian Tradition outcome supposes that the development path and the content, character, and craft aspects of the student's journey will be heavily influenced by their current (or future) vocational/ministry context.

Preliminary Summary

From the two outcome examples given above, demonstrated competency is holistic: the development pathway integrates the content, character, and craft components into each outcome. Furthermore, because of the student-focused nature of CBTE, most assignments can be contextualized to meet the individual needs of each student (and the competencies that need to be demonstrated) for success in their specific ministry context. The following question dominates the CBTE approach: "What does each student need to know (content), be (character), and do (craft) to be competent in their unique ministry context?" Content, character, and craft assignments are distributed throughout the student's journey of discipleship that eventually leads to a degree. All three areas are given equal consideration by the mentor team when assignments are given and outcomes/competencies are assessed. This is a key difference from traditional non-CBTE programs. Most traditional theological education emphasizes content with relatively little room for character (typically some sort of required spiritual formation course) and craft (typically field education). In the CBTE model, while content is still important, it is subservient to the specific competency needs of the individual students in their ministry contexts.

Think of CBTE as a hamburger. The top bun is the outcomes. The bottom bun is the assessments conducted by the mentor team that demonstrate that a particular outcome has been accomplished, that the student is indeed competent in the areas of content, character, and craft related to that outcome as well as to the student's vocational/ministry context. The meat of the hamburger is the contextually driven assignments/targets/indicators for the content, character, and craft needs of the student that can be individualized for them and their specific vocational/ministry context. Again, the depth of necessary content is determined by the student's ministry context. Furthermore, assignments are specifically chosen to enhance and deepen both the student's character and ability to do ministry in their specific context. The student meets regularly with their faculty, vocational/ministry, and personal mentors, as well as occasionally with the entire mentor team, to ensure satisfactory progress is happening.

In the final analysis, CBTE is a journey of discipleship. It is a journey that intimately involves the student, the student's mentor team, and the student's vocational/ministry context.

CBTE and Kairos University

Kairos University today is a global system of competency-based theological education that provides opportunities for students to build entirely customized educational journeys that are affordable, accessible, relevant, and faithful. Everything can be done online, and all courses are offered in synchronous and asynchronous formats or as self-paced learning experiences. The university has a campus in Sioux Falls, South Dakota, offices throughout the United States and Canada, partnerships with organizations around the world, and students from nearly every continent.

This was not always the case. Kairos University began in 1858 when a small group of Baptist church leaders in Rochester, New York, saw the need to develop pastors to serve the German-speaking immigrants flowing into the United States. For 150 years, this North American Baptist seminary was a traditional seminary, with a traditional credit-hour course-based curriculum like most of today's 270 or so accredited seminaries of North America. Then, in 2013, through the guidance of our new president, Greg Henson, we discovered CBTE and made the seismic shift to it.

What's been the result of this shift from traditional theological education to that of CBTE? For Kairos University, the results have been truly phenomenal. When I became chief academic officer and dean in 2015, we were a traditional theological seminary with around 150 students, who averaged $50,000 to $60,000 in debt upon graduation. In 2014, we had just begun a pilot program in CBTE with fifteen students, and honestly, we had little idea what would happen. Today, we have more than 1,500 students who are fully engaged in CBTE at program levels ranging from the BA to the PhD. Our students are located in more than sixty countries. All students pay a monthly subscription fee (that entails all tuition and fees) ranging from $25 to $300 per month, depending on the gross domestic product of the student's local context, thus resulting in little student debt. Some three thousand mentors and more than 150 formal and nonformal partners are distributed around the globe, including several partnerships with theological institutions. In addition to English, we have translated, or are now translating, our CBTE curriculum into Spanish, French, Portuguese, German, and Chinese. More significantly, after ten years of doing CBTE, we now have evidence to show that our CBTE approach to theological education is producing better-equipped graduates (in terms of content, character, and craft) than our former traditional approach did. Furthermore, both the Association of Theological Schools and our regional government accreditor (the Higher Learning Commission) have fully accredited all our CBTE-based master's and doctoral programs. They recognize the value of CBTE.

Why Competency-Based *Missiological* Education?

Contextualized CBTE

CBTE is all about relevancy in relation to the student's specific vocational/ ministry context. By beginning with that end goal in mind, CBTE shapes the content that the student needs to *know*, the character that the student needs to *be*, and the craft that the student needs to *do* in order to be successful in their vocational/ministry contexts. As a result, from readings to assignments, everything is contextualized as much as possible for the student's context.

The contextualized nature of CBTE is *missiological*. As a result, a missiological CBTE is really CBME: competency-based *missiological* education. Substituting the T of CBTE with the M of CBME isn't removing the theological component of being; rather it is enhancing it by making the being element even more missiologically informed since contextualized theology is one of the core elements of missiology. As a result, CBME allows us to shape the educational journey of all of our students, especially our missions students, to equip them in content, character, and craft no matter their contextual missional task.

Since CBME grows out of CBTE, everything said in the first part applies to CBME as well. What's unique to CBME are those components of CBTE that especially lend themselves to contextualization.

Contextualized Components of CBME

There are at least two components of CBME that can be especially helpful for missions students: contextualized mentored teamwork and contextualized learning. Let's examine each in turn.

Contextualized mentored teamwork. Mentor teams are crucial to CBTE and especially to CBME. The missiological nature of CBME allows for faculty mentors to be recruited not only from the realm of academia but from the missions world as well, whether they are indigenous leaders or current or former missionaries. Having a faculty mentor with cross-cultural or multicultural experience coupled with an advanced doctoral degree means that not only is the faculty mentor academically qualified but also missionally qualified to lead the student and mentor team. The vocational/ministry mentor will most likely be an individual (perhaps a veteran missionary or national church leader) who is in the same or similar missional context as the student (currently or in the future). This can result in an especially contextualized development path focused on the competencies needed to do ministry in a missions context. Of course, contextually qualified mentors can also be found in CBTE, as can be contextually focused competencies, but they may more naturally flow out of CBME situations involving missions students.

Contextualized learning. While contextualized learning is possible in CBTE programs, it may more naturally flourish in CBME programs, especially for students serving in or from the Global South. Most Global North cultures tend to be more individualistic, and oftentimes the needs of the individual are stressed over the needs of the group. This is not the case in most Global South cultures. Here the vast majority tend to be more collectivist, meaning that the needs of the group are often stressed over the needs of the individual. That being said the reality is that most Global South educational systems—especially Bible schools and seminaries—were developed by individualistic Global North missionaries and educators (see Caldwell 2010). As a result, most Global South individuals today, though they may be used to an individualist educational system, may prefer the collectivism of their culture if given the opportunity. They may be more open to learning experiences that emphasize group learning, group involvement, and even group assessment.

Furthermore, CBME may be more able to adapt itself to the learning styles and systems of the Global South than CBTE, which tends to be more individualized, especially as it is practiced in North America. Again, this is not to say that CBTE cannot be adapted to Global South contexts, but the missiological basis of CBME may be more flexible in this regard. Some contextualized learning approaches include:

- Assignments can be completed with the learning styles of the student/group in mind (written/oral/video; individual/group);

- Students may form huddle groups to facilitate peer learning, especially in group-oriented cultures;

- Assignments can be divided up among the group with individuals working on specific elements of the assignment (e.g., the chapters of a book can be divided among the individuals of the group to read and then report to the group on what was read instead of requiring everyone to read the entire book);

- Assignments can be presented in the native language of the student;

- Group assessment can be built into mentor-based assessment practices.

Let me give an extended illustration of how a contextualized CBME approach can be worked out. For a few years, I have been mentoring a group of Kairos University students who are a part of our Persian Gulf cohort. These mostly Filipino bi-vocational missionaries are planting aboveground and underground churches throughout the Persian Gulf region, from Saudi Arabia to Qatar to the United Arab Emirates. The CBTE program that we first developed at Kairos University was quite individualistic with a curriculum full of individual assignments. Thus, at the beginning of their CBTE journey, we all (students and mentors alike) defaulted to this individualistic approach to learning. The students in this cohort made slow progress.

After two years of such slow progress, in consultation with Filipino leaders, I totally revamped what we were doing. I went from a CBTE approach to a more missionally focused CBME approach. Instead of an individualistic approach, I followed a collectivist approach based on the culture from which these Filipinos came. Now three or four students were assigned to a huddle group that met weekly either in person or via Zoom. They were encouraged to do their assignments together as a group with each person contributing in their own way to the successful completion of the group's assignments. Most of these assignments involved video presentations, which allowed the creativity of the Filipino people to come to the forefront, resulting in wonderful group presentations. Reading assignments were group based, with various individuals reading parts of an assigned book or article and then coming together to share their insights and learn from one another. When it came to final competency assessments, the other mentors and I used this peer-group format, where members of the huddle group went through the competency assessment process and contributed to the evaluation of each other's competency under the guidance of the mentors. This peer approach proved to be especially fruitful for both students and mentors and often made the competency assessments the highlight of the group's discipleship journey.

Within a year, a significant number of these Persian Gulf cohort students completed their MA program. Some of these graduates are now leading a second generation of huddle groups throughout the Persian Gulf. As a result of the success of this group approach to CBME, I am now encouraging peer huddle groups for other international CBME students that I am mentoring. It is safe to conclude that students from collectivist cultures will flourish if they are allowed to learn according to their cultural preferences. Fortunately, the contextual flexibility of CBME allows mentors to make such learning possible.

Practical Examples of Competency-Based *Missiological* Education

I conclude with two practical examples of competency-based *missiological* education. The first example shows how mission agencies can use CBME with their new missionaries from their initial appointment to ministry on the field. The second example shows how CBME can work in the life and ministry of veteran missionaries, who are already significantly engaged in mission work.

Converge International Ministries and CBME

Through its innovative educational philosophy, revolutionary financial model, and student-centered operating practices, Kairos University's partnership network has expanded to include more than one hundred ministry training organizations and seminaries, including several mission agencies. One of these mission partners is Converge International Ministries (Converge IM). Converge IM is a good example of how CBME can be implemented—building contextually appropriate journeys of missiological education for their new missionary appointees, or global workers, that are affordable, accessible, relevant, and faithful.

Designed by Ann McGhee, Converge IM's director of training, and me, the missiological educational journey for Converge IM's new global workers is called EQUIP:

EQUIP is the onboarding path for all Converge International Ministries global workers. It includes the learning and training experiences that our appointees/commissioned global workers use to prepare for their field of service and is completed by the end of their first 1.5 years on the field (some might complete it faster and some more slowly). This equipping process helps each global worker develop new skills and/or sharpen existing skills to prepare them for the field God is calling them to. (McGhee 2023, 1)

EQUIP incorporates the following into one streamlined, robust, and integrated onboarding path for Converge IM's global workers:

- The list of competencies developed by the worldwide regional directors of Converge IM that they desire our global workers be equipped with prior to deployment to the field;

- The Converge IM vision, values pathway, and central ministry focus;

- The fostering of Converge IM's distinct culture;

- The assurance that all Converge IM appointees have the resources they need to succeed.

EQUIP has seven outcomes that are built on Converge IM's pathway vision, values, and central ministry focus. EQUIP is competency based and includes a pre-field and on-field mentor team that walks alongside each global worker to ensure they receive the unique training they need to thrive in ministry on the field. The seven outcomes include:

- Transformational leadership
- Personal development
- Biblical understanding
- Missiological theology
- History and culture
- Ministry project
- Reflection in community

Each of these seven outcomes incorporates the outcomes of the Master of Arts (intercultural studies) degree at Kairos University. Once global workers demonstrate competency in these seven outcome areas to their mentor team during their pre-field and on-the-field work, they receive the MA degree from Kairos University. The pre-field and on-the-field work that the new global workers will already do in their cross-cultural journey of discipleship (e.g., support raising, language and culture learning, and field strategy development) have been incorporated into the seven outcomes of EQUIP in the three categories of content, character, and craft. All assignments relate directly to specific pre-field and on-the-field requirements to help new global workers become competent for their unique cross-cultural ministry contexts. Furthermore, the costs for EQUIP are built right into the outgoing expenses that the global workers need to raise before their initial field deployment, so no debt is incurred.

As a CBME model, EQUIP is affordable, accessible, relevant, and faithful. It is a great example of how mission agencies, like Converge IM, can incorporate their ethos into their new global workers from the start as well as truly equip them for their future ministry contexts.

Rak Mon and CBME

Mission agencies are one possibility for the implementation of CBME. However, we cannot speak about CBME without speaking about actual students whose lives have been influenced by the flexibility inherent to CBTE and, especially, CBME. One such man is Rak Mon (pseudonym) from Nepal.

Rak Mon grew up outside of Kathmandu. He had some primary education but did not graduate from high school. Instead, he excelled in the local martial arts and became a national champion and later the chief bodyguard to the king of Nepal. Over time he was exposed to Christianity and became a follower of Jesus. He soon demonstrated a gift for evangelism, led many to Jesus in Kathmandu, and started a church there. He became a part of a larger mission organization and through that organization received significant nonformal biblical and theological training. He also perfected his English language skills.

Ten years ago, Rak Mon and his family moved to the United Arab Emirates, where he began evangelizing and planting churches among expatriate Nepalis. His mission organization eventually partnered with Kairos University to give more formal training to their bi-vocational church planters, like Rak Mon, who were scattered throughout the Persian Gulf region. Along with several other pastors within this organization, Rak Mon enrolled in our competency-based Master of Arts (intercultural studies) program. The goal was to help better equip them for their ministries by focusing on the areas of content, character, and craft related to this particular degree.

Though he only had a grade school education, because of the excellent nonformal training of his mission organization combined with his extensive ministry experience, Rak Mon thrived in his MA work, which was built around the core missiological outcomes of spiritual formation, Bible, theology, cultural analysis, and church history. By demonstrating competency from his prior learning and ministry, working with a mentor team, working with peer learning groups, doing joint assignments that were shared among the peer group, submitting video responses instead of written assignments, and participating in verbal final master assessments of his work with his mentor team, Rak Mon completed his MA degree after three years. Today he is a mentor for other bi-vocational pastors and missionaries serving in the Persian Gulf.

Rak Mon is a great example of a proven missions leader who had limited access to formal theological and missiological education but who, through the flexibility of CBME, could still earn a credible, accredited, and master's-level missiological degree. CBME may prove to be one way to help meet the huge missiological training needs of pastors and missionaries in the Global South.

Conclusion

The overview of competency-based theological education coupled with an examination of the missiological nature of competency-based *missiological* education has shown that both are real options for theological and missiological education and training in both the Global North and Global South. Furthermore, it has been shown that CBME is particularly suited for the missiological interests of both missionary training institutions and mission-sending organizations. As a result, there are several reasons to consider CBTE and especially CBME:

- CBTE/CBME will increasingly impact seminaries and how theological and missiological education is done in both the Global North and, increasingly, the Global South;

- The missiological education component of CBME naturally flows from CBTE, with both having much to offer in the doing of theological and missiological education worldwide;

- Missions-related degrees have often been the more practical and relevant degrees, and consequently, they can be adapted most easily to CBME;

- CBME has the potential to revolutionize the missionary training process for both Global North and Global South missionary-sending organizations as well as revolutionizing the training of Global South missionaries and church leaders.

Now is the time to capitalize on the growing interest in CBTE worldwide and build on this interest to develop even more relevant CBME training programs. So, whether you represent a theological and missiological institution or a mission-sending organization, I encourage you to consider what CBTE, and especially CBME, might offer your institution or organization, and especially your students, missionaries, and national leaders. CBME is not the only way to do missiological education, but it is worth examining to see if it might work for you. Competency-based *missiological* education—its time has come!

References

American Institutes for Research. 2019. *State of the Field: Findings from the National Survey Postsecondary Competency-Based Education*. https://www.air.org/sites/default/files/National-Survey-of-Postsecondary-CBE-Lumina-October-2019-rev.pdf.

Anderson, Kenton C., and Gregory J. Henson. 2024. *Theological Education. Principles and Practices of a Competency-Based Approach*. Grand Rapids: Kregel Academic.

Anderson-Levitt, Kathryn, and Meg P. Gardinier. 2021. "Introduction Contextualising Global Flows of Competency-Based Education: Polysemy, Hybridity and Silences." *Comparative Education* 57, no. 1: 1–18. https://doi.org/10.1080/03050068.2020.1852719.

Association of Theological Schools. 2020. "Guidelines on Competency-Based Theological Education (CBTE)." https://www.ats.edu/files/galleries/guidelines-for-cbte-programs_(15_April_2020).pdf.

Caldwell, Larry W. 2010. "How *Asian* Is Asian Theological Education?" In *Tending the Seedbeds: Educational Perspectives on Theological Education in Asia*, edited by Allan Harkness, 23–45. Quezon City: Asia Theological Association. https://kairos.edu/wp-content/uploads/2022/05/Caldwell_-How-Asi...ion_.pdf.

LeBlanc, Paul. 2021. *Students First: Equity, Access, and Opportunity in Higher Education*. Cambridge: Harvard Education Press.

Lurie, Howard. 2019. "State of the Field: Findings from the 2018 National Survey of Postsecondary CBE." January 29, 2019. https://encoura.org/state-of-the-field-findings-from-the-2018-national-survey-of-postsecondary-cbe/.

McGhee, Ann. 2023. "Converge International Ministries EQUIP Path: Information Brief." Internal document. Converge International Ministries.

McGillivray, Ruth. 2020. "Competency-Based Theological Education: Origins of the *Immerse* MDiv at Northwest Baptist Seminary." Northwest Institute for Ministry Education Research. https://nimer.ca/wp-content/uploads/2020/04/McGillivray-New-Model-PDF-Pub-Copy-1.pdf.

Nodine, T. R. 2016. "How Did We Get Here? A Brief History of Competency-Based Higher Education in the United States." *Competency-based Education* 1, no. 1: 1–11. https://onlinelibrary.wiley.com/doi/epdf/10.1002/cbe2.1004.

Chapter 8

Digital Transformation for the Next Generation

Learning by Doing

Andrew Feng and Nick Wu

Introduction

"One in three terrorists are technologists and only one in 1,500 Christian missionaries are technologists" (Preston, 2020). This alarming contrast underscores the disparity in which technology achieves pain and destruction instead of redemptive purposes. The secular world has leveraged media and digital strategies as a key to its success, whereas many Christians have lagged in adopting technology to share the gospel effectively. Implementing technological changes in ministry can appear daunting, but to be cultural and societal leaders, Christians must keep up with the evolving digital landscape. The church needs to embrace digital technology to deliver the good news to the unreached and engage the next generation in the Great Commission.

The next generation—Generation Z (Gen Z)—is in touch with the digital world but often out of touch with global missions. Born in the late 1990s to early 2010s, the oldest members of Gen Z are now entering the workforce. As digital natives, they have had access to smartphones and computers before they were teenagers. In a 2018 study in the United States, only 17 percent of Christians were familiar with the Great Commission, and only one in ten Christians knew of their responsibility to share the gospel (Barna Group 2018). If the church as a whole has not realized the need for global missions, then it is unlikely to expect the church's next generation to take on the work of cross-cultural missions. The growing generation gap has led to the absence of workers willing to engage and serve unreached people.

Digital spaces present new opportunities to connect Christians to the Great Commission and the unreached. The next generation uses digital platforms daily, permeating various places such as school, professional work, entertainment, shopping, and social networks. With only 1 percent of Christians in professional ministry, the remaining 99 percent can use digital skills to support and supplement frontline workers.

However, the digital landscape comes with its challenges. The sheer volume and variety of learning opportunities can be overwhelming, and individuals need help to validate the information they encounter. Within digital spaces, online learning models and platforms can also exacerbate feelings of isolation and loneliness. These difficulties with technology cannot be overlooked; rather, there must be an approach to redeem technology for global missions.

In this chapter, virtual cohorts are presented as a method for the next generation to learn by doing and to use their digital skills to engage in global missions. Through this mission-infused avenue of experiential learning, they can apply their faith and work together to advance the gospel. The virtual cohort creates an accessible yet engaging experience to collaborate with like-minded peers. Through this approach, the next generation can go beyond the traditional boundaries of ministry, regardless of location, and take a step toward the future of long-term missions involvement.

Technology in Missions

Technological advances have historically helped spread the gospel to new people and places. Several key tools that impacted evangelism include the network of Roman roads built in 300 BC, the printing press in AD 1436, television evangelism in 1950, the internet in 1983, and the mobile phone, now with 5.4 billion users (Kemp 2023). In every missions era, technology helped missionaries go where the gospel had not yet gone. For example, William Carey realized the compass provided new possibilities for reaching people. In 1792, Carey wrote, "Use every lawful method to spread the knowledge of his name" (3). In this current era of missions, every disciple of Christ is called to make disciples of all nations anywhere and everywhere, including through the available tools and technology. D. Ray Davis (2017) wrote, "We are relationally connected and networked like never before. We should seize this moment to build toward limitless impact." Christians living in this modern era of missions now have a greater responsibility to utilize technology in a way that reflects Christ.

In the Bible, Paul used an important medium—letters. He wrote in Ephesians: "For we are God's handiwork, created in Christ Jesus to do good works, which God prepared in advance for us to do" (2:10 NIV). Paul indicated that God has given every person a specific plan, purpose, and skills needed to follow Christ in doing good works. Through technology, Christians can do good in sharing the gospel via online evangelism, social media outreach, or using technology to take part in charitable efforts. Paul also wrote, "I have become all things to all people so that by all possible means I might save some" (1 Cor 9:22 NIV). Christians are called to be near the culture of the people they are reaching so that souls may hear of Jesus. This mindset also applies in modern technology, where digital spaces and knowledge are ubiquitous in daily life. Digital channels, including social media, blogs, and other online platforms, enable followers to take part in representing Christ in their personal faith journey. In this way, technology is a vehicle for evangelism, and the sharing of testimonies is a vehicle for building up the church.

Internet Users in the 10/40 Window

Today, more than 5.1 billion people have internet access, and about 65 percent of global internet users live in North Africa, Central Asia, South Asia, East Asia, and Southeast Asia (fig. 8.1). These regions overlap with the 10/40 window, a key target for missions work because so few believers live there. The slow progression of the gospel in these regions indicates a disparity of Christian efforts in fully using the internet to engage with people in the region. Their greatest spiritual need is often emphasized because many people in these regions will never hear the gospel or meet a Christian in their lifetime (Joshua Project n.d.). However, many people who are considered unreached are online. The internet and digital spaces provide an opportunity to learn about Jesus for the first time, whether through online evangelism, social media ads, or other digital strategies. Before a few missionaries follow their calling to go to these regions, there is an opportunity for all believers with digital access to initiate reaching out to the unreached online, which also includes the potential for digital discipleship. This can be a strategic choice for digital natives, in which case the internet has taken on globalization and crossed traditional cultural boundaries. People online may find more in common with each other in this new culture than with people in their ethnolinguistic localities.

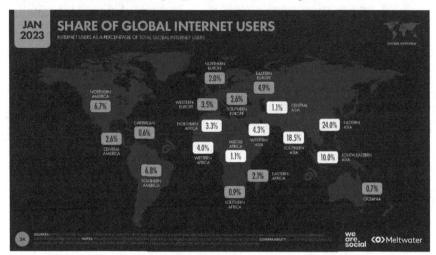

Figure 8.1: Share of Global Internet Users
Areas represented in white show 65 percent of the total 5.16 billion global internet users (Kemp 2023). This indicates that the majority of internet users are located in the 10/40 window, where there is an urgent need for pioneering missions work.

The Missions World Needs Digital Transformation

In a rapidly changing digital landscape, the missions world needs digital transformation to adopt and utilize new strategies to reach a digitally connected world that is disconnected from Jesus. Digital transformation is the adoption of digital technology for innovation, invention, user experience, or efficiency. The term is widely used in the tech industry to describe "the continuous process by which enterprises adapt to or drive disruptive changes leveraging digital competencies, customer experiences, and operational processes" (Fitzgerald et al. 2020).

Digital transformation includes both the practice and mindset of Christians to engage in digital technology as a valuable medium for communication and evangelism. In practice, it can transform work and daily tasks to be more streamlined or automated, thus saving resources like time and money. It is also crucial for Christians to be thinking about the future, where there will be a need for continual adaptation and innovation. Missions leaders need to be pioneers of innovation to be culturally relevant in reaching a wider audience undergoing digital globalization.

Digital transformation also enables Christians to collaborate effectively. Where there are digital needs, ministries can share their resources and work together online. Instant communication has become an accessible way for Christians to connect with the rest of the world. Staying on top of the digital landscape also helps them to address the challenges of cybersecurity, misinformation, cyberbullying, and mental health.

As for the next generation, digital transformation can bridge the gap in digital knowledge and experience between generations. Experienced leaders in global missions have the opportunity to activate digital native Christians to be involved in global missions in their culture and for their future. The hope is for the next generation to learn how they are urgently needed in missions, find their place and how they fit, and discover their identity at the intersection of faith, work, and missions.

Missions Premortem

Rapid changes in digital transformation, staying ahead of the curve, and adopting new technology can be daunting for many Christians. The world is now digital and will only become increasingly digital. The global pandemic in 2020 proved how far behind many ministries were in adapting to digital strategies. However, one positive outcome was the movement of ministries to go online, providing remote access to content and theological education. Now, a student from India can join a seminary online without extracting themselves from their community or local ministry. Other current digital strategies include outreach via social media and media content. Now that multiple generations have adopted video conferencing, digital discipleship has also become more prevalent. Across oceans and borders, Christians provide holistic training and development for those with technological access and simultaneously open avenues for the gospel.

While the church has significantly improved in digital transformation and using technology for good in this post-pandemic period, Christians must continuously adapt and learn. John Dyer (2011) notes that as technology advances, more time and education are required to use it. While hot topics like artificial intelligence, cybersecurity, and big data have existed for decades, they have become mainstream rather than limited to a subset of users. Even the most skilled industry professionals require academic and corporate resources to learn about new technology, but learning is an investment in improving productivity and knowledge.

Christians in any setting require the same time and effort to stay ahead of the curve when adopting technologies. Artificial intelligence (AI) is one of the mainstream technology topics that require the church's attention. AI can be applied in a variety of contexts, but it raises ethical challenges as well. In the past year, ChatGPT, which is an AI-text generator tool developed by OpenAI, emerged as a powerful chatbot due to its conversational responses and broad expertise. More than the typical one-liner fact checks, ChatGPT can generate essays within seconds, thus raising the subject of academic integrity. AI art generators that create full digital renders from text prompts have also challenged the art community, where data permissions and copyrights are compromised. For the Great Commission, AI has also been used to great effect for Bible translation, such as with SIL and Wycliffe, where translators can analyze large data sets on language to produce more accurate translations. These tools have great potential but require careful discernment, which Christians are encouraged to navigate to guide the church in following God's will.

These new digital technologies are indicative of where the world is heading. The digital landscape shapes this missions era where traditional methods will no longer be the most effective strategies. Similar to the frog in the kettle metaphor, a similar phenomenon is at play with the decline of Christianity in the US. Church attendance and influence have slowly declined in recent decades, with fewer members from each generation. Pew Research Center (2019) conducted a survey identifying the large generation gap in American religion, as seen in figure 2. This decline has been attributed to various factors over the past few decades, but many Christians have failed to adapt to these changes, especially when the church relies on outdated strategies of evangelism and discipleship. When Christians do not respond to the cultural and generational changes around them they become like a boiling frog, leading to Christianity's overall decline and loss of influence.

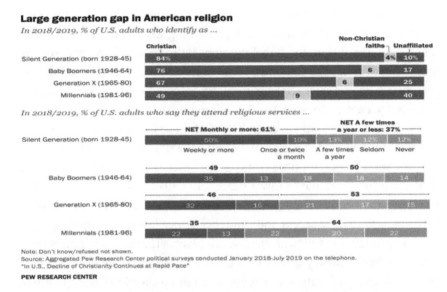

Large generation gap in American religion
In 2018/2019, % of U.S. adults who identify as ...

Figure 8.2: Large Generation Gap in American Religion
This survey was conducted by Pew Research Center (2019) from January 2018
to July 2019 by telephone. At this rate, the younger generation, including
Generation Z, can be projected to show even less religious affiliation.

Innovation in practice is to discover through the unknown. Innovating in
missions work, like using digital technology and engaging the next
generation, can be a daunting task. It can also be compared to a "blizzard"
as Andy Crouch, Kurt Keilhacker, and Dave Blanchard (2020) wrote:

> As leaders we must react swiftly to the blizzard that is already upon us ...
> pivot to survive ... and reimagine our organizations to outlast the rigors of
> a possible little ice age. ... We are, for reasons only God knows, on the front
> line, on the starting team. Let us act boldly, today, to build as best we can,
> for the love of our neighbor and the glory of God.

This is the task for current and future ministry leaders, especially when there
is a dire need for the next generation to help fulfill the Great Commission.
Getting to the front of the adoption curve is essential in preventing the
loss of the next generation in this digital age. Before young adults become
fully disengaged from the church, digital transformation, innovation, and
collaboration must be implemented to address the challenges of spreading
the gospel. If organizations pivot to a posture of change, it may circumvent
any need for a painful postmortem (Klein 2007). Conducting a premortem

examination in a business project is helpful compared to a postmortem for the sake of looking ahead and preventing disastrous consequences. Likewise, a premortem for global missions indicates a task that will remain unfinished without the full body of believers and the next generation. The premortem model is crucial for ministry leaders because their influence alone is not enough to reach the 3.2 billion unreached people in the world. Michael Oh (2019) apologizes on behalf of those in professional ministry, "Global mission partnerships mobilizing the 1% and the 99% to go to peoples and places with little or no gospel witness or community are the strategic need of our day." Only 1 percent of Christians are in professional ministry. The need is to empower the ministry of the other 99 percent of Christians, who have access and influence to disciple people in all spheres of society, including the hardest-to-reach places. The next generation must step into their ministry role of evangelism and discipleship, whether they enter a professional ministry or remain in a nonprofessional occupation to be a light.

Opportunities for the Next Generation

The next generation has been culturally transformed by digital technology, and it will continue to influence and shape their future. David Bourgeois (2013) indicates how society has evolved in the usage of the internet, moving away from just using digital media for informational purposes, but for relational purposes, where top sites are social networks and platforms. Online social skills affect the culture of the next generation and how they engage with the world around them. Relationships, entertainment, education, and work are now fully available online. Ninety-two percent of jobs now require digital skills (National Skills Coalition 2023). Thirty-nine percent of US knowledge workers will work in a hybrid function, both in an onsite environment and remotely, by the end of 2023 (Gartner 2023). Computer science and communication degrees have two of the highest job growth rates projected for 2020–2030, at 13 percent and 14 percent, respectively (BestColleges 2021).

While young adults are learning digital methodologies, streamlining, and automation in the marketplace, ministry work often forgoes those practices or lacks the knowledge and resources to properly implement their digital skills. Whether or not they desire to serve in missions in any capacity, many young adults do not know how their digital skills can be impactful for global missions. However, there are many digital opportunities and needs in the missions world, where many missions organizations are implementing digital strategies and providing cross-cultural content and training resources online. For contemporary missions, the next generation has vast amounts of digital resources available, including online theological education, to learn about global missions and strategies.

Virtual Cohorts and Learning by Doing

Online learning became popular with the growth of the internet in the late 1990s and early 2000s. Jones International University launched the first fully online degree program in 1999, and then many other colleges and universities began to offer their own (Allen and Seaman 2016). In recent years and as a result of COVID-19, online education has become more popular at all grade levels. Many seminaries have also begun to offer complete programs online.

There are both benefits and challenges to online learning. Some advantages include the accessibility of courses from anywhere, customization for students to learn based on their interests, and saving on costs that come with in-person tuition and expenses. However, online learning can also result in thinner relationships between students, lower commitments, higher drop-out rates, and other technical challenges like slow internet connectivity. Some hesitate with online learning due to arguments of it being both "disembodied" and "sedentary" (Graber 2021). FaithTech addressed this objection in its report on digital learning platforms:

> Given the example of footwashing, which involves active participation, some might object that virtual education does not engage the whole person. However, we must distinguish "disembodied" from "sedentary." While virtual learning can be quite sedentary, it is still fully embodied. Virtual education involves the whole person at some level, even if it looks quite different from a learner raising their hand in a classroom, speaking passionately during a seminar, or doing experiments in a lab. Each is embodied in different ways. If the "disembodied" objection is actually a "sedentary" objection, how might that concern be addressed? The better we articulate these varieties of embodiment, the better we may be able to decide what forms of education are best applied in each case. (Graber 2021)

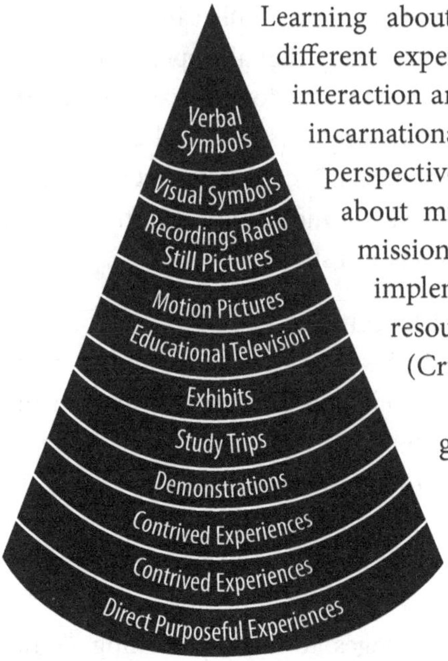

Learning about missions will also look like a different experience. It cannot replace physical interaction and relationships that are needed for incarnational ministry. From an educational perspective, it provides many inroads to learn about missions and be involved in digital missions, which include the creation or implementation of tools, strategies, and resources for the spread of the gospel (Cru n.d.).

To address the need for the next generation to be involved in global missions, virtual cohorts can be an effective program for the long-term advancement of the gospel. Christian pedagogy is also exemplified through a cohort-based learning model (1 Cor 4:15; Gal 3:24–25). The Bible shows how various teaching methods are used, such as Jesus teaching his disciples and the crowds through parables. The disciples then practiced Jesus's teachings and taught new believers to follow Christ. Jesus's pedagogy is influential for the cohort-based learning model, where Christians can foster community support between peers and mentors, actively serve others using their God-given talents and abilities, grow and develop personally and spiritually, and model missional engagement to those around them. A virtual cohort integrates this in learning by doing, which may be best described as "Direct Purposeful Experiences," represented in Edgar Dale's "Cone of Experience" (fig. 8.3). With new technology and digital platforms, "Direct Purposeful Experiences" can be blended with multiple media and formats to engage learners in a virtual cohort, including verbal and visual symbiosis and videos (motion pictures and demonstrations) to reinforce what they have learned. Increased learning retention across today's multimedia digital platforms can enable the next generation to be informed and involved in global missions.

Verbal
Symbols
Visual Symbols
Recordings Radio
Still Pictures
Motion Pictures
Educational Television
Exhibits
Study Trips
Demonstrations
Contrived Experiences
Contrived Experiences
Direct Purposeful Experiences

Figure 8.3 Cone of Experience
The "Direct Purposeful Experiences" appear at the base of the cone as the most effective pedagogical approach (Dale, 1946).

Cohort-based learning also gains many advantages over traditional online learning. This integrates the Christian pedagogical approach, which promotes a faith-aligned community to collaborate when serving. In traditional online learning, "understanding" and "remembering" are the objectives. However, Bloom's Taxonomy emphasizes that cohort-based learning extends knowledge retention beyond just understanding and remembering to applying, analyzing, evaluating, and creating (fig. 8.4). Virtual cohorts encourage the next generation to apply what they learn in global missions to produce new and original work that meets the needs of the missions world.

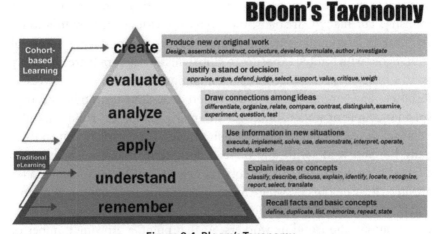

Figure 8.4: Bloom's Taxonomy
The peak of learning is when you create, evaluate, and analyze.
The baseline of learning is when you remember and understand.
Source from vanderbilt.edu. Edited by Teachfloor.com (Solis 2022).

To engage the next generation in missions, a virtual cohort encourages people to learn, ideate, solve problems, and create together. Virtual cohorts given digital missions projects learn about global missions while creating new digital solutions for challenges in the missions world. When virtual cohorts are available to people in different locations or countries, they can have new discussions based on their multiple cultural backgrounds. Learning together in this type of community can also result in higher engagement and retention. This is a direct application of their faith and work, where their skills, including digital affinities and abilities, can be put into practice. The virtual cohort-based model also enables accessibility for

Christians where overseas missions involvement may not yet be feasible. There are opportunities to connect with missionaries and frontline workers through online communication and learn about their needs and challenges firsthand. In many cases, these missionaries also have digital needs, and the help of young digital natives becomes beneficial in both ways. Missionaries receive support, while young adults gain a deeper understanding of their missional calling. Some of the digital needs of the missions world include tools or apps that aid in telling Bible stories, Bible translation, missions information and data analysis, marketing, and social media.

Enabling the next generation to leverage their digital skills will help to activate those among the 99 percent of Christians who are not yet in ministry. For many Christians, their typical missions journey to a long-term missions commitment is a long road. Often, they start as a normal churchgoer with limited exposure to global missions. From there, they may go to a missions conference or take a missions course like Perspectives. If resources and timing line up, they will go on a short-term missions trip, spend a couple of weeks running a summer program for children, build a house, or teach English. At that point, many Christians return to their daily life and work, with any hope of long-term missions involvement delayed for retirement. Virtual cohorts engaged in digital missions offer an alternate user journey, where they can start long-term involvement now and be available remotely to offer their digital expertise to support missions organizations and frontline workers. At that point, a growing number of digital natives in the 99 percent of Christians who are not in professional ministry will have a place in global missions.

For the activation of a young adult, learning by doing in a virtual cohort combines their heart (emotions), head (knowledge), and hands (skills), allowing the student to bring their whole self to God. R. Paul Stevens (2016) wrote: "Orthodoxy. Orthopraxy. Orthopathy. All three point to the marriage of theology and everyday life: theology and life linked in praise (orthodoxy), practice (orthopraxy) and passion (orthopathy). What God therefore has joined together let no theological institution put asunder." When learning about missions involves the whole person, we will see the next generation take ownership of their calling to missions.

Examples of Virtual Cohorts

Virtual cohorts engaged in digital missions projects have been conducted by Indigitous, a name coined from the words indigenous and digital. Indigitous is a global movement engaging believers in their digital and creative skills to take the gospel to new people and places. Indigitous identified this gap for the next generation to learn of the urgent need for global missions, and it gives them a space to use their digital skills to help solve some of the biggest challenges the missions world faces today. Indigitous began in 2016 with #HACK, the largest Christian hackathon, and has since engaged thousands of technologists and creatives in digital missions (Lukens 2022). In 2021, Indigitous US launched its virtual cohort program to engage young adults through digital missions projects in partnership with several missions organizations, including Joshua Project, Pioneers, SIL, and Frontier Ventures.

The virtual cohort program was created during the COVID-19 pandemic as a solution for young adult Christians to be engaged in global missions while they were unable to go overseas for short-term missions. This was an opportunity for like-minded believers to connect across the US, receive mentorship and digital discipleship, and collaborate on a digital missions project. The first iteration of the virtual cohort was made up of young adults from different universities, including Cal Tech, Gordon College, University of California San Diego, and the University of Texas. The cohort met with the Joshua Project and learned about the needs of frontier people groups. They built awareness campaigns through social media and digital content, videos, and websites. Through this cohort experience, young adults brought together their various digital affinities and abilities from computer science, marketing, business, graphic design, and video production to take a step in their missions journey. As part of the program, they also raised funds, recruited prayer partners, wrote newsletter updates, and invited local churches and communities to support them.

Another cohort in 2021 partnered with a ministry of Pioneers to develop a simple Bible story app for a persecuted, unreached people group. This cohort of students developed and designed the mobile app through the mentorship of software developers from Google and missionaries with backgrounds in computer science to answer a real need for this unreached people group. In this way, they learned about this people group's deep struggles and challenges and prayed for the gospel to reach them. Developing a mobile app with several key Bible stories would be a small step with a significant impact on this local community. Through online communication, the cohort received real-time feedback from the local missionary to refine the Bible app. The partnership with Pioneers has now expanded to multiple cohorts throughout the year, where students can contribute their digital skills to help take the Bible to more unreached people who do not yet have translations in their heart language.

The virtual cohorts at Indigitous were also not exclusive to technologists. Another group of young adult art students from a local church in Los Angeles wanted to use their illustration skills to help families pray for unreached people groups. For students who have only ever gone on short-term missions trips to run a Vacation Bible School or an English camp, this was a unique opportunity to activate their artistic skills. For their project, they partnered with the Joshua Project to produce, write, and illustrate a prayer guide for thirty-one of the largest frontier people groups with the fewest pioneering Christian workers. Through illustration and character design, these students depicted these people groups for children and parents to pray together. Through careful research and prayer for each people group, the virtual cohort of art students learned about the different cultures to represent the people groups accurately and appealingly to families. The project has since resulted in a full publication in digital and print, including translations in more than eight major languages, and an audiobook for families to pray together.

The virtual cohort program yielded positive results and feedback from the next generation of young adults:

> The biggest thing I learned is that you don't have to be in vocational ministry to be in the Lord's service. I often fell into the trap of believing that my skillset couldn't be used for the glory of the kingdom. I thought that my skillset was somehow less valuable because it didn't lend itself to on-the-ground, frontline mission work. To put it bluntly, I felt bad that I was a desk jockey by trade. Now, however, I don't feel that way so much. The fall cohort provided an opportunity for me to use the talents God has granted me for the purpose of mission work. (Indigitous cohort member)

> The most important thing I learned about missions was the power and importance of collaboration. I was not familiar with the culture that we

would be working with, but the field team provided us with lots of useful information and feedback. We were able to create something that was specifically designed for the group of people that we were catering to. (Indigitous cohort member)

It was so incredible to see these young technologists engaging with a least-reached people group. We were blessed to have them come alongside us in this work. Sometimes in work among unreached peoples, you can feel a bit alone, and having a group come in with fresh ideas and skills is very life-giving. (Indigitous cohort mentor)

Many of these young adults would have considered themselves part of the 99 percent of Christians who will not pursue professional ministry as their calling. Their heart for ministry has often been confined to traditional ministry defined by their church. At the same time, their most valued skill sets are used in the marketplace, where innovation and digital technology are prioritized. Through digital missions projects in virtual cohorts, these young adults have gained a new sense of their faith and work, where they can contribute beyond the four church walls with a digital reach to support places that have the biggest hurdles to knowing Jesus. The activation of the 99 percent into their calling to missions and in ministry is necessary for finishing the task of the Great Commission and reaching every people group with the gospel.

Conclusion

The current generation finds itself at a critical juncture in fulfilling the Great Commission. Digital transformation is an imperative step toward keeping pace with the rapidly evolving world. Presently, a meager one in 1,500 missionaries possesses technological expertise, making it crucial to incorporate digital transformation to bridge the gap between generations.

Every facet of modern society has become permeated by the digital landscape, with more than 5 billion internet users worldwide, 65 percent of which are concentrated in regions in the 10/40 window. The 1 percent in professional ministry must seize the opportunity for innovation and collaboration with the 99 percent of the church to advance the gospel to new people and places. Failure to take action premortem would be akin to being a metaphorical boiling frog or being unaware of an impending blizzard, leading to the loss of the next generation.

Through virtual cohorts engaged in digital missions projects, the next generation has an opportunity to realign their faith journey toward their missions calling. Whether they eventually go as cross-cultural workers or support missions using their digital skills, they can find their place by taking the first step through digital. In this way, they can become informed of the greatest needs of the missions world and create together. Through purpose-driven work, the next generation can build upon the missions knowledge of their predecessors and innovate strategies to complete the Great Commission. Digital transformation is one step toward the future, where virtual cohorts offer a unique learning experience for the next generation to embrace global missions.

References

Barna Group and the Impact 360 Institute. 2018. *Gen Z: The Culture, Beliefs, and Motivations Shaping the Next Generation*. Barna Group.

BestColleges. 2021. "Most Popular College Majors." *BestColleges* (blog).

Bourgeois, David T. 2013. *Ministry in the Digital Age: Strategies and Best Practices for a Post-Website World*. Downers Grove, IL: InterVarsity Press.

Carey, William. 1792. *An Enquiry into the Obligations of Christians to Use Means for the Conversion of the Heathens*. Leicester: Ann Ireland. https://www.wmcarey.edu/carey/enquiry/anenquiry.pdf.

Crouch, Andy, Kurt Keilhacker, and Dave Blanchard. 2020. "Leading beyond the Blizzard: Why Every Organization Is Now a Startup." *Praxis Journal*. https://journal.praxislabs.org/leading-beyond-the-blizzard-why-every-organization-is-now-a-startup-b7f32fb278ff.

Cru. n.d. "Digital Missions." Cru. Accessed January 11, 2024. https://www.cru.org/digitalmissions/.

Dale, Edgar. 1946. *Audio-Visual Methods in Teaching*. New York: Dryden.

Davis, D. Ray. 2017. "Missions History: On the Cusp of a New Era of Modern Missions?" *International Mission Board*. https://www.imb.org/2017/09/07/have-we-entered-a-new-era-of-modern-missions/.

Dyer, John. 2011. *From the Garden to the City: The Redeeming and Corrupting Power of Technology*. Grand Rapids: Kregel.

Fitzgerald, Shawn, Daniel-Zoe Jimenez, Serge Findling, Yukiharu Yorifuji, Megha Kumar, Lianfeng Wu, Giulia Carosella et al. 2020. "IDC FutureScape: Worldwide Digital Transformation 2021 Predictions." IDC. https://www.idc.com/getdoc.jsp?containerId=US46880818.

Gartner. 2023. "Gartner Forecasts 39% of Global Knowledge Workers Will Work Hybrid by the End of 2023." Gartner Newsroom. https://www.gartner.com/en/newsroom/press-releases/2023-03-01-gartner-forecasts-39-percent-of-global-knowledge-workers-will-work-hybrid-by-the-end-of-2023.

Graber, Adam. 2021. "Digital Learning Platforms." *FaithTech*. https://faithtech.com/product/digital-learning-platforms/.

Helfer, Doris. 1999. "Has the Virtual University Library Truly Arrived?" https://scholarworks.calstate.edu/downloads/kk91fp99v.

Joshua Project. n.d. Accessed January 11, 2024. https://joshuaproject.net/.

Kemp, Simon. 2023. "Digital 2023: Global Overview Report." DataReportal. https://datareportal.com/reports/digital-2023-global-overview-report.

Klein, Gary. 2007. "Performing a Project Premortem." *Harvard Business Review*. https://hbr.org/2007/09/performing-a-project-premortem.

Lukens, Jeremy. 2022. "Indigitous Celebrates 9 Years of Digital Missions." Indigitous. https://indigitous.org/2022/11/11/nine-years-of-indigitous/.

National Skills Coalition. 2023. "New Report: 92% of Jobs Require Digital Skills; One-Third of Workers Have Low or No Digital Skills due to Historic Underinvestment, Structural Inequities." National Skills Coalition. https://nationalskillscoalition.org/news/press-releases/new-report-92-of-jobs-require-digital-skills-one-third-of-workers-have-low-or-no-digital-skills-due-to-historic-underinvestment-structural-inequities/.

Oh, Michael. 2019. "An Apology from the Christian 99%, from the 1%." *Christianity Today*. https://www.christianitytoday.com/ct/2019/june-web-only/apology-christian-99-1-percent-lausanne-gwf-michael-oh.html.

Pew Research Center. 2019. "In U.S., Decline of Christianity Continues at Rapid Pace." https://www.pewresearch.org/religion/2019/10/17/in-u-s-decline-of-christianity-continues-at-rapid-pace/.

Preston, Frank. 2020. "Shortage of Technologists: Reimagining the Future of Missions Training." *Media to Movements*. https://mediatomovements.com/articles/shortage-of-technologists.

Solis, Janica. 2022. "Cohort-Based Learning vs Traditional e-Learning: Which Is Better?" *Teachfloor* (blog). https://www.teachfloor.com/blog/cohort-based-learning-vs-traditional-e-learning-which-is-better.

Stevens, R. Paul. 2016. "Living Theologically: Toward a Theology of Christian Practice. *Themelios* 20, no. 3: 4–8. https://www.thegospelcoalition.org/themelios/article/living-theologically-toward-a-theology-of-christian-practice/.

Chapter 9

Transforming Our Mission Education Methods from Cognitive Teaching to Connected Learning

Sarah K. Lunsford

Everything we do in the field of missiology involves education—from evangelism to leadership training, from life-on-life discipleship to theological education. Vast libraries of information and training are widely available on teaching principles, and most of us are regularly exposed to training on this topic. The information is out there, but the question is—how are we doing? Are we applying the educational principles that we know to our missiological task? Have the facts and concepts about how people learn been able to transform the way that we teach? This chapter will focus on the missiological implications of transformative learning principles with an emphasis on the role of relationships in the holistic learning process. In the interest of practicing what I preach, we will explore this topic not in a purely academic and cognitive-dominant manner but in a holistic, relational, storied way that encourages personal reflection and collegial dialogue.

My undergraduate degree was in missions. I threw myself into my courses and was even granted my school's annual missions award. I confidently (nay, arrogantly) launched my international mission career within a week of my graduation ceremony. Was I a raging success? Not at all. I had no idea what to do, and I messed up the things I thought I knew how to do. It turns out that, despite my ability to *talk about* missions, I was completely unequipped to *do* missions. A few years later, I earned a seminary degree and relaunched my missions career (take two!). This time, though, I knew what I was doing. I felt fully equipped and was able to navigate every unique contextual scenario I encountered. Today, as I've spent the past fifteen years training ministers and missionaries in the US and internationally, I want to know what made the difference between my first and second degrees. What was it about my seminary's educational methods that transformed my mission career? How can I capitalize on that experience to help me transform the lives of my mission students? The analysis and application approach I take in evaluating and integrating these social science theories into our mission education methods follows the framework I previously developed (Lunsford 2023).

Holistic Transformative Learning Principles

In the field of transformative learning, we find that learning is not an entirely linear process. People do not simply receive information and then, as soon as they cognitively apprehend its meaning, go on to apply it to their lives. There's far more to the holistic learning process (see Taylor 2008, 5–15; Cranton 2006; Dirkx, Mezirow, and Cranton 2006, 123–39; Kolb 2015).

In fact, when people hear new information, they react to it emotionally. They evaluate whether the subject is important to their own lives and goals and how it integrates with their existing cognitive framework of facts and experiences. If a person is apathetic or antagonistic toward a topic, then no matter how well they understand it, they will not incorporate it into their lives. Our affective response to a topic has a direct bearing on the way we process, evaluate, and integrate cognitive information. It makes us want to change our perspective. Our emotional response is what motivates us to adjust our lives to accommodate the new information and its implications (see Ott 2016; Smith 2009; Sousa 2017; Shaw 2014).

In addition to the cognitive and affective dimensions of learning, there is also the behavioral element. We tend to think of our actions, behaviors, and applications as the linear consequence of adequate cognitive learning. Behavioral change follows comprehension, right? Not quite. We need to actively engage a subject as *part of* the learning process. We learn by doing (Festinger 1957; Bushnell 1979; Simpson 1966; Issler and Habermas 1994). In my first experience on the mission field, I had more than enough cognitive understanding of missiology, but because I had not practiced any of it, I had not fully learned it.

These three dimensions of learning—cognitive, affective (evaluative), and behavioral (experiential)—occur in a holistic manner with all three elements working together. New information interacts with our whole life when it engages us emotionally and actively (see Smith 2009, 53–59).

Perhaps even more interesting is the discovery that human relationships may be the key ingredient to this holistic learning process. Even when we balance the cognitive, affective, and behavioral elements of learning, we cannot neglect the vital *mode* or vehicle for engaging all three of those elements—the human social connection. When we can receive information through a relationship, when we can process its meaning, significance, and implications in community with others, and when we can witness the variety of applications and outcomes in other people's lives—that is the most ideal, holistic learning scenario for encouraging a life-changing response (see Ott 2016, 228; Shaw 2014; Cranton 2006, 163–67; Marzano 2007; Hwang 2004; Ito et al. 2013).

In fact, recent studies in neuroscience confirm that relationships manage our holistic learning process. The parts of the human brain that regulate data, emotions, behaviors, and relationships are all biologically interconnected systems (see Taylor 2001, 218–36; Zull 2002; Elmer and Elmer 2020; Jones et al. 2011). Curt Thompson explains that the mind "is crucially dependent on the presence of relationships" (Thompson 2015, 40; see also Siegel 2020; Siegel 2010; Thompson 2010).

Studies also show that the human mind even makes relationship connections with people who will never know us personally and who may not even be real, like book or movie characters. Consider the way that Jesus's parables were just as powerful as if the characters were living people or think of the real connection we might feel with a beloved author or a favorite television character. It seems that relationships serve to embody (incarnate) lessons into a natural, holistic, living context. When cognitive information is packaged in a living human connection (whether storied or real, distant or face-to-face, social or parasocial), the affective and behavioral elements are simultaneously engaged (Marzano 2007, 152; see also Rain and Mar 2021; Thomson 2021).

The interpersonal nature of how our minds function reflects the Trinitarian God in whose image we are created. Not only did God create us to need community, even down to our very biology (Thompson 2015, 40), but community is also a core element of the nature of church. When John Hammett describes the five ministries of the church (teaching, fellowship, worship, service, and evangelism), which jointly serve the purpose of glorifying God, he demonstrates that fellowship is the key central ministry that undergirds and unites all others (Hammet 2005, 220, 232–38). The teaching ministry of the church requires *koinonia* (fellowship). Our fundamental need for interpersonal connections and community is far more essential to every part of how we think, learn, and function than we often realize.

The principles of holistic transformative learning through relational connections bear implications for every part of our missiological task. When Thomas Seckler studied the key elements for life change in Cambodian evangelism among Muslim-background believers, he uncovered the significance of these holistic and relational principles. He writes: "The Christian message is not received by humans in a sterile fashion. It comes through the words of humans, often demonstrated by their hands and actions. … This Christian message became personal to many of them because it was communicated to them by those they knew intimately and respected, and because it was lived out in front of them" (Seckler 2020, 129–45). When Lynn Thigpen (2020, 99–100) studied adult learners without formal education, her findings overwhelmingly demonstrated the vital role of connected learning through relationship and socialization for discipleship among oral learners. Alemseged Alemu (2022), who taught me much of what I know about transformative learning, tested and supported that transformative learning principles are key for effective theological education in Ethiopia.

While advances in our educational methods have certainly been made in recent years, we can generalize that the importance of holistic transformative learning through community is not a new topic. As Arthur Lin (2023, 138) pointedly argues, it's not that we don't know these teaching principles, it's that we don't apply them. Perhaps it's safe to say that many of us have not yet allowed our cognitive grasp of holistic and connected learning principles to fully transform our missionary training methods.

Implication One: Beware Cognitive Mastery

Paulo Freire offered a needed rebuke on the paternalistic implications of our traditional cognitive-based teaching methods. When we set up the teacher (or missionary) as the expert or the redeemer on a given topic and use a largely lecture-style teaching model, focused on conveying information, Freire said that we reinforce a master-slave teaching approach (Freire 1996, 45). Instead, he argued for a more dialogical approach, one that respects the experience and reasoning of the learners. He wrote: "The important thing is to help me (and nations) help themselves, to place them in consciously critical confrontation with their problems, to make them the agents of their own recuperation" (Freire 2005, 12).

In a similar vein, Jessica Udall highlights the patronizing approach assumed by the Gospel Coalition's Theological Famine Relief project: "It portrays majority world pastors as helpless, starving, not having what is needed for survival unless relief is brought from outside" (Udall 2022, 151). Darren Carlson likewise challenges the assumption that a specific degree program with a set curriculum of courses is the final word in whether or not someone has been theologically trained. Most Majority World ministers receive discipleship and informal training through a wide variety of sources, but we still refer to them as "untrained" (Carlson 2022, 5–8). Does the future of global theological education require a cognitive-focused commitment to an academic curriculum of topics, or is there a way to train church leaders around the world in a way that is less academically formal and more responsive to their own unique contexts and learning needs? How might a focus on *koinonia* community as a key learning tool guide us in this matter?

Church Planting Movement (CPM) methods like Training for Trainers (T4T) and Disciplemaking Movements (DMM) often recognize the weaknesses of a cognitive approach to discipleship, choosing to focus more on obedience-based (behavioral) discipleship. While the transition from cognitive-based to obedience-based discipleship has revealed new and sometimes better discipleship methods, it has not been without criticism. Mark Rhodes decries the neglect of theological training in obedience-based CPM methods (Rhodes 2022, 79–95). If we assume, as some CPM methods do, that faith and knowledge will follow obedience, we have simply reversed the already problematic linear assumptions about how people learn. Theological teaching is essential to the discipleship process, as is obedience, but they must be holistically balanced. In pursuing a more behavioral and experiential discipleship approach, we have overly neglected the necessary cognitive elements. In holistic transformative learning, discipleship and training are not a matter of *either* cognitive *or* behavioral. Rather, we must incorporate the cognitive, behavioral, *and* emotional in our discipleship methods, and relationships are essential to that process.

Implication Two: Mind Your Relationships

An examination of the universal and common elements in church-planting movements highlights numerous overlaps with communal learning and relational methods of informal training (see Garrison 1999). The natural relationships and shared worldviews within kinship groups have likely played a more influential role than we previously appreciated. House churches tap into several areas for ideal learning. In CPM methods, relationships between church members play a significant role. Friends and family members are able to evaluate and discuss the gospel message and its implications together. They trust the person sharing the gospel with them, and they see living testimony of life change. Their emotions are engaged and connected to the message through these relationships, and they work out the transformative implications actively together. The *koinonia* (fellowship) within a house church is a powerful discipleship force.

While CPM house church methods tap into key discipleship elements for community, Rhodes notes that the way many CPM methods purposely cut off relationship ties with the missionary hinders the discipleship process. He writes: "Discipleship requires personal interaction. We must be present to ask and answer questions until we know that people understand" (Rhodes 2022, 181–82). As effective as CPM methods are, they could be even more effective if they would balance the cognitive and behavioral more holistically and if they would extend their network of relationships to include the missionary and others who are not native to their kinship communities.

In Western education systems, we tend to value a certain amount of professional distance between the teacher and learner. Studies show that students do best when they have a relationship with their teacher and when they can interact with other learners, but as with the neuroscience of parasocial relationships, this does not need to be a warm and affectionate two-way interpersonal relationship (Marzano 2007, 152). A certain amount of distance between the teacher and students is fine, but perhaps greater transparency on the teacher's part can help the learners process their lessons more effectively. We are personally passionate about missions, but does that come across in our teaching? Do we permit ourselves to cry when we are moved, demonstrate anger over injustice, or rejoice in hope and worship when we see the hand of God moving among the nations? Do we tell learners our own stories of how and why we came to hold the positions we hold? Do we authentically share what methods we have tried, both the successes and the failures? A lesson will engage students more holistically and move them to apply key concepts to their own lives and ministries if we are willing to authentically share our own holistic experiences.

Not only can we consider being more transparent in the teacher-learner relationship, but we can work to be more responsive to our students' lives and to the natural learning opportunities with which they are actively engaged. A set curriculum of topics is needed and wise, but what if we leave some flexibility for responsive teaching? When I was a church planter in East Asia, I was teaching through a set T4T curriculum (Smith and Kai 2011), but my new disciples were distracted by questions about the animistic spiritual forces that they grew up fearing. This topic was not addressed in the standard curriculum I had at that time, and I was ill-equipped with any personal experience to guide them toward a contextual theology of animism. This was a ripe learning opportunity, but my curriculum focus and my missionary-expert perspective failed them. I wonder how my group might have been better helped to self-theologize on this issue if, alongside the study of Scripture, I had also connected them with other believers (locally or globally) who had walked through similar questions. What if I had reached across my network of fellow missionaries to find insights or living examples that could benefit my group? I could have facilitated discipleship connections if I had been a little more relationally responsive to their contextual needs.

The teacher-learner relationship can also be enhanced by tapping into active learning methods that not only help them to learn holistically but also encourage bonding. The powerful effects of life-on-life training and mentorship do not have to be limited to an overseas ministry context. Whether in cross-cultural discipleship or a classroom setting, we can think about ways to work on projects together and practice ways of applying a concept. Local ministry projects, short-term mission trips, and even brief group activities within the classroom can facilitate the learning process and build necessary relationship connections between teacher, students, and peers.

Implication Three: Reconceive the Teaching Role

What could happen if the missionary trainer thought of discipleship and theological education less in terms of an information transfer from expert to untrained and more in terms of strategically facilitating discipleship-focused connections (see Steffen 2011)? A subtle shift in perspective about the trainer's role, from expert to facilitator, not only shows more respect to the learner but also grants them active control over their learning process. We can embody cognitive concepts by connecting learners with human beings who have stories and perspectives to share regarding specific issues. This process begins with the teacher-student relationship, includes facilitating community within the learning group, and extends to connecting learners with others outside their group.

We can also work to present abstract concepts incarnationally as living dialogue partners. Most of our teaching objectives tend to be pure cognitive information, unnaturally distilled from a living context. What if we try to embody the abstract content in a particular context so that learners can more easily relate to the concept holistically? If I'm teaching on "The Flaw of the Excluded Middle" (Hiebert 1999, 60, 414–21), can I do so by introducing Paul Hiebert as a conversational partner, giving a brief introduction to his life, his ministry, and the living context that caused him to analyze the topic? If I'm teaching patristic theology, can I embody concepts through the life and context of Saint Augustine (see Reeves 2016)? How might I add missionary examples and biographical stories at key points in my lesson plan to help learners fully engage the concepts in a more holistic and connected manner (see Tucker 2004)?

Virtually every topic in a mission-training curriculum will be enriched by hearing from a Majority World perspective. How can I connect students to a global voice and testimony? My seminary professor taught us the importance of sharing the gospel in a people's heart language by connecting us to a living testimony of a family radically changed by the gospel when they realized that God cared enough to speak their own language. That personal testimony shared by a person I could see and know taught me the curriculum lesson in five minutes rather than through three hours of lecture, and I was forever motivated to learn and use heart-language resources in my mission work.

Similarly, we can take advantage of the missionary's global network of relationships to introduce cross-cultural dialogue partners. A church in Bangladesh might find answers to their challenges when they hear the biblical/theological perspective and testimony from a people group in Indonesia who dealt with a similar challenge. As we fellowship with missionary colleagues from around the world and hear a wide variety of stories and testimonies, perhaps we can listen to those stories with our own learners in mind. How might this movement in China speak to my group in Turkey? How might this missionary training approach in Brazil inspire a contextualized version in Kenya?

Studies in social network theory demonstrate that the way information goes viral does not necessarily depend on key influencers or hub personalities, as previously assumed. Instead, ideas spread widely and take hold when they are spread through "weak link" connections, as people share a concept across several circles of their relatively distant acquaintances (Watts 2003; Watts 1999, 493–527; Berger 2013). Missionaries have a global network of weak link connections. What could happen if we employed that incredible resource for educational purposes? How could the missionary teacher's weak link connections serve the process of global theology?

Implication Four:
Facilitate Global Missiological Partnerships

Anthony Casey makes a strong argument in favor of global theological partnerships and the reciprocal sharing of faculty between the West and Majority World schools. He writes: "Partnerships and faculty mentorship are necessary to spur on majority-world theological institutions. A globalized world necessitates global partnerships. ... These partnerships should continue into the realm of theological education so the global church can in fact benefit from the global church!" (Casey 2022, 19–20). The exchange of faculty helps both schools, as the Western classes also benefit from the enhanced global perspectives that their faculty bring back from their ever-expanding global network of human connections.

A mutual global partnership in theological education and missionary training might involve more Western faculty volunteering to teach in Majority World schools, but it might also invite Majority World Christians and teachers to connect with our Western classrooms. We have much to learn from the Majority World, particularly from the persecuted church. A 2004 Lausanne Occasional Paper emphasizes the importance of networking and partnerships between persecuted and non-persecuted believers for mutual growth, encouragement, and theological development (Sookhdeo 2005). Likewise, Brent Kipler (2019, 23) argues that we have "an underdeveloped awareness that persecuted Christian leaders have spiritual resources—uniquely shaped by their suffering—to contribute to the thriving of the global church." What are some of the many benefits that our students will gain from hearing key concepts from a Majority World perspective? How might we creatively include Majority World leaders in our Western classrooms, whether in person, online, or through recorded media?

Dialogue toward Transformative Application

As I compare my two different mission degree programs in search of the most effective teaching methods, many key elements of holistic transformative learning in community relationships reveal themselves. My first degree was purely classroom learning that relied on textbooks and lectures. Students did not directly engage the topics in classroom discussions; we did not write papers in anticipation of future mission scenarios; nor did we engage in active missional activities together outside the classroom. On the other hand, my seminary degree was driven as a cohort of mission students. We took our classes together and often engaged in class discussions and group projects. Some of our courses involved going out into the community to interact with internationals and those who profess other major world religions. We went on short-term mission trips to our intended region of future ministry service alongside our mission professors who actively modeled and demonstrated contextual evangelism and discipleship methods. Our first few years on the mission field were done through a mentorship program, and we had a network of peers and senior missionaries at our disposal for further discussion and problem-solving. We met together annually with our professors and mentors to receive further instruction and address common issues dialogically. By encouraging fellowship among the students, missionaries, and professors, we were emotionally engaged in each new learning topic, saw the relevance of our intended goals, and were given active experiential learning opportunities.

If we say that transformative learning is holistic and relational, then the only way these principles and their missiological implications will transform our teaching and ultimately transform our students' lives is if we begin by considering the topic in dialogue with others. Let us open conversations with our mission-teaching colleagues and mission disciplers about how and why they apply various transformative learning principles. Let us hear one another's perspectives on how people learn in the community and hear examples of how to revise our lesson plans to address the students' minds, hearts, and hands through human connections.

Here are some questions to ask yourself and others to begin a holistic and relational engagement with these key learning principles:

- What learning experiences have most influenced your ministry today? How might you leverage those learning methods effectively in your own teaching ministry?

- What are some creative ways to incorporate connected learning methods in our curriculum? How can we follow an accreditation-approved syllabus while reserving some flexibility for responsive teaching and strategic relational connections?

- What are some creative ways that we might be able to "incarnate" a distilled cognitive principle? How can we present our learning objectives in a relational manner, in context with human emotions, motivations, challenges, analyses, and applications?

- How might global partnerships for theological education transform our missionary training and facilitate global theology? What is it about global partnerships that could enrich our students' learning experience, spiritual formation, and future ministries?

References

Alemu, Alemseged K. 2022. *Predictive Factors for Transformative Learning within ACTEA-Related Theological Institutions in Ethiopia*. Carlisle, UK: Langham.

Berger, Jonah. 2013. *Contagious: Why Things Catch On*. New York: Simon and Schuster.

Bushnell, Horace. 1979. *Christian Nurture*. Grand Rapids: Baker Book House.

Carlson, Darren M. 2022. "What Does 'Untrained' Mean?" *Journal of Global Christianity* 7, no. 1 (April): 5–8.

Casey, Anthony F. 2022. "Majority-World Theological Education in the Globalized Age." *Journal of Global Christianity* 7, no. 1 (April): 8–20.

Cranton, Patricia. 2006. *Understanding and Promoting Transformative Learning: A Guide for Educators of Adults*. 2nd ed. San Francisco: Jossey-Bass.

Dirkx, John, Jack Mezirow, and Patricia Cranton. 2006. "Musings and Reflections on the Meaning, Context, and Process of Transformative Learning: A Dialogue between John M. Dirkx and Jack Mezirow." *Journal of Transformative Education* 4, no. 2 (April): 123–39.

Elmer, Muriel I., and Duane H. Elmer. 2020. *The Learning Cycle: Insights for Faithful Teaching from Neuroscience and the Social Sciences.* Downers Grove, IL: IVP Academic.

Festinger, Leon. 1957. *A Theory of Cognitive Dissonance.* Stanford: Stanford University Press.

Freire, Paulo. 1996. *Pedagogy of the Oppressed.* London: Penguin Books.

Freire, Paulo. 2005. *Education for Critical Consciousness.* New York: Continuum.

Garrison, David. 1999. *Church Planting Movements: How God Is Redeeming a Lost World.* Richmond, VA: International Mission Board.

Hammett, John S. 2005. *Biblical Foundations for Baptist Churches: A Contemporary Ecclesiology.* Grand Rapids: Kregel Academic.

Hiebert, Paul. 1999. "The Flaw of the Excluded Middle." In *Perspectives on the World Christian Movement: A Reader,* edited by Ralph D. Winter and Steven C. Hawthorne, 414–21. 3rd ed. Pasadena, CA: William Carey Library.

Hwang, I. 2004. "The Relationships between Discipleship Training and Transformative Learning in Korean Presbyterian Congregations." *Dissertation Abstracts International* 65, no. 5, 1625A. UMII No. 31324775.

Issler, Klaus, and Ronald Habermas. 1994. *How We Learn: A Christian Teacher's Guide to Educational Psychology.* Grand Rapids: Baker Books.

Ito, Mizuko, Kris Gutiérrez, Sonia Livingstone, Bill Penuel, Jean Rhodes, Katie Salen, Juliet Schor, Julian Sefton-Green, and S. Craig Watkins. 2013. *Connected Learning: An Agenda for Research and Design.* Irvine, CA: Digital Media and Learning Research Hub.

Jones, Rebecca M., Leah H. Somerville, Jian Li, Erika J. Ruberry, Victoria Libby, Gary Glover, Henning U. Voss, Douglas J. Ballon, and B. J. Casey. 2011. "Behavioral and Neural Properties of Social Reinforcement Learning." *Journal of Neuroscience* 31, no. 37 (September): 13039–45.

Kipler, Brent L. 2019. "Overlooked Mentors: What Can Persecuted Christians Teach Us about Leadership?" *Journal of Global Christianity* 5, no. 1: 16–33.

Kolb, David A. 2015. *Experiential Learning: Experience as the Source of Learning and Development.* 2nd ed. Upper Saddle River, NJ: Pearson Education.

Lin, Arthur. 2023. "The Role of Theological Institutions in Missionary Training." *Journal of the Evangelical Missiological Society* 3, no. 1: 128–46.

Lunsford, Sarah. 2023. *Missiological Triage: A Framework for Integrating Theology and Social Sciences in Missiological Methods.* Evangelical Missiological Society Monograph Series 16. Eugene, OR: Pickwick.

Marzano, Robert J. 2007. *The Art and Science of Teaching: A Comprehensive Framework for Effective Instruction.* Alexandria, VA: Association for Supervision and Curriculum Development.

Ott, Bernhard. 2016. *Understanding and Developing Theological Education.* Carlisle, UK: Langham.

Rain, Marina, and Raymond A. Mar. 2021. "Adult Attachment and Engagement with Fictional Characters." *Journal of Personal and Social Relationships* 38, no. 9 (June): 2792–813.

Reeves, Michael. 2016. *Theologians You Should Know: An Introduction: From the Apostolic Fathers to the 21st Century.* Wheaton: Crossway.

Rhodes, Matt. 2022. *No Shortcut to Success: A Manifesto for Modern Missions.* 9Marks. Wheaton: Crossway.

Seckler, Thomas W. 2020. *Experiencing the Gospel: An Examination of Muslim Conversion to Christianity in Cambodia.* Eugene, OR: Wipf & Stock.

Shaw, Perry. 2014. *Transforming Theological Education: A Practical Handbook for Integrative Learning.* Carlisle, UK: Langham.

Siegel, Daniel J. 2010. *Mindsight: The New Science of Personal Transformation.* New York: Bantam.

Siegel, Daniel J. 2020. *The Developing Mind: How Relationships and the Brain Interact to Shape Who We Are.* 3rd ed. New York: Guilford.

Simpson, Elizabeth J. 1966. "The Classification of Educational Objectives, Psychomotor Domain." Urbana, IL: University of Illinois.

Smith, James K. A. 2009. *Desiring the Kingdom: Worship, Worldview, and Cultural Formation.* Grand Rapids: Baker Academic.

Smith, Steve, and Ying Kai. 2011. *T4T: A Discipleship Re-Revolution.* Monument, CO: WIGTake Resources.

Sookhdeo, Patrick. 2005. "The Persecuted Church." *Lausanne Occasional Paper* 32. Pattaya, Thailand: Lausanne Committee for World Evangelization.

Sousa, David A. 2017. *How the Brain Learns.* 5th ed. Thousand Oaks, CA: SAGE.

Steffen, Tom. 2011. *The Facilitator Era: Beyond Pioneer Church Multiplication.* Eugene, OR: Wipf & Stock.

Taylor, Edward W. 2001. "Transformative Learning Theory: A Neurobiological Perspective of the Role of Emotions and Unconscious Ways of Knowing." *International Journal of Lifelong Education* 20, no. 3: 218–36.

Taylor, Edward W. 2008. "Transformative Learning Theory." *New Directions for Adult and Continuing Education*, no. 119 (September): 5–15. https:doi.org/10.1002/ace.301.

Thigpen, L. Lynn. 2020. *Connected Learning: How Adults with Limited Formal Education Learn*. Eugene, OR: Pickwick.

Thompson, Curt. 2010. *Anatomy of the Soul: Surprising Connections between Neuroscience and Spiritual Practices That Can Transform Your Life and Relationships*. Carol Stream, IL: Tyndale House.

Thompson, Curt. 2015. *Soul of Shame: Retelling the Stories We Believe about Ourselves*. Downers Grove, IL: InterVarsity Press.

Thomson, Jonny. 2021. "Parasocial Relationships: How People Form Eerily Intimate Bonds with TV Characters." Big Think. October 4, 2021.

Tucker, Ruth. 2004. *From Jerusalem to Irian Jaya: A Biographical History of Christian Missions*. 2nd ed. Grand Rapids: Zondervan.

Udall, Jessica. 2022. "Faithful Fundraising: Communicating Needs without Sacrificing Dignity or Short-Circuiting Discipleship." In *Communication in Mission: Global Opportunities and Challenges*, 149–59, edited by Marcus Dean, Scott Moreau, Sue Russell, and Rochelle Scheuermann. Evangelical Missiological Society Series 30. Littleton, CO: William Carey Publishing.

Watts, Duncan J. 1999. "Networks, Dynamics, and the Small-World Phenomenon." *American Journal of Sociology* 105, no. 2: 493–527.

Watts, Duncan J. 2003. *Six Degrees: The Science of a Connected Age*. New York: Norton.

Zull, James E. 2002. *The Art of Changing the Brain: Enriching the Practice of Teaching by Exploring the Biology of Learning*. Sterling, VA: Stylus.

Chapter 10

"Are You Prepared to Eat with Us Our Theology?"

Preventing Resource Righteousness in Theological Education

Jessica A. Udall

In 1974, the prolific Kenyan intellectual and theologian Dr. John S. Mbiti wrote an article entitled "Theological Impotence and the Universality of the Church," arguing that "theological reciprocity and mutuality [is] necessary" for the global church and that this could be accomplished through "theological pilgrimage," not just as it had been carried out in the past—that is, those from the Majority World making the effort to learn from and about the theological context and process of the West—but also vice versa. He asserted his reasoning as follows:

> There cannot be theological conversation or dialogue between North and South, East and West, until we can embrace each other's concerns and stretch to each other's horizons. Theologians from the southern continents believe that they know about most of the constantly changing concerns of older Christendom. They would also like their counterparts from the older Christendom to come to know about their concerns of human survival. (Mbiti 1974, 17)

He asked:

> We have eaten with you your theology. Are you prepared to eat with us our theology? ... The question is, do you know us theologically? Would you like to know us theologically? Can you know us theologically? And how can there be true theological reciprocity and mutuality, if only one side knows the other fairly well, while the other side either does not know or does not want to know the first side? (17)

To continue with Mbiti's metaphor, this article will envision the global church as a large dining room filled with people, and global theological conversations as get-togethers where the extended family comes from near and far to gather around a table simply because they value being together. Who sits at the head of the table in this scenario? If we view Christians around the world as our brothers and sisters, then it would seem logical that the seat at the head of the table would be reserved for our heavenly Father, but this article explores what happens when—fifty years after Mbiti's article was written—someone from a globally dominant culture sits in that head-of-the-table chair instead.

The Presuppositions of the Resource Righteousness Approach

If someone from a dominant culture sits in the head-of-the-table chair, he is buying into a fallacy with a long history that I have begun to call *resource righteousness*, which is the belief that the group with the most power, infrastructure, or resources must necessarily have the best theology and should be listened to more closely and given leadership over all things with which they are involved. This fallacious resource righteousness springs from several deep-seated (often unconscious) biblically contrary presuppositions that are killers of true intercultural partnership in mission.

Presupposition of Historical Centrality

The head of the table has likely been taught a Eurocentric story of Christian history, which, while containing elements of the truth, often leaves out more than it includes. Ethiopian theologian Samuel Deressa explains the history of African Christianity from ancient times as an example of an equally valid form of Christian history worthy of study and reflection:

> For many decades, they have generally been treating Christianity in other parts of the world as an appendix to the history of European Christianity. The Christian faith that existed outside the Western hemisphere is being generally understood and described as what has been brought there by missionaries. However, this Eurocentric reading of Christian history neglects the fact that Christianity existed in Africa beginning early in the patristic period (perhaps even before then in the cases of Ethiopia and Egypt), and that Christianity existed in Asia before the arrival of western missionaries. After Christianity began in the Near East, Christianity was mainly spread throughout North Africa and Asia. In the first and second centuries, the area comprising Syria, Egypt, Tunisia, and Mesopotamia

was considered the center of Christianity. Tunisia was home to the great church fathers such as Cyprian, Tertullian, and Augustine—the three main theologians who laid the foundation for western theology to emerge as it did. Already by the second century, Egypt and North Africa were also part of the Christian Roman Empire, playing a major role in the formation of global Christian theology. (Deressa 2021, 37–38)

Flowing from this Eurocentric mentality, Deressa extrapolates,

For some western scholars, southern Christianity is a creation of western missionaries, and therefore there is nothing new to learn from them. In other words, there is not much to learn from southern Christianity since it is a duplicate of western Christianity. This assumption is founded on western scholars' emphasis on the role of missionaries in the spread of Christianity in the Global South. In recent scholarship, however, in response to such erroneous conclusions, some have started to emphasize the role of indigenous missionaries in the spread and development of Christianity in the South. (38–39)

Indeed, Deressa concludes, quoting Andrew Walls, "Christianity has [existed] in Africa for far longer than it has in Scotland, and infinitely longer than it has in the United States. African Christianity can assert their right to the whole history of Christianity in Africa, stretching back almost to the apostolic age" (38). While this insight from Deressa is offered as a corrective to an overly Euro-American perspective on Christian history, Amos Yong's reminder is also pertinent and balancing: "In the Pentecost economy, *center and periphery are already overturned.* The world's conventions of power are reorganized so much so that the outpouring of the Spirit had produced 'people who have been turning the world upside down' (17:6). *There are no marginal cultures or languages* in God's salvation history" (Yong 2021, 34, emphasis added).

In the same way that it is no longer expected that the majority of theological reflection would come from Palestine (because of the theological contributions of the apostles) or North Africa (because of the theological contributions of Augustine and his contemporaries), it should not be expected that the majority of theological reflection should come from an area of the world where church membership and growth is in steady decline. Instead, the gospel has been present globally (while certainly not in every people group) for a large swath of Christian history with ebbs and flows according to the Spirit's will, which should encourage those around the table to view each other as equal teammates, without hierarchy, in theological reflection and disciple-making. Certainly today, the mission of God is taking place from everywhere to everywhere, from the people of God to the not-yet-people of God, and the global church can only function as a healthy team of disciple-makers if we truly value each others' contributions.

Presupposition of Aculturality

The person sitting at the head of the table likely believes that his theology is acultural and is therefore qualitatively different and superior as compared to the "cultural" theology practiced by the majority of the guests at the table. Indeed, there is "a strongly rooted construction of thought that the true pattern of Christianity is the Western pattern" despite "the fact … that Christianity was actually born on the Asian continent" (Kolimon 2016, 100). This way of thinking leads to an often unconscious cultural hegemony in theological practice, which requires Christians from other cultures to conform to the dominant cultural norms to gain theological approval and acceptance in the global church. Keon-Sang An, a Korean trained in the West who worked as a theology professor in Ethiopia, describes this phenomenon as a "theological monopoly [that] is prevalent in many different places in the world" (An 2016, 2), which assumes that those from (or at least trained in) the West should do the talking and teaching, while others should do the listening and learning. There is no mutuality in this model since "genuine interdependence is possible only when the entities in a relationship are independent. A healthy relationship is not one-sided—the 'give' of one side and the 'take' of the other side—but reciprocal—the 'give and take' of both sides" (2).

For mutuality to be possible, previous "maps" of Christian history and theology will have to be recognized as too small and remade with praise for a God who is bigger than our previous conception of him, says Andrew Walls, because

> conventional theological education too often employs pre-Columbian maps of the church. Everyone is aware, of course, that there is a New World, that there are Christians—perhaps many Christians—beyond the Western world. But the pre-Columbian theological space. That map no

longer reflects [author's note: or perhaps, see Deressa, never did reflect] reality. It is little use to draw new insets to put into its corners; it will have to be thrown away. And mission studies are essential for the redrawing of the theological map. (Walls 1996, 18)

For those who are concerned that the essence of the gospel will be lost in the process of contextualization, Amos Yong offers this assurance:

Although some of the more radical approaches are calling for a relativization of historic creeds and confessions to Christianities in the West due to their contextual situatedness, most scholars are simply urging that there be a more substantive dialogue between the West and Majority World churches regarding how to understand Christian faith (including theologies and dogmatic confessions) afresh in the newly emerging world Christianity. (Yong 2021, 34)

Sadly, when exported without reciprocity or a possibility for balancing dialogue, unconscious Western cultural norms are noticeably discordant in many other cultures and may even unnecessarily hinder evangelism and discipleship efforts because of the perception that the gospel is a foreign import. In this situation, people—whether those from other cultures hearing the gospel for the first time or those from other cultures who become deeply involved in a Western-slanted discipleship process and eventually become disillusioned—believe that they are rejecting the gospel when they may, in fact, be rejecting the Western trappings and framings that have clung to it due to a resource righteousness that refuses to see or is blind to the need to contextualize because of a spiritual superiority complex.

Presupposition of Theological Oligarchy

If someone from the dominant culture sits at the head of the table, he is, in light of current demographic and religious realities, condoning a theological oligarchy that ensures the governing of the many by the few according to the cultural norms, preferences, and emphases of the few. This leads to theological reflection that majors on a certain small context—and that context's particular needs, pressing issues, and perspective on the rest of the world. This kind of theological reflection often does not reflect the contexts of the majority at the table, thereby missing relevant areas and issues that need robust theological reflection and missionary praxis in the multiple contexts where the gospel finds itself. Indeed, Philip Jenkins notes that "the types of Christianity that have thrived most successfully in the global South have been very different from what many Europeans and North Americans consider mainstream," and thus, "If we are to live in a world where only one Christian in five is a non-Hispanic White, then the views of that small minority are ever less likely to claim mainstream status, however desperately the old world order clings to its hegemony over the control of information and opinion" (Jenkins 2009, 391).

Illustrative of the need for Majority World Christians to be given seats at the table of theological conversation is the fact that demographically speaking, if one were to try to find a representative sample of Christianity in the modern day, it would be more accurate to envision a young "woman living in a village in Nigeria, or in a Brazilian favela" (Jenkins 2011, 1–2) rather than an elderly man from Britain or the United States. Correspondingly, "Third World theology is [more] likely to be the representative Christian theology" (Deressa 2021, 33). This is not to suggest that the theological reflections of elderly British and American men are unneeded; instead, it is to suggest that they are simply insufficient for the numerous diverse contexts and contemporary challenges and opportunities facing the global church. Recognizing and eschewing Western theological oligarchy has benefits for theological education in non-Western contexts from a philosophical and pedagogical perspective as well, says Perry Shaw, since "intercultural research ... suggests that the linear-analytical thinking of Greek philosophy and the Enlightenment, which has so shaped Western educational systems, is globally atypical. While the specifics differ, the general pattern of information-processing throughout most of the non-Western world tends toward holism and networked thinking, in contrast to the tight specificity so typical in Western academia" (Shaw 2014, 238).

If we are to face challenges with resilience, take opportunities with wisdom, and proclaim God's word with relevance in a globalized world, we must theologically reflect together for the co-edification of the diverse body of Christ. Practically speaking, this means allowing the table fellowship of believers from around the world to reflect global faith demographic realities, such that there is not simply a token non-Westerner invited into table fellowship, but the table is crowded and even expanded to include many from diverse cultural backgrounds that reflect the diverse global church itself.

Presupposition of Lack of Blindspots

Third, if someone from the dominant culture sits in the head-of the-table chair, their blindspots become barriers to the gospel in other contexts since those spots are not examined with the light of the gospel. These blindspots certainly have repercussions even in the dominant culture of the head of the table, but they can turn into disastrous chasms in other contexts where the area of the blindspot is of larger cultural concern. Neglect of theological reflection and missionary praxis in the missionary's cultural blindspots prop open the door for shallow religion and syncretism to creep into the lives of their disciples from other cultures.

A quintessential example of a blindspot common to Westerners, including Western missionaries, is the "excluded middle"—the neglect of which has caused huge issues in the discipleship of those from other cultures. This blindspot is present in a worldview that only has two categories: a transcendent, supernatural God and a natural world governed by science. This typically Western worldview has no category for or thought given to the existence of "supernatural but this-worldly beings and forces" (Hiebert 1982, 43) and how Christians should interact with them. In the past and even still today, the strategy is to "[deny] the existence of the spirits rather than claim the power of Christ over them" (44).

Cultural blindspots are unconsciously transmitted where resource righteousness and cultural superiority are found because of a refusal to meaningfully engage with contextual concerns. Thus, there is a missed opportunity for mutual theologizing and together discovering God and his truth anew in a new cultural context. An observes: "A local reading of the Bible reveals certain aspects of God's truth. The biblical interpretations of local faith communities throughout the world contribute together to enrich our understanding of God's truth in the Bible" (An 2016, 32). Whether new believers or those who have been walking with God for a long time, brothers and sisters from different backgrounds can help alleviate each others' blindspots as they each bring their own cultural perspectives to the table.

Stephen Strauss shares his own experience with realizing and remedying his own excluded middle blindspot through interaction with non-Western believers:

When I (Steve) was a new missionary in Ethiopia, I was asked to serve as pastor of an international church for a time. One of my first sermon series was on the book of Ephesians. I preached through Ephesians, primarily using notes that I had from my recent seminary studies. Years later, while still serving in Ethiopia, I was asked to lead a Bible study on Ephesians. As I studied through the book again, I was amazed at all that was in the text that I had not seen when I was a new missionary. I particularly noticed Paul's emphasis on Christ's lordship over the spirit world and its impact in the believer's life. Living in a new context had opened my eyes to see things already in the biblical text that I had previously missed. (Ott and Strauss 2010, 279)

Presupposition of Wealth as Purely Asset

Fourth, if someone from the dominant culture sits at the head of the table, they are assuming that the relative wealth of their culture is purely a net asset, when in fact, in a biblical understanding, their prosperity is more likely a net drawback in terms of faith and spiritual maturity. While the righteous rich are certainly present in the biblical narrative (e.g., Abraham, Joseph of Arimathea, Lydia), it appears that they are more the exception than the rule. Likewise, though the Bible shows that there are appropriate ways to use wealth well (1 Tim 6:17–19), there are far more warnings of the problems it brings. The love of money is identified as "the root of all kinds of evil" (1 Tim 6:10 ESV), and the idol of wealth accumulation is portrayed as an ever-present temptation that must be continually guarded against by those experiencing prosperity (Matt 6:24).

I am not suggesting that Western cultures are the only prosperous cultures or that there are not wealthy people in Majority World cultures, but I am seeking to generalize somewhat in this case in order to observe the resource righteousness phenomenon from a key angle. It should also be noted that by wealth, I do not simply mean cash on hand but rather having more than most in terms of any resource that matters in terms of this-world Christian clout: influence, prestige, connections in terms of theological education or publishing, infrastructure, availability of books, availability of online resources, and this list goes on.

The potential problem with wealth, it becomes clear, is that it makes people feel self-sufficient, thereby deceiving themselves and becoming out of touch with their need for God. The poor are much less likely to suffer such a delusion simply due to their life circumstances. While being poor is not inherently sanctifying and being rich is not necessarily sinful, it should be noted that those who are poor are often shown by Scripture to have a particularly solid grasp on theological realities as compared to the rich, who are often prone to struggle with "the deceitfulness of riches" (Mark 4:19 ESV). Those whose culture is generally prosperous tend to have a culture-wide temptation toward the pitfalls of wealth (as well as attendant blindspots), and this shows up in their theologizing. Conversely, those whose culture generally lacks prosperity have different challenges, but their low socioeconomic status also allows them to experience more naturally and be oriented by the promises of God for the poor.

Those in the church are strongly cautioned by James not to be overawed by rich people or show partiality toward them to the detriment of those who have less wealth. James used table imagery, which is particularly relevant to our framing of the theological conversation in this chapter:

> If a man wearing a gold ring and fine clothing comes into your assembly, and a poor man in shabby clothing also comes in, and if you pay attention to the one who wears the fine clothing and say, "You sit here in a good place," while you say to the poor man, "You stand over there," or, "Sit down at my feet," have you not then made distinctions among yourselves and become judges with evil thoughts? (Jas 2:2–4 ESV)

James went on to defend his bold accusation with the following assertion that echoes Jesus's Sermon on the Mount: "Listen, my beloved brothers, has not God chosen those who are poor in the world to be rich in faith and heirs of the kingdom, which he has promised to those who love him?" (v. 5 ESV). Though James reminded them that it is the rich who oppress them and make their lives difficult, the believers "have dishonored the poor man" (v. 6) by assuming that he was not worthy of a legitimate seat at their table. In the same way, those from cultures with a sense of resource righteousness dishonor those from cultures with a lower socioeconomic status when they equate that status with a lack of theological vitality and depth. In reality, the opposite is more likely true.

Away from Resource Righteousness: The Alternative Approach of Theological Global Table Fellowship

There is an alternative to resource righteousness, and it necessitates that the head of the table from the dominant culture instead sits among his brothers and sisters around the table, leaving the head chair for their heavenly Father. It also requires space to be made for those who come from cultures that appear to have less in worldly terms, knowing that God's grace is not bound by appearances: "For the Lord sees not as man sees: man looks on the outward appearance, but the Lord looks on the heart" (1 Sam 16:7 ESV).

A relationship that involves mutual theologizing, it should be noted, involves neither "a transcending set of truth claims" held perfectly by the dominant culture "acting as a referee to other opinions" nor a "simple pluralism that uncritically accepts all truth claims." Rather, "critical pluralism," that is, a thoughtful conversation between multiple perspectives equally seated around the theological table, is preferred as a method of co-edification (Soh 2016, 72). This kind of conversation that presupposes equality enables "mature relationships," observes Kolimon, which

> encourage the exchange of criticism, and both parties [are] able both to accept and to give it without being offended. ... Within the relationship of equality, both parties can acknowledge that they are not perfect and therefore need one another, just as they also need God. They can also affirm that they each have energy and capabilities that can be shared in support of one another in the practice of mission. (Kolimon 2016, 107)

Theologians from all over the world must have a seat at the table that is equal to those who hail from the most wealthy cultures. Their histories ought to be taken seriously, and their perspectives ought to be actively sought out as valuable, such that they are invited to speak and not only to listen. Thus situated, Mbiti's biblically resonant vision for "theological reciprocity and mutuality" is possible and even plausible for God's people. Such a theological table conversation will raise previously neglected questions, challenge assumptions, and expose blindspots—which will admittedly cause discomfort for all involved—but it will be in the context of table fellowship, will ultimately result in co-edification, and will serve the upbuilding of the global church.

Logistically, it is important to consider how to make the theological reflections of those in the Majority World more accessible globally. The work of Langham Partnership is admirable in this regard. Yet it must be remembered that "some of the documentation will remain inaccessible to scholars who read European languages exclusively. This is why documentation is needed on grassroots Christianity in Africa written in African languages or on Chinese Christianity written in Chinese" (Tiénou 2006, 41). Tiénou goes on to explain that much of Christian theology in the non-Western world, particularly in oral cultures, may not be written down but is still valid and worthy of note.

Application of the Two Approaches in Theological Education

In the West

In theological educational institutions in the West, resource righteousness manifests itself in several ways, and its antidote is giving value and attention to theological reciprocity and mutuality in conversation with the global body of Christ, of which Westerners are but a part. When little or no attention is paid to including voices from the nondominant culture as required reading or listening for Western students who attend Western Bible schools and seminaries, there will likely be a variety of negative consequences in the students' future ministries, especially for those who plan to work outside the West. It should be noted that non-Western students who attend Western Bible schools and seminaries will likely experience some combination of the situations described in the "In the West" and "In the Majority World" sections.

Western students may continue to hold the common but patently untrue idea that when they go to another culture, they are single-handedly bringing God to that culture, thus predisposing themselves to grandiose and off-putting behavior. If, however, they have been exposed to the edifying experience of learning from people who are from the culture they plan to go to (or a near-culture neighbor), they are more likely to instead view themselves as just one member of a multicultural team of missional believers, some international and some local, who work together to bring the not-yet people of God to the Savior, for his glory alone. It is particularly helpful to comfortably take the role of the learner (not always insisting on being the teacher) when living cross-culturally, as it is necessary to become like a child in order to truly adjust and acculturate for fruitful long-term ministry work.

In addition, if Western seminarians are not exposed to the teachings and writings of Majority World believers while in school, then they will likely persist in their belief that they themselves are acultural and will be confused and stymied in ministry without knowing why. By contrast, if they are made aware of their own culture through exposure to other Christian perspectives that are culturally different, then they will avoid becoming conquistadors who war against other cultures or colonizers who gradually destroy other cultures. Instead, they will become farmers who plant the seed of the gospel, which can grow organically in the soil where it was planted. It is tended by and benefits the local community as well as the missionary through co-edification.

If those receiving theological education are only given resources that feel culturally comfortable to them, then they may also fall prey to naïve realism, the idea that everything they believe is in one-to-one correspondence with what is true and they are therefore right about everything. Interacting with Christian voices that hold to the truth of the gospel but come at it from a different cultural perspective will helpfully call into question the Western seminarian's sense of having mastered a set of doctrines. It will instead open them up to a more humble stance of an ongoing relationship with God, who speaks all languages and is the fullness of truth, as well as a relationship with people from different cultures, who can help us grasp different aspects of God's character and expose blindspots of which we would be unaware on our own.

In the Majority World

In theological education institutions in the Majority World, there still tends to be an emphasis on Western voices, and this has several negative effects as well. First, as mentioned above, Western theology has culturally specific blind spots, which means that key areas of theology and praxis may be left out of required readings, professor lectures, classroom discussion, and student reflection, leading to a lack of relevance in their seminary education. This has ramifications for real-life ministry, weighing students down and requiring extra time to digest and "translate" if the student is going to apply Western-oriented teaching to a non-Western setting. Students who are unable to or unaware of the need to digest and translate what they are taught will be unprepared for real-life ministry situations and cultural issues in their contexts. This too often leads to a disconnect with their own culture and a lack of effectiveness in engaging their countrymen where they are, culturally speaking, in evangelistic and discipleship efforts. The above is true for all theological training in the Majority World, but contextualized resources are particularly important when training non-Westerners to be missionaries in another non-Western setting. They will already deal with cultural stress and struggle to translate the gospel from their own culture to their host culture, so imagine the extra confusion of having Western-oriented teaching, strategies, and styles floating around in their heads at the same time!

The accusation of unbelievers in many nations calling Christianity a foreign religion has a grain of truth to it, at least in the current practice of theological education in those nations. Conversely, empowering non-Western Christian leaders to create contextualized theological training materials for non-Western classrooms will have a virtuous cycle effect. The non-Western Christian leaders of today will be reminded that they are capable of and responsible for creating helpful resources to train the next generation, and the non-Western Christian leaders of tomorrow (students) will be exposed to non-Western theologians at a formative time in their lives and will internalize a better message: *God also uses people from my culture to speak powerfully to the world about the message of Christ and the holy truths from his word. God will also use me. I can contribute. I will contribute.*

How much better to give significant attention to being as culturally relevant as possible for students, most of whom will never live in the West. This includes finding same-culture or near-culture resources whenever feasible to inculcate the reality that people can still be authentically from their culture while being authentically Christian at the same time, thus preventing unnecessary disapproval that graduates will encounter from non-believers as well as mitigating graduates' discouragement and disillusionment due to overly Western curriculum that was billed as aculturally Christian with the implicit and insidious message that *the only people worth listening to in matters of theology are Westerners.* Practically speaking, this means prioritizing equipping local believers for theological reflection and publishing over the translation of outside resources.

Second, Majority World students who are only or mostly exposed to Western voices in class and in readings may easily start to manifest an inferiority complex since they do not see themselves represented as contributors to the global theological conversation. After all, the absence of non-Western resources speaks as loudly as the presence of Western ones: *Materials from your own culture are not good enough to be used here.* Requiring Majority World students to be formed in their education by only or mostly Western voices is reminiscent of James 2, referenced above, when the poor man is told to sit on the floor while the rich man is given the seat of honor: it is dishonoring to the students and regards them as less-than when nothing could be further from the truth.

How much better to find same-culture or near-culture resources whenever possible to inspire and empower students both in school and beyond graduation with the reality that they can become theologians in their own right, sitting down at the theological table and joining the global church's conversation with humble confidence for the purpose of co-edification. As I have personally attempted to practice what I preach in this area, it has been thrilling to see students engage (many for the first time) with non-Westerners who write for a global audience. Through this exposure as well as through the many exhortations given as asides during my lectures, several students have shared with me that they are now in the process of writing books or articles, having been inspired that, by God's grace, it was within their ability to do so, and it was also their God-given responsibility to use their gifts to bless the church in this way.

References

An, Keon-Sang. 2016. *An Ethiopian Reading of the Bible: Biblical Interpretation of the Ethiopian Orthodox Tewahido Church.* Cambridge: James Clarke & Co.

Deressa, Samuel. 2021. "What Can the Rest Learn from the Rest? Nurturing the Culture of Global Conversation." *Concordia Journal* 47, no. 4: 33–44.

Hagley, Scott. 2019. *Eat What Is Set before You: A Missiology of the Congregation in Context.* Skyforest, CA: Urban Loft.

Hiebert, Paul G. 1982. "The Flaw of the Excluded Middle." *Missiology* 10, no. 1 (January): 35–47.

Jenkins, Philip. 2009. "The Next Christendom: The Coming of Global Christianity." In *Perspectives on the World Christian Movement: A Reader,* edited by Ralph D. Winter and Steven C. Hawthorne, 390–91. 4th ed. Pasadena, CA: William Carey Library.

Jenkins, Philip. 2011. *The Next Christendom: The Coming of Global Christianity.* 3rd ed. New York: Oxford University Press.

Kolimon, Mery. 2016. "Mutuality in Mission." *Review and Expositor* 113, no. 1: 99–109.

Mbiti, John M. 1976. "Theological Impotence and Universality of the Church." In *Mission Trends 3: Third World Theologies*, edited by Gerald H. Anderson and Thomas F. Stransky, 6–18. Third World Theologies. New York: Paulist.

Ott, Craig, and Harold A. Netland, eds. 2006. *Globalizing Theology: Belief and Practice in an Era of World Christianity*. Grand Rapids: Baker Academic.

Ott, Craig, and Stephen J. Strauss. 2010. *Encountering Theology of Mission: Biblical Foundations, Historical Developments, and Contemporary Issues*. Grand Rapids: Baker Academic.

Shaw, Perry. 2014. *Transforming Theological Education: A Practical Handbook for Integrative Learning*. Carlisle, UK: Langham.

Soh, Hui Leng Davina. 2016. *The Motif of Hospitality in Theological Education: A Critical Appraisal with Implications for Application in Theological Education*. ICETE. Carlisle, UK: Langham.

Tiénou, Tite. 2006. "Christian Theology in an Era of World Christianity." In *Globalizing Theology: Belief and Practice in an Era of World Christianity*, edited Craig Ott and Harold A. Netland, 37–51. Grand Rapids: Baker Academic.

Udall, Jessica A. 2023. "Lives That Welcome: How a Non-Western Understanding of Hospitality Can Revitalize the American Church's Fellowship and Outreach." *Journal of the Evangelical Missiological Society* 3, no. 1: 20–34.

Walls, Andrew F. 1996. "Missiological Education in Historical Perspective." In *Missiological Education for the Twenty-First Century: The Book, the Circle, and the Sandals (Essays in Honor of Paul E. Pierson)*, edited by J. Dudley Woodberry, Charles Van Engen, and Edgar J. Elliston, 11–22. American Society of Missiology 23. Maryknoll, NY: Orbis Books.

Yong, Amos. 2021. "Theological Education between the West and the 'Rest': A Reverse 'Reverse Missionary' and Pentecost Perspective." *Asian Journal of Pentecostal Studies* 24, no. 1 (February): 21–37.

Part
III

Case Studies from the Global Church

Chapter 11

Incorporating Apologetics into Contemporary Missions Education in North America

Matt Cook and Matthew Sokoloski

Introduction

In a recent national conference for evangelicals, I (MC) presented a paper on the experience of Muslim Americans as demonstrated in recent memoirs. My goal was to hear the voices of Muslim Americans and then develop missiological strategies based on those experiences. This was my first real foray into presenting at an academic conference, and I was a bit naïve. I had assumed that my well-intentioned diaspora missiological reflections would be appreciated by everyone. Unfortunately, I was also in a session with a philosophy and apologetics professor who had presented on the philosophical problems of Islam. My paper attempted to highlight Muslim American experiences and concluded with ways to share the gospel in light of these experiences. The philosopher's paper was a bit harsher, though it made a valuable contribution. I was not expecting that he would attack my paper's intentions as an attempt to intentionally elevate Islam and the political leanings of the majority of Muslim Americans. I was simply trying to think missiologically. Alas, it was an unfortunate meeting between missiology and apologetics.

Educating undergraduate missions students at a small-town, conservative, evangelical liberal arts university presents multiple opportunities and challenges. Students at Freed-Hardeman University tend to be morally and theologically conservative but monolithic in their exposure to traditional evangelism and apologetics methodologies, despite their increased exposure to cultural diversity. My upper undergraduate-level world religions course is often the student's first significant exposure to other faith traditions in their diverse world. In previous semesters at both the undergraduate and graduate levels, my tendency has been to focus on contextualized evangelistic strategies and strategies of diaspora missiology in the missiological component of the course. Upon reflection, more emphasis was needed from an apologetics perspective. Despite my negative interaction at the academic conference, I realized that missiology and apologetics need each other.

Given Matt Cook's experience, you may wonder how I (MS) as this apologetics professor became a collaborator with him in a missiology effort. International short-term missions in college, as well as several years working in international higher education, have contributed to my interest in missions. My academic work in philosophy has focused on religious epistemology and apologetics, and I teach courses in Christian evidences, the problem of suffering, and advanced apologetics. Cook and I discovered in conversation that there was an opportunity for collaboration to strengthen both our classes and to address topics of missiology and apologetics more holistically with our students. My apologetics training was classical and so my teaching follows a similar model: beginning with the rational foundations of theism, moving to a case for the reliability of the Bible, and pointing to the divinity and resurrection of Jesus. Over the last few years, I have tried to address meta-apologetic questions by examining different methodologies and moving toward an eclectic model, while also working to incorporate a discussion of *how* to communicate an apologetic in my courses (see Koukl 2009; Chatraw and Allen, 2018). Collaborating with Cook has allowed me to examine my own approach to apologetics by filtering it through a lens of missiology in the classroom. Looking more closely at world religions and missiology has allowed me to reduce blind spots in my Western approach to apologetics and pushed me to continue to seek eclectic models that incorporate a holistic approach both in method and pedagogy.

Cook's training in missiology and world religions and Sokoloski's training in philosophy created a unique opportunity for interdisciplinary collaboration. For our initial collaboration (spring 2023), Sokoloski co-taught three eighty-minute class sessions in Cook's world religions course. Specifically, we integrated world religions and apologetics using the model proposed by Benno van den Toren and Kang-San Tan in their newly published work *Humble Confidence: A Model for Interfaith Apologetics* (2022). In this chapter, we explain how we used Toren and Tan's model as a framework for the class. Next, we describe our pedagogical plan for each of the three classes we conducted and reflect on the effectiveness and student involvement of each class session. To conclude, we make some final observations and suggestions for improvement, followed by a description of further cross-disciplinary engagement we have done (fall 2023).

The desire to create a more interactive learning environment is an ongoing trend in the scholarship of teaching and learning. Huber and Hutchings (2005, x) explain, "Today's scholars of teaching and learning treat their classrooms and programs as a source of interesting questions about learning; find ways to explore and shed light on these questions; use this evidence in designing and refining new activities, assignments, and assessments; and share what they've found with colleagues who can comment, critique, and build on new insights." At our institution, we are encouraged to view the classroom as a learning laboratory. Teaching and learning studies emphasize the integration of academic fields to enhance learning. Our collaboration for this project is an example of "collaboration and cross-fertilization" that "builds relationships among individuals with common interests" in ways that enhance student learning (Hutchings, Huber, and Ciccone 2011, xx).

Further, at Freed-Hardeman, all classes are viewed through the lens of faith, but specifically in the College of Biblical Studies, our teaching is fueled by the *missio Dei* since this is the grand theme of Scripture. The mission of God—when understood as the story of mission in the biblical narrative through creation, the fall, redemption, and future hope—serves as a foundation for missiology, missional living, *and* the undergraduate classroom (Ashford 2011, loc. 212 of 8500; also Richebacher 2003). George R. Knight affirms: "The goals of Christian education go beyond the accumulation of cognitive knowledge, self-awareness, and coping successfully with the environment. To be sure, Christian education includes those aspects of learning, but beyond that, it has the more far-reaching goals of reconciling fallen individuals to God and one another and restoring the image of God in them" (2006, loc. 4470 of 5577). If teaching has the goal of reconciling fallen individuals back to God, then the classroom provides a daily opportunity to participate in the *missio Dei*, especially classes engaged in missiology and apologetics.

An Overview of Humble Confidence:
A Model for Interfaith Apologetics

Toren and Tan (2022) intend for *Humble Confidence* to contribute to the need for more contextual interfaith apologetics. As such, their book became a springboard for our collaborative project. Toren and Tan observe that while Western apologetics often interacts within the modern and postmodern worldviews, there is a need to incorporate interreligious dialogue (recognizing the complex social structures of religion) and interfaith dialogue (recognizing that people populate these structures and derive significant meaning in relation to the transcendent). The book is divided into two parts: the first explores the possibility of reimagining interfaith apologetics, while the second is an application of these insights into particular contexts of world religions or worldviews. For our project, part one informed part of the background for our collaboration, while part two provided practical suggestions that we incorporated into classroom pedagogy.

For our collaboration, the book confirmed the need for the exploration of ways in which missions education and apologetics can mutually benefit one another. Toren and Tan develop their understanding of holistic apologetics that addresses "body, mind, and soul, all embedded in their histories, relationships, communities, and societies" (28) while also searching for ways in which worldviews coincide or clash so that space is created for dialogue (6). These spaces are created by looking for dissonance within or between worldviews, as well as considering how such worldviews line up with a person's lived experiences (49). From clarifying how Christians can theologically understand non-Christian religious traditions to constructing bridges for interreligious and interfaith dialogue, Toren and Tan remind us of the need for bold humility as we engage in interfaith apologetics (6, 124–27). Applying this to missions education, this is the attitude we seek to instill in our students as we encourage the disposition of confidence and courage, along with humility and openness, to share the good news of Jesus Christ.

Pedagogical Plans and the Classroom Experience

Since Freed-Hardeman is a liberal arts institution, the semester's section of world religions included students from across the university. Because it is not a required class for any major or minor and is a 400-level course, most students enrolled because of an interest in world religions. A diverse group from a variety of backgrounds and academic interests, most seemed interested in learning about world religions for the sake of missions and evangelism. Their required reading for the course was Charles E. Farhadian's *Introducing World Religions* (2015).

Islam Session

After reading the textbook chapter on Islam and having two traditional discussion-based class sessions exploring the beliefs and practices of Islam, we turned to the conversation of missiology and apologetics with Sokoloski as our guest in class. Because this was the first combined session, we asked the students to define both missiology and apologetics and explored how these two fields might mutually benefit from one another. From my perspective in missiology (MC), the average southern evangelical student needs a heavy dose of the basics of diaspora missiology: neighbor love and the golden rule, hospitality, service, and simple awareness of diaspora realities (see Anyabwile 2010; Van Rheenen 2016). Further, we emphasized the strategic importance of creative access missions in many Muslim-majority countries and contextualization strategies, specifically exploring the C1 to C6 Spectrum (Travis 1998, 407–10).

Insights from Toren and Tan. In Toren and Tan's (2022) chapter on Islam, they begin by pointing out that since it is the only major world religion with post-Christian origins, it has commonalities and also fundamental disagreements about Jesus and the Christian Scriptures. In addition, given the troubled history between Muslims and Christians and anti-Christian polemics developed by Muslims, we recognize that there are significant obstacles to overcome but also possibilities for building bridges (190). The most helpful parts of the chapter for our class were the perspective of Islam as the natural religion of humanity and the importance of having a developed view of the doctrine of the Trinity (192–95, 198–202).

Results. The session on Islam set the tone for the collaboration to follow and was welcomed by the students. After discussing the meaning of missiology and apologetics, we turned our attention to some areas of apologetics. For example, we imagined how a Muslim would present Islam as a rational natural religion with one simple God (rather than a triune

God) who forgives because he can and would not allow the shameful death of Jesus. We determined that an apologetic witness needs to address a variety of concerns and Christian doctrines. We explored the reliability of Scripture and the reality of Jesus's crucifixion and resurrection. Regarding the Trinity, we pointed out that this teaching is revealed in Scripture and not from a later corruption. Though some Islamic teachings are simpler, we should be open to greater complexities of reality, especially when revealed from a transcendent source, rather than limiting ourselves to what seems most natural or rational from our limited perspective.

This class session also incorporated more of a missiological focus, and we continued to look for points of connection to draw a Muslim to consider other religious possibilities. For example, we used the idea of ceremonial cleansing observed by Muslims as a way to build a bridge to the need for cleansing and atonement made possible through the sacrifice of Jesus. The students continued to think of potential connections to express the resulting existential impact that accepting the complexities of the Christian faith would have on the life of an individual. While there were no definitive answers of what exactly an apologetic witness would look like, the students became more aware of the points of conflict and the need to be prepared to defend the doctrine of the Trinity, the reliability of Scripture, and the deity of Christ.

Hinduism Session

Our students struggled to grasp Hinduism more than any other religion we studied. In his classic work, Robert Zaehner (1983, loc. 2558) affirms why the religion is difficult to understand: "What, then, is the message of Hinduism? If it has a message at all, it would seem to be this: to live out your dharma which is embedded in the conscience … and thereby to live in harmony with the dharma of all things, so that in the end you may see all things in yourself and yourself in all things and thereby enter into the eternal and timeless peace which is the dharma of moksha, the 'law' of 'freedom' that has its being outside space and time yet comprises and hallows both." At the end of a doctoral seminar on Hinduism, my (MC) own professor added "If you feel like you don't 'get' Hinduism, then you 'get' it." While Hinduism was the most difficult religion to explain to undergrads, this difficulty also revealed the need for a Christian apologetic.

I (MC) spent one full day explaining the basics of Hinduism. On the second day, we discussed the development, adaptation, and practice of Hinduism in the United States and then evangelistic methods for reaching Hindus. I tend to focus on strategies related to diaspora missions practice (Lausanne Movement and Global Diaspora Network 2017, 31–35). Pathickal (2012, 120) reminds readers that fruitful outreach among Hindus begins with our availability: "Very few Christians take the time and make the effort to become profoundly available to a Hindu. However, wherever someone has taken the time and effort, the results have been astonishing. This is the core of friendship evangelism."

Insights from Toren and Tan. In their chapter on Hinduism, Toren and Tan (2022) use the example of a religious celebration in Nepal, Bhai Tika, to introduce the challenge of a holistic apologetic. Religion is embedded in culture, and the challenge of deciding what needs to be left behind and what can be kept (but perhaps untangled) is discussed at some length. Much of the chapter considers the notion that "Christ is the fulfillment of the Hindu quest," particularly by using the more narrow Bhakti tradition— religious devotion to just one god (156).

After considering the possibility of a "fulfillment structure" in which "Christ is uniquely unique because of who he is and what he accomplishes" (163), we explored the possibility of subversive fulfillment. That is, Christ and the Trinitarian Godhead could be critical of false elements of Hinduism but also provide true fulfillment. Returning to the question of participating in festivals and celebrations that are entwined with religious meaning, Toren and Tan discuss practical concerns regarding "dual belonging" in which someone is converted to Christianity but also maintains ties to their community of origin and the positive influence they can be as "a subversive presence witnessing to their new Lord" (171).

Because of these insights, we focused our apologetics on the possibility of a fulfillment or subversive fulfillment framework, and we used Bhakti as a model for apologetic bridge building while also acknowledging the limited scope of the example in the broader context of Hinduism.

Results. This class session was the least productive for a few reasons. First, since the students had so many questions about Hinduism, we allowed their questions to prompt our discussion. Despite that, an in-depth discussion never took off. Second, Toren and Tan's chapter on Hinduism was less helpful because it was limited in scope. For example, they took an example from

Hinduism that was so close to Christianity and did not represent mainstream Hinduism. Third, we did not spend as much time defining important religious terms for apologetics (e.g., fulfillment structure, subversive fulfillment). Because of these reasons and Hindu's overall foreignness to the students, the impact of this class session was limited.

Buddhism Session

Because of the schedule, Cook conducted only one class session on Buddhism before Sokoloski joined to discuss Buddhism and apologetics. This class session summarized the story of Siddharta Gautama, his teachings, the major sects of Buddhism, and Western Buddhism. Buddha's teachings are easy to organize because of their numbered nature, though like Hinduism, Eastern thought is difficult for Western students to comprehend. Beyond the distinct characteristics of Theravada and Mahayana Buddhism, we merely introduced the many subsects of Buddhism since the course text provided an adequate description of them.

In the classes following the collaborative session, we focused on mission strategies for reaching Buddhist immigrants in the US and abroad. We particularly talked about reaching Buddhists with an honor-shame worldview. I (MC) also discussed in more detail the philosophical questions of epistemology and suffering.

Insights from Toren and Tan. From Toren and Tan's chapter (2022), we are reminded again of the diversity found within one religion. Unlike Christianity and Islam, Buddhism can be a part of a multireligious identity; however, like Christianity and Islam, it is a missionary faith because it offers answers to problems of the human condition (172).

What most informed our teaching was an exploration into the "deep resonances and radical differences" between Christianity and Buddhism (176). For example, in Buddhism, desire can be a root cause of suffering, but for the Christian, desire is not necessarily wrong though it must be properly ordered or directed. Likewise, in Buddhism, understanding the true nature of life and reality is crucial for liberation; however, for the Christian, it is forgiveness that provides freedom from sin and death (176–77).

Indeed, there are radical differences between Christianity and Buddhism regarding the nature of God, the self, and the world. Buddhism can also present itself as a rational or spiritual alternative to religion, free from doctrinal demands. This can be particularly attractive to freethinkers in the West who are drawn to spirituality without the implications of a personal God or particular doctrine. Therefore, the challenge for a holistic apologetic is to create a triadic encounter between the two individuals in dialogue, along with the experience of reality, while providing a deep and existentially relevant alternative. This Christian alternative conveys (1) that our experience of ourselves is not an illusion but that we are most truly ourselves when relating to a personal God; (2) that our desires can be well-ordered and shape us by loving God and loving our neighbor; and (3) that true hope is found in Christ, which leads to ultimate fulfillment (178–81, 187–89).

In this chapter, Toren and Tan write more about missiological matters than in their chapters on Islam and Hinduism. For example, their discussion of the parallels between the four noble truths and the eightfold path offers possibilities for positive conversation about bridges to Buddhism. They also compare Christian compassion to Buddhist compassion based on epistemological understandings of suffering (176–79).

Results. The lively engagement and discussion from this class session were encouraging given how flat the Hinduism discussion had been. A few things contributed to this experience. First, insights from Toren and Tan were easier to practically implement into the session. Despite the pronounced differences in worldviews, the potential bridges to Christianity were more obvious and representative of the core of Buddhism, compared to the more limited focus of Hindu Bhaktism. Also, it seemed that the students could more easily imagine an encounter with a Westerner who had adopted Buddhism and thus have more potential cultural connections. This led to a deeper discussion of different ways to present an apologetic witness to different Buddhists from Southeast Asia versus an American Buddhist living in California. The students creatively considered ways to offer a better narrative to the problem of suffering and concepts of the self while also acknowledging how someone could find spirituality appealing without doctrine. In the end, they found their own way to express the beauty of the Christian message and the hope found in Christ.

Second, our preparation was an important factor. Learning from the challenges of our previous class session on Hindium, we prepared better questions and more directed discussions that would better connect with the students.

Third, we discovered a better order for class sessions. For Islam and Hinduism, I (MC) taught two class sessions of content, including some missiological implications, before doing the collaborative session with Sokoloski. For Buddhism, however, I led one full class session on content followed by our collaborative session on apologetics, and then I led the practical class session on mission strategies toward Buddhists last. This order seemed to create the best environment for engaged discussion.

Final Observations, Suggestions for Improvement, and Future Plans

Overall, we were pleased with this teaching experiment. The class sessions were fun and created significant student dialogue. These collaborative sessions seemed to enrich the learning experience for the students and will probably be the part of the class that they remember most. The students expressed their appreciation for the collaborative experiment. Most importantly, every collaborative class session focused on the beauty of Jesus and the hope of the gospel—key qualities of apologetic and missional engagement with adherents of world religions.

We feel we can improve the collaborative sessions with a few suggestions. First, small groups would be an effective way to create discussion, especially when the discussion is lagging. Svinicki and McKeachie remark, "Students are more likely to talk in small groups than in large ones" (2013, 194). Second, since our conversations were more robust when we combined missiology and apologetics, rather than solely focusing on apologetics, we want to continue doing that.

Third, regarding Toren and Tan, several concepts stand out for framing future discussions. The metaphor of pull and push factors could be used to better organize potential attractions and tensions between, and within, worldviews. Concepts such as fulfillment structure and subversive fulfillment are worth clarifying and considering further. Interfaith dialogue as a triadic shape could also be emphasized more to shape examples of apologetic witness. As Toren and Tan (2022, 241) write: "Together, we are relating to a world beyond ourselves, a God beyond ourselves, whom Christians believe is supremely revealed in Jesus of Nazareth. Because of this shared world, we can communicate, bridges can be built, and we can be reminded of the inadequacy of our own views and attitudes towards life."

Given the testimony at play from Scripture and our apologetic witness, it would also be relevant to explore the epistemology of testimony and the role it plays in both apologetics and missions. Finally, student learning would be enhanced through more concrete engagement with adherents of these world religions. If possible, we plan to seek out adherents to visit as guests to dialogue with students. Though this will be more challenging in our small town than it would be in an urban context, it is still possible. Further, we plan to implement field trips to Muslim, Buddhist, and Hindu places of worship and meditation to enhance the student learning experience.

Since our initial collaboration (spring 2023), we have combined two classes that were coincidentally meeting at the same time. Cook's missionary anthropology class and Sokoloski's Christian evidences class combined for four fifty-minute sessions in the fall of 2023. In session one, we introduced the missiological concept of contextualization and challenged students, through small group discussions, to imagine contextualizing apologetics conversations in several different global settings. In session two, Cook introduced worldview concepts related to honor-shame, fear-power, and guilt-innocence cultures. In session three, students explored case studies in which they developed ideas for evangelistic conversations with individuals from cultures that emphasize honor-shame and fear-power worldviews. Finally, in session four, we led a class discussion on the value of narrative as a contextualized tool for both learning about cultures and sharing faith in a secular culture. This semester, we have discovered that using small groups that explore case studies has created excellent class discussions and learning opportunities.

We plan to continue this collaboration in future semesters. Perhaps this will become a new tradition each semester, but regardless, we each plan to better incorporate aspects of apologetics and missiology into our courses that benefit and complement the goals of each class. It is our hope that our collaboration for incorporating apologetics into contemporary missions education continues to yield more fruit in the future.

References

Anyabwile, Thabiti. 2010. *The Gospel for Muslims: An Encouragement to Share Christ with Confidence*. Chicago: Moody.

Ashford, Bruce, ed. 2011. *Theology and Practice of Mission: God, the Church, and the Nations*. Nashville: B&H Academic. Kindle.

Chatraw, Joshua D., and Mark D. Allen. 2018. *Apologetics at the Cross: An Introduction for Christian Witness*. Grand Rapids: Zondervan.

Huber, Mary Taylor, and Pat Hutchings. 2005. *The Advancement of Learning: Building the Teaching Commons*. San Francisco: Jossey-Bass.

Hutchings, Pat, Mary Taylor Huber, and Anthony Ciccone. 2011. *The Scholarship of Teaching and Learning Reconsidered: Institutional Integration and Impact*. San Francisco: Jossey-Bass.

Farhadian, Charles E. 2015. *Introducing World Religions: A Christian Engagement*. Grand Rapids: Baker Academic.

Knight, George R. 2006. *Philosophy and Education: An Introduction in Christian Education*. 4th ed. Berrien Springs, MI: Andrews University Press. Kindle.

Koukl, Gregory. 2009. *Tactics: A Game Plan for Discussing Your Christian Convictions*. Grand Rapids: Zondervan.

Lausanne Movement and Global Diaspora Network. 2017. *Scattered to Gather: Embracing the Global Trend of Diaspora*. Rev. ed. Vernon Hills, IL: Parivar.

Pathickal, Paul. 2012. *Christ and the Hindu Diaspora*. Bloomington, IN: WestBow Press.

Pratt, Zane. 2011. "The Heart of Mission: Redemption." In *Theology and Practice of Mission: God, the Church, and the Nations*, edited by Bruce Ashford, location 1279–540. Nashville: B&H Academic.

Richebächer, Wilhelm. 2009. "*Missio Dei*: The Basis of Mission Theology or a Wrong Path?" *International Review of Mission* 92, no. 367 (October): 588–605.

Svinicki, Marilla, and Wilbert J. McKeachie. 2013. *McKeachie's Teaching Tips: Strategies, Research, and Theory for College and University Teachers*. 14th ed. Belmont: Wadsworth.

Toren, Benno van den, and Kang-San Tan. 2022. *Humble Confidence: A Model for Interfaith Apologetics*. Downers Grove, IL: InterVarsity Press.

Travis, John, 1998. "The C1 to C6 Spectrum." *Evangelical Missions Quarterly* 34, no. 4 (October): 407–10. https://missionexus.org/the-c1-to-c6-spectrum/.

Van Rheenen, Gailyn. 2016. "Is Missional a Fad?" *Missio Dei: A Journal of Missional Theology and Praxis* 7 (Summer-Fall). https://missiodeijournal.com/issues/md-7/authors/md-7-van-rheenen.

Zaehner, R. C. 1983. *Hinduism*. 2nd ed. New York: Oxford University Press. Kindle.

Chapter 12

Cultivating African American Missionaries

A Discipleship Model for Churches

Mimsie Robinson

In recent years, several Christian missions leaders have raised the question, "Why are there so few African American missionaries?" (Zylstra 2013, 14). Others have commented on how the unique experiences and suffering of African Americans allow them to receive a warmer welcome in some international contexts than many White missionaries might receive (Kwon 2010). Indeed, the socioeconomic struggle and racial discrimination experienced by most African Americans give them the ability to identify with the world's hurting and oppressed people.

According to a study of 750 African American churches in urban areas, many churches do reasonably well in the areas of providing food (71 percent) and clothing (66 percent), ministering to prisoners (56 percent) and those struggling with substance abuse (46 percent), and other holistic ministries (Bositis 2006, 7–8). In addition to meeting physical needs in the community, some African American churches are meaningfully engaged in local evangelism. However, the biggest challenge has been mobilizing and equipping African American believers for global missions service.

We are striving to develop a discipleship model that will cause many African American Christians to experience a shift in worldview that makes cross-cultural ministry a viable and achievable life calling. Many African Americans have participated in short-term missions efforts and witnessed firsthand the meaningful impact they can have in these cross-cultural contexts. How can these experiences play a greater role in helping African American believers develop a greater vision for the world? What discipleship strategies can African American churches adopt to raise up long-term African American missionaries to serve among the world's least-reached peoples?

Raising the Issue for African American Churches

African American churches need a global missions discipleship strategy that addresses the unique context of its members. In keeping with Van Rheenan's missional helix (2011), it must be provocative enough to confront the strongholds of safety and security that have become a critical element of the African American worldview (see Sutherland 1998). At the same time, it must be sensitive enough to honestly portray history, including the dehumanizing racial discrimination experienced by African Americans, while also providing believers with the tenacity to obey the Great Commission at whatever cost. Such a discipleship program should be contextual to African American church culture and also be undergirded by a holistic and practical theology. Such a strategy will prepare African American missionaries to thrive and be fruitful in challenging places around the world.

In reality, there are very few African American churches with established missions programs that have commissioned international missionaries. I am fortunate to be the missions pastor at one such church, and I can attest that the harvest is plentiful, but the laborers are few (Matt 9:37–38). As we ask the Lord of the harvest to send out laborers, we must also ask him for an effective discipleship strategy that will ultimately lead to more African American global missionaries. Given the challenges we have mentioned, this is not an easy task, but we must remember that the Lord is the ultimate sender.

Instead of writing off African American sending as an impossibility, we must start the conversation. When I asked one pastor if his church had a goal to send members out as long-term missionaries, he responded not at this time. His church's missions involvement took place primarily through the denominational missions structures. If a member asked the church leadership to prepare them for a long-term missions assignment, the pastor would surely be surprised and need to rely on the denominational structures as the primary means for preparing the candidate. If more African American local churches had direct relationships with missionaries and a missions-oriented discipleship program, then there might be more African American missionaries being raised up to serve long term.

A Missionary Candidate Discipleship Program

Why shouldn't each local African American church develop a discipleship plan to cultivate prospective missionaries to make disciples among unreached peoples? What would this program look like?

Inspired by the model developed under the leadership of John Piper at Bethlehem Baptist Church in Minneapolis (see Piper and Stellar 1998), our church has developed a strategy called the Bethel Nurture Program for Missionary Candidates. I would like to express sincere gratitude to Pastor Tom Stellar for his mentorship and support by sharing the primary document that helped me develop this model.

Building off of Jesus's words to "ask the Lord of the harvest to send out workers into his harvest field" (Matt 9:38 NIV), all of our recruitment begins and ends in prayer. Prayer for the global harvest is the responsibility of church leaders and members.

Missionary mobilization has both an individual and corporate dimension. In his sovereignty, God speaks to his people who are praying and in his word. God will put a desire for missions on the heart of individual believers as they are seeking him (Phil 2:13). Sometimes, the Lord will use a persuasive appeal from a godly person (Acts 11:25–26). Other times, a person may receive a vision or guidance through a word of prophecy (Acts 16:9–10).

On a corporate level, church leaders, whether lay or ordained, should prayerfully take the initiative to approach church members about considering missionary service. This should not be limited to those believers who demonstrate skills in preaching and teaching. Many believers in a local church have professional skills that could be a tremendous asset on the mission field. Sometimes these are overlooked because they do not have the obvious gifts that we associate with ministry. Like the church in Antioch, church leaders must lead the congregation in confirming a potential missionary's calling, preparing them, and then sending them off (Acts 13:3). Paul reminds us that the role of church leadership is to equip God's people for service at home and abroad (Eph 4:11–16).

A missionary training program should include the training necessary to send someone out as a witness for Jesus Christ. All missionary candidates entering the missionary nurture program must be saved and baptized in water and with the Holy Spirit (John 3:5; Acts 1:8; 2:1–4, 38–39).

The ministry of the Holy Spirit is indispensable in the believer's life. A believer who is a missionary candidate must be devoted to ministry in the local assembly.

For candidates preparing to serve in fields directly associated with the home church, the church itself may serve as the primary training and sending arm. For those interested in fields where the church is not presently engaged, an appropriate missions agency should be identified. In addition to taking part in the church's training program, the candidate will also take part in that organization's training experience. In this case, the church's primary goal should be to provide a candidate who is Christ-centered, compassionate, well-prepared, and highly motivated. While a church-centered nurture program ought to be contextualized to address the needs of missionary candidates from a variety of backgrounds, our program is particularly geared to prepare African American candidates for missions. Our missionary nurture program focuses on five dimensions.

A Growing Maturity—Spiritual, Emotional, and Relational

The most important dimension of missionary preparation relates to the candidate's relationship with God and their growth in Christlikeness. Missionary candidates should demonstrate a consistent devotional life of prayer, Bible study, and meditation. They should be men and women shaped by the word of God (2 Tim 3:16–17) and led by the Holy Spirit in every area of their lives (Acts 16:7–10). In addition to these spiritual disciplines, we have them read and reflect on some important books, including *How to Be a World-Class Christian* (Borthwick 2010), *The Purpose Driven Life* (Warren 2012), and *Out of the Comfort Zone* (Verwer 2000).

Since Christian workers may be assigned to areas where there is less accountability than they would experience at home, we want to ensure that they are spiritually mature, so we hold them to the standard of spiritual leaders laid out in 1 Timothy 3 and Titus 1. For those who will primarily preach the word on the mission field, we regard them as an elder; for those doing support ministries, we hold them to the standard of a deacon.

We also want to ensure that our missionary candidates are emotionally healthy. Prospective missionaries joining missions agencies are usually given a battery of psychological tests. At the church level, we do a preliminary evaluation of the candidate's emotional health. These screenings may determine that candidates, individuals and couples, may require professional counseling before they are released to missionary service. For others, we require them to read books on inner healing and emotional growth, such as Pete Scazzero's *Emotionally Healthy Spirituality* (2006).

During the first six months of the program, the candidate fills out a preparedness questionnaire. This is designed to help the candidate take an honest look at his or her life, relationship with God, self-awareness, relationships with others, and perspectives on cross-cultural issues. In addition, married couples will take the Prepare/Enrich survey to indicate their strengths and areas of needed growth in their marriage (Olson, Olson, and Larson 2012). To evaluate the missionary candidate's relational skills and needs, the Myers-Briggs Type Indicator (2015) may also be administered. Once these questionnaires and surveys are completed, the missions pastor or another member of the ministerial or counseling staff will sit down with the candidate, talk through the results, and make appropriate recommendations.

A Growing Commitment to the Local Church

A believer who responds to a call to missionary service should be a person who demonstrates a growing commitment to the life and ministry of the local church. If someone desires to minister cross-culturally, they should demonstrate commitment to the church's outreach ministries, including neighborhood evangelism, coffee house ministry, or visitation. The candidate should also be regularly involved in the church's missions prayer meetings. Whether a person is being sent out by the church directly or is working through a missions agency, his or her meaningful participation and use of gifts in our local assembly allow the leadership and the congregation to confirm the calling of the individual or couple in question.

It is also important to encourage the potential missionary to pursue a local cross-cultural learning experience by attending a French- or Spanish-speaking church service. We would especially encourage the candidate to serve in a ministry in the language of the people they hope to serve overseas. These efforts can be coordinated with the missions leadership of the church, which would increase the accountability for the candidate's local ministry and allow it to possibly turn into an internship. This might also result in some formal pre-field language learning classes.

A Growing Knowledge of God's Word

Since Christian workers and potential missionaries will be witnessing, preaching, and teaching at least as part of their job description, a working knowledge of the Bible is indispensable. While some missions agencies require formal Bible training, others require that candidates be able to demonstrate a good grasp of Scripture. In addition to the daily disciplines of reading, studying, and memorizing Scripture, some formal or informal Bible training may also be necessary. Some courses may be taken through the church's Christian education ministry, while other formal courses can be taken through a Bible college, seminary, or an approved online program (see e.g., Thirdmill's online courses). Candidates should have a solid grasp of Bible study methods and Old and New Testaments surveys. They could also benefit from a discipleship course such as MasterLife (Willis 1997).

All missions candidates should also take a Perspectives on the World Christian Movement course, generally offered as a fifteen-week face-to-face class and sometimes online. Perspectives provides an introduction to the biblical, historical, cultural, and strategic dimensions of the missionary movement. If an African American church is hosting Perspectives, then the instructors should be African American missionaries or mobilizers who can contextualize the content for the Black church, addressing issues such as historic racial discrimination, safety, security, and fundraising. A supplementary bibliography of resources for African American missionaries ought to be provided with texts such as Walston and Stevens's *African-American Experience in World Mission: A Call beyond Community* (2002).

A Growing Application of God's Word through Ministry

There is an old adage that says, "If you're not doing it here, what makes you think you'll do it over there?" This is a probing question. Mission agencies rightfully ask it all the time. They insist that missionary candidates demonstrate a significant degree of inclination and effectiveness in ministry here, which will be relevant ministry experience for the mission field. Certainly, there may be significant methodological differences. For example, street evangelism in Spanish Harlem and doing evangelism among the Baka people in Cameroon require significantly different approaches. Despite this, there are similarities and the missionary's greatest need is to

develop a heart for lost people. Both situations are cross-cultural, and both give you the experience of depending on the Holy Spirit to empower you to move out of your comfort zone and communicate the gospel in terms that can be understood. All churches should want their candidates to go to the field with enough experience of God working through them that they leave with a well-grounded confidence that he will continue to do so in the future wherever they go (Phil 2:13; Acts 1:8). Most of all, preparatory prayer and a heart of love and compassion are required. Consider the response of Jesus to the multitudes in Matthew 9:36. In the next two verses, he incited his disciples to develop a similar heartfelt response by encouraging them to pray for laborers. They became the answer to their own prayers. God will often work this way in our lives.

At this point in the missionary candidate's development, a ministry internship in a context that is closest to what will eventually become the long-term assignment would be best. In New York, especially in Harlem, there is a sizable community of West African Muslims, so much so that a certain area is referred to as "Little Africa." Through partnership with organizations like Global Gates or the International Project, a ministry internship can be developed that may bring the prospective missionary into contact with members of the *Fulani* or another intended target population (Global Gates 2023). Another kind of ministry that all missionary candidates should be trained for and become engaged in is hands-on prayer ministry. They need to learn how to pray for the sick, the hurting, and the demonized in a way that communicates the compassion and power of the kingdom of God. This might be obtained through formal deliverance classes or through involvement with the intercessory prayer ministry of the church, if they have the maturity to provide such an internship experience.

A Growing Relationship with Senders

A sender is anyone who helps a missionary on his or her way and tires to "see that they have everything they need" (Tit 3:13b NIV). All missionaries, whether sent out by the church directly or by a missions agency, should have healthy relationships with a network of senders. These senders aim to offer help to the missionary during his or her time of preparation, ministry on the field, and home ministry assignment. They advocate for the missionary by encouraging the sending church to partner through prayer, giving financially, and by sharing a vision for why missionaries among the unreached are needed. For many African American churches, this might be the first time they have been challenged to serve as senders. Here is a brief survey of six categories of senders.

Accountability partner. Every missionary candidate entering the nurture program should have an accountability partner. They should seek out a partner from their home church who is a mature believer. Often an accountability partner can be found among the church's ministers, deacons, auxiliary leaders, Sunday school teachers, Bible study leaders, evangelists, or other committed believers. The missions pastor or director can be a resource for suggested mentors. Candidates should meet with their partner once a month to report on their progress in the program, to establish goals for the coming month, and to pray.

Missionary mentor. This is a missionary who is presently on the field, on sabbatical, or retired who can play a critical role in assisting the prospective missionary, especially helping them answer personal and practical questions related to missionary living. The church missions team will attempt to match the candidate with someone who serves the same people group (or a similar people group) whom the candidate is hoping to serve. The nature of the interactions will, of course, be determined by the proximity of the mentor and candidate. In some cases, virtual meetings must suffice. The church will also strive to arrange a short-term missions trip so the candidate can interact with the mentor on the field. For churches lacking missionary mentors in their congregation, often a missions organization might be willing to suggest mentors for a missionary candidate.

The missions staff or board. This group is composed of pastors and elders, the missions pastor or director, missions prayer leaders, and other various board members. They are the ones tasked with rallying the church to intercede for and support global missions. They also make crucial decisions about policies, including whether or not to recommend a candidate to the church to receive financial support. They are a critical body for helping the prospective missionary make it to the field. The tasks of the missions board's work in sending the new missionary include:

- Sharing monthly or bimonthly prayer points with the missions prayer leaders to be circulated to the church membership.

- Reviewing a missionary candidate's request for financial support once they are appointed by the church or a missions organization. As part of this process, they interview the candidate.

- Communicating with the candidate once they make it to the field. At least once a quarter, the missionary should update the board about their work and share prayer requests. The mission board keeps the missionary up to date on happenings in the church.

- Debriefing and praying with the missionary once they return from the field for a home assignment or possibly a termination of service.

The missions agency. Another critical part of the sending network is the missions agency. Their role is particularly important for missionaries being sent to a field where the church has no previous involvement. The relationship between the missionary candidate and the mission agency generally develops in four stages: (1) exploration—the potential missionary candidate communicates their interests, and the agency shares mission opportunities; (2) application and screening; (3) candidate orientation school; and (4) ongoing accountability and direction. These stages will look different depending on the missions organization.

The missionary support team. In addition to the pastoral and missions board leadership, this is a small group of people chosen by the missionary to be confidants, advocates, prayer supporters, and practical supporters while the missionary is on the field. They are a vital link between the missionary and the church. Again, the missions pastor can recommend to the missionary who ought to serve on such a team.

The pastoral staff and elders. The missionary also needs relationships with the church's pastor and elders. As leaders of the flock, they will given an account for the well-being of missionaries—both local and international workers. Church leaders must be available to teach, encourage, and counsel during the missionary's term of service.

Missional Capacity Building

In addition to this missionary nurture program, African American churches need to build a greater capacity for global missions. I suggest the following next steps.

- Develop a network of African American missionaries who are presently on the field or retired from the field. They could serve as a mentoring network for prospective missionaries considering global service.

- Connect African American churches with missions agencies and parachurch organizations with a vision for mobilizing African American missionaries. For example, churches and organizations might come together to work on a strategic plan to reach an unreached people group in an African country.

- Cultivate partnerships between African American churches and missions-minded White congregations. White churches could learn from Black churches that have strong evangelism and compassion ministries, while African American churches might benefit from missions training, fundraising practices, and approaches to supporting missionaries.

- Locate opportunities where African American professionals might work as tentmakers for two to three years in an unreached context.

- Encourage missions agencies to set apart African American missionaries and mobilizers for the executive leadership team of their organizations.

- Identify African American church multiplication facilitators who can mentor and empower indigenous pastors in countries with unreached peoples. Not only will this bless these indigenous pastors, but it will also involve African American churches more in the work of global missions.

- Through virtual meetings and digital platforms, cultivate relationships between African American Christians and church leaders with indigenous international church leaders.

- Encourage African American churches to connect with the National African American Missions Council's (NAAMC) annual conference and excellent resources.

Conclusion

African American churches must adopt mobilization, training, and sending strategies that are meaningful in the Black church context and that will result in Black churches making global disciple-making a top priority. Following Van Rheenan's missional helix (2011), the strategy must be comprehensive and relevant enough to confront the strongholds of safety and security that have characterized the African American worldview (Sutherland 1998). At the same time, it must be sensitive enough to honestly engage the real history of racial discrimination but also challenge the African American church to obey the Great Commission at whatever cost. A contextualized African American training program that is holistic and practical can help accomplish this. My hope is that these programs will become normative in African American churches. Now is the time to blow the trumpet for missions in African American churches throughout our country.

References

Borthwick, Paul. 2009. *How to Be a World-Class Christian: Becoming Part of God's Global Kingdom.* Downers Grove, IL: InterVarsity Press.

Bositis, David A. 2006. "Black Churches and the Faith-Based Initiative: Findings from a National Survey." Washington, DC: Joint Center for Political and Economic Studies.

Briggs, Katharine. C., and Isabel Briggs Myers. 2015. The Myers-Briggs Type Indicator. https://www.themyersbriggs.com.

Global Gates. 2023. "Get Training." Global Gates. www.globalgates.info/.

Kwon, Lillian. 2010. "Black Christians Largely Absent from U.S. Missionary Force." Christian Post. http://www.christianpost.com/news/black-christians-largely-absent-from-us-missionary-force-47088/.

Olson, David H., Amy K. Olson, and Peter J. Larson. 2012. "Prepare-Enrich Program: Overview and New Discoveries about Couples." *Journal of Family and Community Ministries* 25, no. 1: 30–44.

Piper, John, and Tom Stellar. 1998. "Bethlehem Nurture Program for Missionary Candidates Handbook." Unpublished document.

Scazzero, Pete. 2006. *Emotionally Healthy Spirituality.* Nashville: Thomas Nelson.

Sutherland, James W. 1998. "African American Underrepresentation in Intercultural Missions: Perceptions of Black Missionaries and the Theory of Survival/Security." PhD diss., Trinity Evangelical Divinity School. https://www.rmni.org/african-american-missions/dissertation-why-so-few-afam-missionaries.html.

Van Rheenan, Gailyn. 2011. "MR #26: The Missional Helix: Example of Church Planting." http://www.missiology.org/blog/GVR-MR-26-The-Missional-Helix-Example-of-Church-Planting.

Verwer, George. 2000. *Out of the Comfort Zone: A Compelling Vision for the Transforming Global Missions*. Bloomington, IN: Bethany House.

Walston, Vaughn J., and Robert J. Stevens, eds. 2002. *African American Experience in World Mission: A Call beyond Community*. Pasadena, CA: William Carey Library.

Warren, Rick. 2012. *The Purpose Driven Life: What on Earth Am I Here For?* Expanded ed. Grand Rapids: Zondervan.

Willis, Avery T. 1997. *MasterLife: A Biblical Process for Growing Disciples.* Nashville: Lifeway.

Winter, Ralph D., and Steve C. Hawthorne, eds. 2009. *Perspectives on the World Christian Movement: A Reader.* 4th ed. Pasadena, CA: William Carey Library.

Zylstra, Sarah Eekhoff. 2013. "Black Churches' Missing Missionaries." *Christianity Today.* April 2. https://www.christianitytoday.com/ct/2013/april/missing-missionaries.html.

Chapter 13

Mission Training on the Move

A Case Study of All Nations Christian College

Richard Evans

Bringing Two "Small Worlds" Together

Social network theory expert Charles Kadushin (2012, 27) speaks of our "small worlds." I live in two. My first small world contains my network of friends and acquaintances in the United Kingdom (my country of birth) and across other parts of the Global North who are involved in an ever-shrinking world of mission training provision. Declining interest in mission sending means fewer formal missionaries. And fewer formal missionaries means fewer, or downsized, mission agencies. This means that would-be missionaries are now a rarer and more powerful species, in a stronger position to call the shots vis-à-vis their agency regarding the need for training, which, due to reasons of cost, time, and "not knowing what they do not know," often leads to less training or none. Diminished demand for traditional mission training presents the institutions where I serve and study with a difficult trilemma—die gracefully, merge defensively, or change proactively.

More positively, some agencies and training institutions have begun to engage their domestic markets by tapping into the multicultural world on their doorsteps and engaging growing Christian diaspora communities. Nevertheless, the overall picture is still one of gradual decline, rationalization, and increasing uncertainty concerning the future, which raises challenging questions. Can Western churches be reconvinced that sending members beyond their local situation is still commendable and commensurate with the gospel (Adeney 2010, 71–72)? Is there still a role for mission agencies (Arthur 2017; Harley 2019)? Are (traditional) Western mission training institutions willing to radically respond to persistent and pressing demands for change?

My second small world comprises a network of friends and acquaintances involved in mission training across the continents of the Global South. Here, a completely different set of realities are playing out. Burgeoning numbers of potential missionaries have increased the need for new sending structures. Increasing numbers of potential missionaries have heightened the demand for mission training and new opportunities for its provision. However, this demand often goes untapped due to a lack of supply (Lee 2022, 205) and want of innovation (Hoke 1999, 46), leaving individuals, families, and churches missionally unfulfilled. In this context, the questions asked are different. How can churches, mission agencies, and mission training institutions work together to meet this need? What creative means can they employ to release the necessary resources, produce the necessary content, and develop new mission trainers? Here, the contrasting picture is one of growth, possibility, originality, and the potential for cooperation within a framework of interdependence between institutions at every level (Cueva 2015, 188ff.).

Of course, my depiction of these two worlds is blunt, formed with partial information, and devoid of notable exceptions. Some Western mission agencies *are* thriving, often because they can bring their own small worlds together by successfully internationalizing (Smallman 2000, 28; Harley and Harley 2022, 178–83) or by attractively positioning themselves as niche players within their domestic markets. Both efforts mercifully serve to prolong the life of training institutions dependent on agency candidates. At the same time, in the Global South, many agencies and mission training schools have been flourishing for decades (Ferris 1990; Windsor 1995; Brynjolfson and Lewis 2006, 142–70, 189–94; Lawanson 2009; Lygunda li-M 2009). They are by no means a new phenomenon.

Despite these exceptions, I contend these broad-brush portrayals of my divergent small worlds are sufficiently accurate to inform the shaping of a new, emergent, mission training strategy (Mintzberg, Ahlstrand, and Lampel 2009, 199–210). For All Nations Christian College (ANCC) in the United Kingdom, this has been tentatively termed: *All Nations On-The-Move* (ANOTM).

Working from the economic hypothesis that there is a deficient demand for and oversupply of mission training in the Global North, and a deficient supply of and over demand for mission training in the Global South, ANCC envisions collaborating in the provision of mission training in new ways and contexts and through new friendships. But while this initiative is underpinned by an economic imbalance of demand and supply, it has not been realized through economic exchange. Instead, the underlying pattern has been entirely relational (Wan and Hedinger 2017, 11), with mission understood as "serving together as friends to release one another to fulfill the callings that we believe God has for each of us, our families, our organizations, His church, and our nations" (Evans 2021, slide 25). The ANOTM initiative works on the premise that the catalytic potential of connecting our many small worlds fosters the development of grassroots global networks dedicated to designing and delivering appropriate, affordable, and accessible mission training in situations of high demand and limited supply.

From a Polycentric to an Omnicentric Paradigm

Such training does not occur within a vacuum. Witness the remarkable numerical shift in Christian adherence "from the North and West to the South and East" (Prior 2022, 167) and the corresponding mission movements emanating from these latter directions (Zurlo, Johnson, Crossing 2020, 12–13). These developments have deeply challenged the Western paradigm that mission is "from the 'Christian' West to the non-Christian, non-West" (Goheen 2014, 144–45). I hesitate to add the word former to the Western paradigm because, as with any paradigmatic shift, there is overlap, often for several generations. Indeed, I would contend, from my own lived experience, that this mindset is still deeply embedded in the psyche of many, not only missions decision-makers in the Global North but unconscientized minds in the Global South. Western mission has done an effective job convincing others of their limited place in missions. As to probable cause, I would concur with Thomas Kuhn that paradigm shifts often precipitate "pronounced professional insecurity" (2012, 67) that can lead to "considerable resistance" (62). As for the emerging paradigm, Sam George articulates its expression most lucidly when he contends that, "The focus, resources, and personnel for [the] missionary task are [now] arising from different parts of the world as much as from the former heartlands of Christianity. … Such redirection and flow of missionary, personnel resources, and *training* are making Christianity *polycentric* and transforming the margins as the new centers of Christianity" (2022b, 9, emphases added).

From here, there are three points worth noting, the first being the instructive nature of polycentric development. In 1991, Michael Nazir-Ali described polycentric mission as "from everywhere to everywhere" (208). In 2003, Samuel Escobar adopted the expression "from everywhere to *everyone*" (3). More recently, in 2016, Allen Yeh proposed, "From *everyone* to everywhere" (21). While it is tempting to write a volume subtitled "From *everyone* to *everyone*," the final word goes to Daniel Ahn, who in a 2022 lecture usefully combined all these terms to generate "from everywhere to everywhere, *through* everyone to everyone." This latter version deftly captures the geographical situatedness and people-focused dynamism of polycentric mission, together with its "polydirectional" nature (Yeh 2016, 9, 216), as manifested in the imperative, intercultural relationships that it journeys across.

Second, my observation is that describing missiology as polycentric and polydirectional is generally seen as liberating and progressive. However, I would contend this nomenclature does not go far enough. Many-centered is not the same as all-centered. And many directions are not the same as all directions. My concern is that polycentric and polydirectional are only partially emancipating—with mission under this terminology still perceived to originate from the major urban centers and larger organizations and churches within the Global South. I propose that the terms omnicentric (all-centered) and omnidirectional (all directions) serve as useful bulwarks against such thinking. My experiences with the ANOTM project confirm that mission can arise from anyone, any family, any church, and anywhere.

Third, I wholeheartedly welcome George's inclusion of training in his description of polycentric missiology. The dearth of mission training in the Global South, in the face of unprecedented growth and huge missions potential, has long been observed by commentators (Pate 1991, 37; Kim 2009, 36), and it persists despite the best efforts of many churches, agencies, and institutions. Perhaps the time is right to seriously explore the potential of omnicentric, omnidirectional mission training movements. This is a new term I have coined and defined as *the development and delivery of a physical or virtual cross-cultural mission training course in one context, which via social networks catalyzes multiple expressions of new mission training courses in additional contexts.* Here, movement can be across geographic, denominational, generational, and cultural cleavages, with the potential to effect reconciliation and transformation—as well as address some of the previously noted deficiencies in mission training supply in the Global South.

Toward Omnicentric, Omnidirectional Relationships

When I inherited the foundational, ten-week mission training course called En Route from its principal designer and developer in 2015, I confess to being completely unaware of the potential that God had placed in my hands. At that point, the course seemed destined to continue running three times a year in a 150-year-old manor house in the middle of the English countryside—the home of ANCC since 1964 (Oakley 1997, 15). That was until I began receiving requests to develop En Route in different locations around the world.

But how could ANCC respond to these invitations in a culturally appropriate way? Certainly not in a paternalistic and Eurocentric manner that cultivates dependency on a college located twenty miles from the capital of a former global empire (Hyam 2010, 17, 133). Formally, this empire forfeited these territories during the independence movements of the mid- to late-twentieth century. However, informally, this ignoble history remains, subconsciously embodied in the lives of succeeding generations of both colonizer and colonized (Puri 2021; Memmi 2006) and reenacted via contemporary geopolitical, sociocultural, and economic channels (Gildea 2021, Ngũgĩ 1986). As a White, middle-aged Englishman, I continue to be aware that, to many of the people I serve alongside, I can look and smell of a colonial spirit that has lingered well beyond its time. Beyond appearance, however, my real challenge continues to be decolonized thinking and practice (Tuhiwai Smith 2021, 51). Fortunately, ANCC realizes that ANOTM requires a new *modus operandi*—how can we be, behave, and do differently? How can Kadushin's small worlds be brought together for the *genuine* benefit of all? A collaborative work in progress has begun.

Principles of Partnership

First, this involves an *absence* of strategy, at least on ANCC's part. ANCC must not run the risk of recruiting others to fulfill any plan of its own. Establishing relationships takes priority—and any joint activity should naturally flow from these, not the other way around. We must resist the temptation to do something, have numbers, make reports, implement systems, and develop organizations. Thankfully, many have been surprised and even relieved by this attitude—except those already locked into the well-framed "managerial missiology" mindset (Escobar 2000, 109–12) for whom such thinking is anathema. I remember being rightfully quizzed by one long-suffering and skeptical Global South leader concerning which Global North vision I had come to impart and cause him to implement. I passed this test by sharing that I had no such plans, and I was duly invited to participate in his plans. Thankfully, this genuinely empty-handed approach seems to facilitate more open and energetic conversation, as well as release others into the vision that the Lord has impressed upon their hearts (Phil 2:4).

Second, this involves *minimal* financial exchange. Generally speaking, beyond the Global North, ANCC does not charge for its contribution to joint activities and does not pay its partners to secure its involvement. Furthermore, ANCC does not charge potential partners for their contribution and is not paid by its partners to secure their involvement (Rom 15:7). These arrangements attempt to circumvent historical tensions concerning monetary dependency and accountability in all directions (Lausanne Committee for World Evangelization 2011, 102–3). Such an approach has a way of reducing resource anxieties, focusing resource expectations, minimizing costs, and promoting course accessibility through increased affordability.

Third, this involves each party contributing *what they are content to provide* (2 Cor 9:7)—whether churches, mission organizations and agencies, missiological-theological training institutions, retreat centers, sponsors, students, families, or individuals. This support can take the form of a training venue, facilitation expertise, stationery, board and lodging, transportation, worship and prayer ministry, hospitality, equipment, marketing, and administration, with the overwhelming majority of the resources and expertise coming from within the local context. J. Andrew Kirk (1999, 192) wisely counsels that "the ideal would be for resources to be pooled and mutual decisions taken about how they are used." Going further, ANCC is slow to involve itself in local decision-making, leaving local decisions on pooling and administering resources to be mutually made by those best positioned to do so—our local friends. So far, such an approach appears to fuel the generosity of all (1 Pet 4:10).

Fourth, this new way of working involves written agreements, if requested, and if so, the shorter the better. It quickly became clear that the overly complex, legalistic, multipage contracts that beset trust-deprived Western interactions were not appropriate. However, if resourcing is well distributed, and if relationships are sufficiently transparent, the risks such agreements seek to mitigate are proportionately lowered for all. Admittedly, concerns around the potential for relational breakdown and reputational damage still exist, but these are risks worth taking if ANCC is to break from its *centripetal* ("come to us") mode of existence into this brave new world of *centrifugal* ("join with others where they are") mission (Moynagh 2018, 166). Such an approach, perhaps idealistic in the eyes of some, moves all parties to rely on one another, rather than contracts, to sustain collaborative ministry.

Fifth, this involves *maximum flexibility and adaptability* in terms of course construction. The need for mission training depends on the context, as determined by a mixture of historical, sociocultural, political, spiritual, missiological, and geographical factors. As I have indicated previously, in the Global North, these factors currently combine to create a negative outlook for mission training. However, in the Global South, where "the greatest creativity and effectiveness in missionary training comes from ... whether Argentina, Korea, Nigeria, Philippines, South Africa, Singapore, India or China" (Taylor 2008, 80), ANCC recognizes the need to see training solutions developed that best fit a given locality—not solutions that we think would best fit a given locality. Ultimately, this means that solutions need to emanate from the context. This realization often comes from painful lessons that I am still learning (sadly, the colonial desire to tell, inform, shape, and do runs deep) with undesirable, unhelpful, and ultimately, counterproductive consequences. Hence the necessity of a different approach that moves in the opposite spirit.

Sixth, this encourages the *movement of training expressions* across multicultural, multilingual, interdenominational, and geopolitical boundaries. Christian cooperation has often been an unfulfilled ideal. Dietrich Werner (2015, 12) laments that the "vision and hope" of the World Missionary Conference held in Edinburgh in 1910 is "that co-operation in Christian mission would also lead to more unity and solidarity in theological education, [which has] obviously not been fulfilled in major segments of world Christianity one hundred years later." However, we often witness the reverse—missiological education, or mission training, leading to greater unity and solidarity between denominations. Indeed, appropriately designed mission training events provide a space to birth future training collaborations involving different partners in new contexts. Such an approach often has John 13:35 consequences.

Finally, this involves *trust*. The call on the Western church and Western mission organizations like ANCC is changing due to the emergence of the new missions paradigm. They need to refind their place within the current *motus Dei* (movement of God)— for which the initiative rests squarely with the new centers of missiological gravity, the churches in the Global South (George 2022a, 114; Walls 1996, 190). In seizing this initiative, Christian friends in Africa, Asia, and Latin America are rightly asking, Can the Global North be trusted (Borthwick 2012, 139)? Instrumentalized relationships, individualism, quantification, arrogance, "us and them" discourses, contracts, "yet another program," and imperialistic attitudes combine to provoke a wise and understandable wariness.

Consequently, such concerns require a new manner of engagement— one that acknowledges a fractious past, provides a mutually acceptable tenor for the conduct of current conversations, and demonstrates the intercultural, interracial, interhemispheric sensitivity that will train God's people to "deal effectively with an increasingly diverse and global world ... [and] enable them to traverse and transgress borders with ease" (Martell-Otero 2015, 144). However, delivering this kind of training, using the principles I have tentatively outlined, requires trust between everyone involved (partners, facilitators, and students) and also in the Lord—to work in and through all of these relationships.

Toward Omnicentric, Omnidirectional Mission Training

While these emerging principles may form a preliminary foundation for the development of omnicentric and omnidirectional relationships, a coincidental and co-related set of embryonic characteristics concerning the delivery of mission training has also become apparent. In no particular order, these characteristics include the presence of cross-cultural training *facilitators,* serving in a cross-cultural *context(s),* with a cross-cultural *cohort,* to form a cross-cultural learning *community,* navigating cross-cultural *relationships* while wrestling with cross-cultural *content* in cross-cultural *training,* and embodying a cross-cultural *ethos,* which is brought together by cross-cultural *partners.* While I concede that it is not always possible to enact all these characteristics to their fullest extent in every context and that these characteristics are not exhaustive or necessarily new, my thesis is that the more fully present these are, the greater the potential to realize interculturally transformative learning (Makoelle 2018, 61–72) and to better prepare to "deal with [the] difference[s]" that contemporary mission involves (Pierce 2008, 47).

For an initial assessment of this argument, I initiated conversations with five mission training leaders around the world with whom I've served alongside as friends over the past five years. They represent countries located in Central Africa (Burundi), Central America (Guatemala), Northern Africa, Scandinavia (Norway), and South Asia. Four of the five leaders are female, and all have cross-cultural missions experience. All five leaders are significantly involved in establishing mission training courses within their home contexts but also harbor visions to develop and deliver training elsewhere in line with mission training movements. ANCC is currently serving alongside these individuals and their respective organizations on various mission training projects in different ways, across a variety of contexts. I will consider their reflections on each of the mission training characteristics in turn.

Cross-Cultural Facilitators

Global education mobilities researcher Anatoly Oleksiyenko (2018, 94) states that in a cross-cultural education context, "the appearance of even one 'different other' [teacher] may stimulate excitement and generate questions [in the classroom]." And while my conversation partners would likely agree with this sentiment, they go beyond it. According to North African mission trainer David R. (2023), it is not just about enthusiasm and curiosity but the "different experiences, backgrounds, perspectives, values, and expertise" that a diverse team of facilitators can bring into his "challenging context." For him, this is an "essential element" of any successful mission training effort. Meanwhile, Tai L. (2023) from Guatemala, while acknowledging that a diverse team can be "one of the riches" of a mission training course, builds on David's reflections by emphasizing the advantage of including local missionaries with professional backgrounds who can inspire others, especially those from rural areas, to take up a profession and then use it for the Lord in the context where he puts them—working and witnessing, either locally or globally.

A different focus comes from Pascasie N. (2023), a Burundian missionary and mission trainer from Bujumbura, who highlights the importance of local teachers. From within her context, their involvement "demonstrates that mission teaching is not only for [Western/Eastern] expats." Her words are a telling reminder not only of the persistence of paternalistic attitudes but also of how these establish discriminatory practices in terms of accessibility to opportunity, as well as negate prospects for collaboration and rightful, local leadership. As Pascasie also emphasizes, "We want the challenge, stretch, and push of teaching missions too!" Encouragingly, through cross-cultural friendships developed during the training course in Burundi, opportunities for her to teach in other national contexts have opened up—a good example of mission trainers on the move.

Finally, Synnøve A. B. (2023), a Norwegian missionary-trainer, comments that the "more diverse [the facilitation team], the more *challenging*" (in a pedagogical sense) this is for her students (emphasis added). At the same time, she describes how trainers within her context also needed to demonstrate "vulnerability and honesty," being "able to share life" and disclose how they have "faced its challenges" as they have engaged in mission. Such a posture, she notes, is often then reciprocated by the students who "share things they have never shared before," frequently affecting relational healing in their own lives that contributes to the comprehensiveness of their overall preparation. Pascasie N. (2023) reinforces this view by application to her own context, commenting that training rooted in missionary practice and experience, rather than just missiological theory, was not only more credible but, in her context, more trustworthy.

Theological educator César Lopes (2021, 131) contends that the fundamental characteristic of cross-cultural teachers should be "humility," a character trait seemingly demanded by all the contributions considered in this section. In summary, they point toward the need for missiologist-missionary-trainers who are discerning enough to build and participate in diverse teams of mutually submissive subject specialists, courageous enough to promote and release others into training ministry, and secure enough to reveal their heart for God's mission through their weaknesses as well as their strengths (of character), their failures, as well as their successes (in life).

Cross-Cultural Cohort Context

In considering the benefits of the multicultural classroom, Nigerian Christian educator Chinwe Ikpeze (2015, 96) comments that "the more variety and differences in the others that prospective teachers are exposed to, the more perspectives they will be able to gain [for development of their cross-cultural teaching skills]." However, as my conversation partners demonstrate, the synergetic gains from diverse training cohorts interacting with diverse facilitation teams go far beyond this.

Indira T. (2023), a mission leader and trainer from South Asia, hosts mission training groups containing "a wide-age range of people [18–40], from many different churches, with different levels of education, [representing] many of the diverse cultural groups" from within her context. Such variety often leads to confusion over words, actions, expectations, and behaviors, resulting in "group culture shock," which she regards as ideal cross-cultural preparation. Two other conversation partners highlighted "culture shock" as part of the training process. Synnøve A. B. (2023) recognized that "even with students [only] coming from different parts of Norway, it was often enough to generate issues of difference sufficient to induce culture shock," while Pascasie M. (2023) observed that intrinsic to mission training in the Burundian context is "exposure to difference [in the group] … meaning that we [all] get to experience [low-level] culture shock together." Evidently, learning to navigate diversity not only stretches students intellectually, but it can also take them to the "edge … of [their] emotional comfort zone" (Kärkkäinen 2015, 51).

It was also apparent that different contexts need to navigate considerable diversities in the classroom. Tai L. (2023) recognizes the potential for cultural friction between the urban and rural participants who engage with her courses, and tensions exist between the in-person preference of older participants versus the greater openness to and desire for online learning of younger generations. Meanwhile, the disparate and conflicted religious backgrounds represented by some of his now-Christian trainees play a significant role in how David R. (2023) assists his groups to "mix together and form one body." Acknowledging and addressing antagonistic histories is critical for a group to develop a genuine "sense of community" (McMillan and Chavis 1986, 8–9).

More generally, David R. (2023) also appreciates that "everybody brings their flavor" and needs space to impact and influence the group, particularly through their "gifts, talents and [life] stories." Such a perspective acknowledges that "we worship the same God, have the same purpose in Him, but are different in so many other ways!" Practically speaking, Indira T. (2023) epitomizes this disposition, going to considerable lengths to recruit students from marginalized groups in terms of caste, gender, disability, and geographic isolation—while also ensuring that resources are intentionally set aside to maintain this level of accessibility. These negotiations often involve protracted meetings with authorities and in-person visits to remote locations as a means of providing reassurance to local church leaders, family, and friends concerning the content of the program and the care these students will receive.

As part of his new "missional model" of learning, Robert Banks (1999, 195–96) challenged the American Christian education community to incorporate "variety in the kinds and vocations of students" accepted into missiological-theological programs. My conversation partners enact this aspiration within global mission training provision. Their contributions point toward the need for mission trainers to value the intrinsic opportunities for cross-cultural learning that a diverse group provides, including experiences of culture shock to cultivate a sense of community in which all students can mutually invest themselves (despite conflicting religious or national backgrounds) and to intentionally promote, motivate, and resource participation from marginalized groups. I would consider this to be a hallmark of omnicentric and omnidirectional mission.

Cross-Cultural Community Relationships

The debate concerning the efficacy of residential versus online mission training has loitered in the literature (Wan and Hedinger 2017, 165–68; Behera 2015, 119–20). The lack of consensus and conclusion points to the need for more empirical research. Tai L. (2023) introduced this issue when referring to the intergenerational aspect of this debate, as noted above.

However, my conversation partners, including Tai, were of one mind in their own strongly stated preference for residential and face-to-face preparation, particularly for shorter courses.

For instance, a vital element of Synnøve A. B.'s (2023) program is that the young people she trains first "live together in the teams that they will serve with overseas." This "challenges people to be honest" and to "really deal with the personality differences in their groups *before* they engage in cross-cultural ministry." In terms of dealing with differences, "you have 'them' *amongst* 'us' to become 'we.'" Likewise, Indira T. (2023) propounds the advantages of "cooking together, eating together, and working together" so that participants can "practice what they have been learning on each other!" However, it is possible to squander these formational opportunities. Learning from a negative training experience in which all the participants had stayed in single rooms, David R. (2023) ensures, along gender lines and families/couples aside, that his students share rooms as part of the community building process. "This often creates problems that they need to solve [together]," he says, as they progress during the two weeks of his intensive course from "beginning as strangers to becoming one community in which members *really* love one another (1 John 4:7)." Finally, returning to Tai L. (2023), while she concedes that mission training is "more tiring in person," she nevertheless remains convinced, like David R., that face-to-face interaction nurtures "deeper, real friendships" where you can "really *see* a person ... their emotions, [and] true feelings."

Such conviction and feelings also surfaced when conversation partners discussed the interdenominational nature of the training that they provide. Connecting repentance with theological clarity, Synnøve A. B. (2023) submits that mission training provides the opportunity to "regret the unkind words that we [all] may have shared about each other's [denominations]," following which "it becomes clearer who God is ... and that we can let go of the lesser issues and focus on the more important things—like mission." Building on this critical insight, Tai L. (2023) contends that interdenominational groups have the potential to "widen people's perspectives about mission" in contrast to the limiting alternative where each denomination hosts its own mission seminars. Sadly, she rues "the lack of relationships, often due to prejudice," which has meant "people have not been sent [as missionaries] because of an inability [of the church] to work together." In this way, she hopes "sitting together in a class, building friendships, discussing together, and praying for each other's churches" should serve to advance God's mission *from* Guatemala. Pascasie N. (2023) wholeheartedly agrees. Reflecting on the "very hard background" from which the Burundian church is emerging, she considers it "a miracle to see people from different denominations training together with the same purpose, the same vision, for the same cause." Witnessing people "letting go of differences" and overcoming historical divisions "that the enemy has used to keep churches apart and working alone" has been a "sign concerning what God is doing, and his desire to heal the church of Burundi and the Nation." With profundity, she lays down the challenge that "we will not get to where God wants us to be without working together."

While the global church retains its distinctive streams and separate expressions of faith within those streams, mission training appears to be capable of offering a viable "third space" (Panotto and Lopes 2021, 107) in which to foster ecumenical understanding and missional collaboration (Esterline 2010, 14). In this regard, the community concerns of my conversation partners centered around the apparent necessity of in-person training for effective cross-cultural mission preparation—coming from a deep-seated relational desire to see Christians from across the church serving together locally and internationally for the good of God's people and their witness to others.

Cross-Cultural Content and Ethos

Over the years, mission training literature has become replete with course content templates (Hibbert and Hibbert 2016, 278–432; Liberty 2012, 141–58). Nevertheless, my intuitive conviction has been that content needs to simultaneously comfort (affirming a participant's context) and challenge (moving the same participants beyond their context). However, Synnøve A. B. (2023) counsels that in her situation, "if you start *too* challengingly … people will fall off [drop out]." She advises the deployment of "spiral learning … sharing and revisiting [in cycles] … starting with the familiar and little by little introducing the new and different." Apart from the discourse on content, there has been less focused discussion on the importance of a learning ethos and how this might vary between contexts. Given the contrast in academic weight given to these two concepts, it was instructive to reflect on the thoughts of my conversation partners.

In line with the flexibility offered by a modular program like En Route, David R. (2023) retains the program's "basic structure and learning ethos" but reconfigures the balance of the content to best suit his context. David's course thus combines "[missional] content from All Nations [En Route course], together with the [more focused] spiritual content from another [UK-based] training center," as well as material that reflects his gifting for biblical-devotional teaching and "love of the Scriptures." Reflective of David R.'s missional milieu, and those of his students, there is also heightened attention paid to apologetics. This flexibility to contextually reconstruct teaching material was also exercised by Pascasie N. (2023), who shares how she recreated a class to "match [and include her] own personal experience" while rightly shedding the Western framework that organized the content she inherited. The educational destination was similar, but the journey was contextually distinctive.

Pascasie N. (2023) also affirms the importance of developing and communicating a distinctive "learning ethos." Within her context, this "put everyone on the same page ... setting the ground first, so that [as a group] we know who we are and where we are going." Focusing on one particular element of the learning ethos that he imparts, David R. (2023) reports that an adapted version of the much-utilized "Head [knowledge and skills], Heart [character and attitudes], and Hands [relationships and community]" approach (Sills 2016; Addison 2015, 51) had proved extremely effective with his students. Accordingly, "each lecture must have a balance of all three ... this is very important, [as well as] be Jesus-Bible centered," with the learning ethos being augmented by "meditation on the Scriptures every day [of the course]."

Tai L. (2023) reinforced this theological perspective, noting the En Route material was "biblical and organized around Christ-centered principles that were also practical and clear. ... You don't have to guess what is going on!" Referring to the adult-learning philosophies underpinning the En Route course (Freire 1970; Mezirow 1991; Vella 2008; Knowles, Holton, and Swanson 2015; Illeris 2014), she noted the andragogical accents on "building from people's experiences" and intensively and intentionally "focusing on smaller groups." In this regard, one of her students had mentioned that (relative to what is normative within that context) they had "never been in a seminar with so few people" (there were twenty-three students). "Working in small groups" was also critical for disclosure and group bonding within Indira T.'s (2023) context with "groups that were either too big or too small being intimidating for some students." This meant that having students share their life stories during the first week of the course required careful and sensitive planning.

Finally, Synnøve A. B. (2023) returned to and expanded upon the importance of the Head, Heart, and Hands approach, explaining that her course has built-in emphases on the "cognitive, practical [over academic], relational, and empathetical domains." The addition of the latter reflects an increasing emphasis on the affective within the cross-cultural teaching and learning literature (Hinga 2015, 133; Heaton 2021, 29–30) and, for Synnøve, works to ensure that the training "helps students remain close to life and close to God." This is a fitting caption to close the conversational reflections on course content and ethos as I turn my attention to the concluding topic of partnerships.

Cross-Cultural Partnerships

Establishing locally based training courses appears key for releasing the global church into its missional calling (Aylett and Green 2015, 84; Saracco 1988, 33–34). Not having to travel internationally for training was important for Pascasie N. (2023), who shared that "God [had] said Burundi should rise up and go for missions ... but people were not being trained [locally], [and] things were not in place. But God's been doing things in the background [in bringing different organizations together] and things are [now] surfacing." Referencing her previous comments, she said being in a partnership where "the content could be contextualized" was key. "Some programs are rigid and don't fit with the context ... [and they] become useless ... often leading to [the] failure" of the program and the dissolution of any associated partnerships. However, the fact that students were also encouraged to partner together and establish their own courses modeled the potential of mission training on the move. These comments resonated strongly with ANCC's desire to release rather than restrict new expressions of mission training.

In terms of institutional agreements, David R. (2023) said that "we are together [with ANCC] because of friendship, not because of paper. We love each other and love to see God's kingdom extended. We build the kingdom together because we are friends, not because we are obligated to do so." He went further to say that "no one can do [mission] alone. If you are doing anything alone you are doing your mission, building your own kingdom rather than God's kingdom." However, having suffered at the hands of Western relationships where "people used connection for [their own] personal gain and at my expense," he warned that "there can be no hidden agendas ... everything must be clear and transparent."

Tai L. (2023) also recognized Western partners' tendency toward paternalism and local groups' tendency to say "[the Westerners] have the money, [and if they give it to us] we can do the rest." While emphasizing the ongoing importance of "being very clear regarding financing," she preferred to advocate for *interdependence* (Reese 2010, 160–61; Padilla 2016, 53–55), declaring that "*we* are all *us*, wherever we are from and whatever we have or don't have. *All* is *all* of *us*—and we do it together."

Conclusion

The Christian world is shifting, and God is on the move, but the global mission training fraternity is playing catch up. In this regard, I pray for the knitting together of our small worlds, as we remain dependent on the Lord while seeking to be *interdependent* on each other. My conversation partners have proved that such coalescence and mutuality are possible. In terms of mission training movements, I hope that by seeking to offer high-quality, accessible, affordable, and appropriate programs—developed locally by teams, spread geographically through relationships, and resourced by all—they will contribute to realizing the omnicentric and omnidirectional mission paradigm into which we are moving. With this future in view, it is a joy and a privilege to be serving alongside like-minded conversation partners and, most importantly, friends.

References

Addison, Steve. 2015. *Pioneering Movements: Leadership That Multiplies Disciples and Churches*. Downers Grove, IL: InterVarsity Press.

Adeney, Frances S. 2010. *Graceful Evangelism: Christian Witness in a Complex World*. Grand Rapids: Baker Academic.

Ahn, Daniel. 2022. "Diaspora Missiology and Mission Training." L6.303: Global Migration and Diaspora Studies. Class lecture at All Nations Christian College, Ware, UK, June 6.

Arthur, Eddie. 2017. "The Future of Mission Agencies." *Mission Round Table* 12, no. 1: 4–12. https://omf.org/the-future-of-mission-agencies/.

Aylett, Graham, and Tim Green. 2015. "Theological Education by Extension (TEE) as a Tool for Twenty-First Century Mission." In *Reflecting on and Equipping for Christian Mission*, edited by Stephen Bevans, Teresa Chai, J. Nelson Jennings, Knud Jørgensen, and Dietrich Werner, 59–78. Regnum Edinburgh Centenary Series 27. Oxford: Regnum.

Banks, Robert. 1999. *Reenvisioning Theological Education: Exploring a Missional Alternative to Current Models*. Grand Rapids: Eerdmans.

Behera, Marina Ngursangzeli. 2015. "Inequality in Theological Education between the North and the South." In *Reflecting on and Equipping for Christian Mission*, edited by Stephen Bevans, Teresa Chai, J. Nelson Jennings, Knud Jørgensen, and Dietrich Werner, 116–28. Regnum Edinburgh Centenary Series 27. Oxford: Regnum.

Borthwick, Paul. 2012. *Western Christians in Global Mission: What's the Role of the North American Church?* Downers Grove, IL: InterVarsity Press.

Brynjolfson, Robert, and Jonathan Lewis, eds. 2006. *Integral Ministry Training: Design and Evaluation*. Pasadena, CA: William Carey Library.

Cueva, Samuel. 2015. *Mission Partnership in Creative Tension: An Analysis of the Relationships in Mission within the Evangelical Movement with Special Reference to Peru and Britain between 1987 and 2006*. Carlisle, UK: Langham.

Escobar, Samuel. 2000. "Evangelical Missiology: Peering into the Future at the Turn of the Century." In *Global Missiology for the 21st Century: The Iguassu Dialogue*, edited by William David Taylor, 101–22. Grand Rapids: Baker Academic.

Escobar, Samuel. 2003. *The New Global Mission: The Gospel from Everywhere to Everyone*. Downers Grove, IL: IVP Academic.

Esterline, David. 2010. "From Western Church to World Christianity: Developments in Theological Education in the Ecumenical Movement." In *Handbook of Theological Education in World Christianity: Theological Perspectives, Ecumenical Trends, Regional Surveys*, edited by Dietrich Werner, David Esterline, Namsoon Kang, and Joshva Raja, 13–22. Eugene, OR: Wipf & Stock.

Evans, Richard. 2021. "God's Mission—Everyone, Everywhere." Presentation at midweek service of Asamblea De Dios La Hermosa, Panajachel, Guatemala, August 21.

Ferris, Robert W. 1990. *Renewal in Theological Education: Strategies for Change*. Wheaton: Billy Graham Center.

Freire, Paulo. 1970. *Pedagogy of the Oppressed*, translated by Myra Bergman Ramos. New York: Seabury.

George, Sam. 2022a. "Motus Dei (The Move of God): A Theology and Missiology for a Moving World." In *Reflections of Asian Diaspora: Mapping Theologies and Ministries*, edited by Sam George, 95–122. Asian Diaspora Christianity Series 3. Minneapolis: Fortress.

George, Sam. 2022b. "The Past, Present, and Future of Evangelical Missiology." In *The Past, Present, and Future of Evangelical Mission: Academy, Agency, Assembly, and Agora Perspectives from Canada*, edited by Narry F. Santos and Xenia Ling-Yee Chan, 3–14. Evangelical Missiological Society Monograph Series 15. Eugene, OR: Pickwick.

Gildea, Robert. 2021. *Empires of the Mind: The Colonial Past and the Politics of the Present*. The Wiles Lectures. Cambridge: Cambridge University Press.

Goheen, Michael W. 2014. *Introducing Christian Mission Today: Scripture, History, and Issues*. Downers Grove, IL: IVP Academic

Harley, David. 2019. "Do We Need Missionary Societies?" *Mission Round Table* 14, no. 1 (January): 4–9. https://omf.org/do-we-need-missionary-societies/.

Harley, David, and Rosemary Harley. 2022. *Together in Mission: From All Nations to All Nations*. London: Monarch.

Heaton, Bob. 2021. "Thinking Theologically about Teaching and Culture." In *Teaching across Cultures: A Global Christian Perspective*, edited by Perry Shaw, César Lopes, Joanna Feliciano-Soberano, and Bob Heaton, 19–32. Carlisle, UK: Langham.

Hibbert, Evelyn, and Richard Hibbert. 2016. *Training Missionaries: Principles and Possibilities*. Pasadena, CA: William Carey Library.

Hinga, Teresa. 2015. "Teaching to Transform: Theological Education, Global Consciousness, and the Making of Global Citizens." In *Teaching Global Theologies: Power and Praxis*, edited by Kwok Pui-Lan, Cecilia González-Andrieu, and Dwight N. Hopkins, 125–42. Waco, TX: Baylor University Press.

Hoke, Stephen T. 1999. "Paradigm Shifts and Trends in Missions Training—A Call to Servant-Teaching, a Ministry of Humility." *Evangelical Review of Theology* 23, no. 4 (October): 33–47.

Hyam, Ronald. 2010. *Understanding the British Empire*. Cambridge: Cambridge University Press.

Ikpeze, Chinwe H. 2015. *Teaching across Cultures: Building Pedagogical Relationships in Diverse Contexts*. Rotterdam: Sense Publishers.

Illeris, Knud. 2014. *Transformative Learning and Identity*. Abingdon: Routledge.

Kadushin, Charles. 2012. *Understanding Social Networks: Theories, Concepts, and Findings*. New York: Oxford University Press.

Kärkkäinen, Veli-Matti. 2015. "Teaching Global Theology in a Comparative Mode." In *Teaching Global Theologies: Power and Praxis*, edited by Kwok Pui-Lan, Cecilia González-Andrieu, and Dwight N. Hopkins, 45–54. Waco, TX: Baylor University Press.

Kim, Steve (Heung Chan). 2009. "A Newer Missions Paradigm and the Growth of Missions from the Majority World." In *Missions from the Majority World: Progress, Challenges, and Case Studies*, edited by Enoch Wan and Michael Pocock, 1–34. Evangelical Missiological Society Series 17. Pasadena, CA: William Carey Library.

Kirk, J. Andrew. 1999. *What Is Mission? Theological Explorations*. Minneapolis: Fortress.

Knowles, Malcolm S., Elwood F. Holton III, and Richard A. Swanson. 2015. *The Adult Learner: The Definitive Classic in Adult Education and Human Resource Development*. 8th ed. London: Taylor & Francis.

Kuhn, Thomas S. 2012. *The Structure of Scientific Revolutions*. 4th ed. Chicago: University of Chicago Press.

Lausanne Committee for World Evangelization. 2011. *The Cape Town Commitment: A Confession of Faith and a Call to Action*. South Hamilton, MA: Lausanne Movement.

Lawanson, Tesilimi Aderemi (Remi). 2009. "Calvary Ministries (CAPRO): A Case Study on a Model of Majority World Initiatives in Christian Mission." In *Missions from the Majority World: Progress, Challenges, and Case Studies*, edited by Enoch Wan and Michael Pocock, 339–70. Evangelical Missiological Society Series 17. Pasadena, CA: William Carey Library.

Lee, Paul Sungro. 2022. "Cross-Cultural Training of Missionary Candidates in the Global South." In *Reflections of Asian Diaspora: Mapping Theologies and Ministries*, edited by Sam George, 205–24. Asian Diaspora Christianity Series 3. Minneapolis: Fortress.

Liberty, R. Zarwulugbo. 2012. *Growing Missionaries Biblically: A Fresh Look at Missions in an African Context*. Bloomington, IN: iUniverse.

Lopes, César. 2021. "Theological Humility in Cross-Cultural Teaching." In *Teaching across Cultures: A Global Christian Perspective*, edited by Perry Shaw, César Lopes, Joanna Feliciano-Soberano, and Bob Heaton, 119–32. Carlisle, UK: Langham.

Lygunda li-M, Fohle. 2009. "Stakes of Mission Engagement: Reflection on Remodelling Mission in the Central African Region." In *Missions from the Majority World: Progress, Challenges, and Case Studies*, edited by Enoch Wan and Michael Pocock, 181–203. Evangelical Missiological Society Series 17. Pasadena, CA: William Carey Library.

Makoelle, Tsediso M. 2018. "Multiculturalism through Transformative Teaching and Learning Approaches." In *Integrating Multicultural Education into the Curriculum for Decolonisation: Benefits and Challenges*, edited by Lloyd Nkoli Tlale Daniel and Thabo Makhalemele, 61–72. New York: Nova Science.

Martell-Otero, Loida I. 2015. "Hablando Se Entiende la Gente: Tower of Babble or Gift of Tongues?" In *Teaching Global Theologies: Power and Praxis*, edited by Kwok Pui-Lan, Cecilia González-Andrieu, and Dwight N. Hopkins, 143–62. Waco, TX: Baylor University Press.

McMillan, David W., and David M. Chavis. 1986. "Sense of Community: A Definition and Theory." *Journal of Community Psychology* 14, no. 1: 6–23.

Memmi, Albert. 2006. *Decolonization and the Decolonized*, translated by Robert Bononno. Minneapolis: University of Minnesota Press.

Mezirow, Jack. 1991. *Transformative Dimensions of Adult Learning*. San Francisco: Jossey-Bass.

Mintzberg, Henry, Bruce Ahlstrand, and Joseph Lampel. 2009. *Strategy Safari: Your Complete Guide through the Wilds of Strategic Management*. 2nd ed. Harlow: Prentice Hall.

Moynagh, Michael. 2018. *Church in Life: Innovation, Mission, and Ecclesiology*. Eugene, OR: Cascade.

Nazir-Ali, Michael. 1991. *From Everywhere to Everywhere: A World View of Christian Witness*. London: Collins Flame.

Ngũgĩ wa Thiong'o. 1986. *Decolonising the Mind: The Politics of Language in African Literature*. Studies in African Literature. London: James Currey.

Oakley, Nigel W. 1997. *The Story of Easneye*. Ware, UK: All Nations.

Oleksiyenko, Anatoly V. 2018. *Global Mobility and Higher Learning*. Abingdon: Routledge.

Padilla, C. René. 2016. "Global Partnership and Integral Mission." In *Mission in Context: Explorations Inspired by J. Andrew Kirk*, edited by John Corrie and Cathy Ross, 47–60. Farnham, UK: Ashgate.

Panotto, Nicolás, and César Lopes. 2021. "Emancipating Cross-Cultural Teaching." In *Teaching across Cultures: A Global Christian Perspective*, edited by Perry Shaw, César Lopes, Joanna Feliciano-Soberano, and Bob Heaton, 101–18. Carlisle, UK: Langham.

Pate, Larry D. 1991. "The Dramatic Growth of Two-Thirds World Mission." In *Internationalizing Missionary Training*, edited by William David Taylor, 27–40. Grand Rapids: Baker Book House.

Pierce, Kathryn T. 2008. "A Holistic View of the Missioning Process." *Missiology* 36, no. 1 (January): 33–51.

Prior, John Mansford. 2022. "Practical Theology and Mission Studies." In *The Oxford Handbook of Mission Studies*, edited by Kirsteen Kim, Knud Jørgensen, and Alison Fitchett-Climenhaga, 165–83. Oxford: Oxford University Press.

Puri, Samir. 2021. *The Shadows of Empire: How Imperial History Shapes Our World*. New York: Pegasus.

Reese, Robert. 2010. *Roots and Remedies of the Dependency Syndrome in World Missions*. Pasadena, CA: William Carey Library.

Saracco, J. Norberto. 1988. "Search for New Models of Theological Education." In *New Alternatives in Theological Education*, edited by C. René Padilla, 25–36. Oxford: Regnum.

Sills, M. David. 2016. *Hearts, Heads, and Hands: A Manual for Teaching Others to Teach Others*. Nashville: B&H.

Smallman, William H. 2000. "Missions—Personnel with a Purpose: A Survey of Contemporary Missions Principles." In *Missions in a New Millennium: Change and Challenges in World Missions*, edited by W. Edward Glenny and William H. Smallman, 17–39. Grand Rapids: Kregel.

Taylor, William D. 2008. "Global and Personal Reflections on Training/Equipping for Cross-Cultural Ministry Today." *Missiology* 36, no. 1 (January): 75–86.

Tuhiwai Smith, Linda. 2021. *Decolonizing Methodologies: Research and Indigenous Peoples*. 3rd ed. London: Bloomsbury.

Vella, Jane. 2008. *On Teaching and Learning: Putting the Principles and Practices of Dialogue Education into Action*. San Francisco: Jossey-Bass.

Walls, Andrew F. 1996. *The Missionary Movement in Christian History: Studies in the Transmission of Faith*. Maryknoll, NY: Orbis Books.

Wan, Enoch, and Mark Hedinger. 2017. *Relational Mission Training: Theology, Theory and Practice*. Skyforest: Urban Loft.

Werner, Dietrich. 2015. "Theological Education in the Changing Context of World Christianity: An Unfinished Agenda." In *Reflecting on and Equipping for Christian Mission*, edited by Stephen Bevans, Teresa Chai, J. Nelson Jennings, Knud Jørgensen, and Dietrich Werner, 3–20. Regnum Edinburgh Centenary Series 27. Oxford: Regnum.

Windsor, Raymond V. J. 1995. *World Directory of Missionary Training Programmes: A Catalogue of over 500 Missionary Training Programmes from around the World*. 2nd ed. Pasadena, CA: William Carey Library.

Yeh, Allen L. 2016. *Polycentric Missiology: 21st-Century Mission from Everyone to Everywhere*. Downers Grove, IL: IVP Academic.

Zurlo, Gina A., Todd M. Johnson, and Peter F. Crossing. 2020. "World Christianity and Mission 2020: Ongoing Shift to the Global South." *International Bulletin of Mission Research* 44, no. 1 (January): 8–19.

Chapter 14

Collaboration

Accelerating Formal and Nonformal Pastor Training

Joseph W. Handley Jr.

As we approach the topic of educating for contemporary mission, one important element is the question of formal and nonformal pastoral training and how practitioners in both spheres may collaborate. To define some terms:

> Non-formal learning is normally defined as "learning which takes place through planned activities (in terms of learning objectives, learning time) where some form of learning support is present." However, it typically occurs apart from institutionalized, programme-based and degree-oriented (academic) education. "Informal" learning refers to "learning resulting from daily activities related to work, family or leisure. It is not organised or structured in terms of objectives, time or learning support. Informal learning is in most cases unintentional from the learner's perspective." (ICETE 2022, 10)

In this chapter, I sketch out how this conversation has developed in recent years, and I consider some case studies for collaboration.

In 2014, Jason Ferenczi of Cornerstone Trust gathered a group in Chicago to begin conversations about collaborating on formal and nonformal theological education efforts (Jason Ferenczi, email, February 24, 2023). Ongoing conversations continued despite a strong sense of tension as each side did not respect or trust the other. Formal theological education (FTE) groups believed that quality control was a significant issue for those in nonformal training. They saw the accreditation standards and processes as a critical affirmation of their quality. Plus, some had concerns about issues of truth. On the flip side, the non-formal theological education (NFTE) groups saw the FTE groups as increasingly irrelevant, teaching material that was unnecessary to pastors and real church life and distanced from the realities of congregations. They also saw teaching that created "elitism" versus "servant-heartedness" was completely impractical. They pressed forward and the next official gathering occurred in Antalya, Turkey, during the International Council of Evangelical Theological Education (ICETE) meeting in 2015.

At the same time, because of changing global conditions, particularly economic, churches were sending fewer pastoral candidates to seminary or were sending them for shorter degrees (e.g., MA instead of MDiv). Also, independent and nondenominational churches began relying less on traditional education, opting for nonformal, pragmatic approaches to equipping pastors and leaders.

Following ICETE 2015, a greater desire for collaboration was developing. Craig Parro (2016) stated, "We need to break down the wall between f[ormal] and n[on]-formal] training and identify the commonalities between the two." The meeting's conclusion was, "We need one another, but what that looks like remains to be seen" (Parro 2016). In 2016, a small gathering occurred at the Global Proclamation Congress for Pastoral Trainers in Bangkok, which kickstarted a process of collecting case studies and identifying who was working in both the formal and nonformal spheres. The following year at the Leadership Development Consultation in Chiang Mai, Thailand—led by Craig Parro (Leadership Resources International), Jason Ferenczi (Cornerstone Trust), Malcolm Webber (LeaderSource), and Riad Kassis (ICETE)—they gathered further case studies and examples of formal and nonformal education partnerships.

ICETE 2022

The ICETE 2022[1] consultation as a whole focused on collaboration in theological education. The final challenge included a call to action to better reflect the hope of Christ: "I have given them the glory that you gave me, that they may be one as we are one—I in them and you in me—so that they may be brought to complete unity. Then the world will know that you sent me and have loved them even as you have loved me" (John 17:22–23 NIV). This call to action was followed by a mandate that spoke to the realities of formal and nonformal training (see ICETE 2022, 8–9). Affirming that "the purpose of theological education must be defined within the framework of

---

1 This ICETE consultation was led by a new executive director, Dr. Michael A. Ortiz. The original Manifesto was drafted in 1981. Dr. Ortiz commissioned Dr. Bernhard Ott to revise the Manifesto, and it took two years in collaboration with leaders from around the world to develop the draft for ICETE 2022.

the *missio Dei* and a missional self-understanding of the church" (8), the authors recognized that "the academization of theological education has opened a gap between the needs of the church in mission and the agenda of academia" (8). They also noted, "Information Technology revolutionizes education" (8), and "Traditional forms of residential full-time studies are being replaced more and more by flexible and modular Diversified Education and Open Distance Learning and Education" (8). Finally, they affirmed the place of both approaches to global theological education: "Formal and non-formal theological education are equally important for church and mission. They should be offered in mutual respect and partnership" (8).

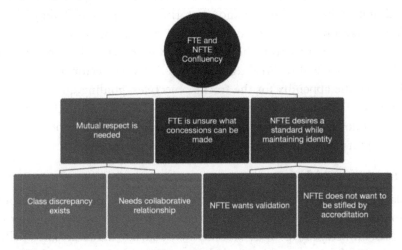

Figure 14.1
Formal theological education (FTE) and nonformal theological education (NFTE)

The chart above (developed by Julie Shoemaker following multiple forums) shows the state of partnerships between formal and nonformal advocates prior to ICETE 2022. The stakeholders concluded, "There is not a mutual respect allowing collaboration to take place [and] the data shows a lack of direction in how to make this happen while still maintaining distinctives." (Tendero et al. 2023).

Formal and Nonformal Training Collaboration Track
In planning the ICETE consultation, the organizers took these realities to heart and invited a track focused on accelerating collaboration between formal and nonformal training practitioners (facilitated by Tendero et al.

2023). This ended up being the second-highest-attended track at ICETE, and it encouraged good interaction throughout the week. I will briefly sketch out the track, its objectives, and the case studies presented.

We first acknowledged that global pastoral training has failed to keep up with church-planting successes. Far too many churches are led by pastors with little or no Bible training. This creates huge vulnerabilities for these churches, including false teaching, syncretism, lack of maturity, and biblical illiteracy. Many have recognized this pastoral leadership crisis and responded with literally thousands of training initiatives. Though formal theological institutions equip many pastors, a far greater number of pastors are equipped by nonformal means. Second, we again recognized the lack of collaboration between formal and nonformal equippers, including a lack of understanding and appreciation for what each sector does.

The aims of this workshop then were to unpack the strengths of each sector while also revealing the biases that each sector holds for the other (see the appendix for the track's objectives, guiding questions, and activities). The hope was to encourage robust interaction and the primary means of doing this was through presenting case studies for collaborating between formal and nonformal training. I summarize these here.

Asian Access (A3)

Asian Access (now called A3) shared how their approach to pastoral training began with the felt need of pastors in Japan. After a number of years of ministry in Japan, A3's founder went back to his alma mater, Fuller Theological Seminary, asking for help from Donald McGavran. McGavran referred him to Bobby Clinton, who designed the original curriculum that incorporated elements of McGavran's church growth theory and Clinton's leadership development philosophy. Eventually, this strategy impacted 95 percent of church growth in Japan (Handley 2022).

A3's model involves a two-to-three-year journey where learning communities of twelve to eighteen leaders are formed. They commit to meet three to four times a year, for four days each time. They strive to develop learning communities that are Christ-centered and community-oriented. The goal is to mirror the model that Jesus employed when he raised up the Twelve.

The leaders who form these communities are intentionally drawn from an array of denominations, theological traditions, and people groups to develop, strengthen, and increase unity among the greater body of Christ in the country. They are leaders with potential—veteran pastors and kingdom leaders who have experienced ministry in the trenches. They are ready for a life-on-life discipleship experience that will empower them not only to survive the stresses of ministry but also to help them and their families thrive as they journey to the next levels of effectiveness and impact.

The training topics covered fall under four categories that comprise A3's primary outcomes. The goal is for each graduate to appropriate these outcomes for the duration of their life and ministry: (1) live in a love relationship with Jesus; (2) grow in Christlike leadership (predominantly character) (3) reproduce disciple-making leaders; and (4) catalyze Christ-centered movements (often church-planting initiatives).

A3's leader-development program partners with Fuller Theological Seminary. Every graduate receives a certificate from Fuller. Though students do not receive academic credit for the training, they value Fuller's endorsement of their training with A3. Recently, Fuller and A3 have signed an agreement where A3 alumni can receive advanced standing in Fuller's Doctor of Ministry program if they are admitted to the program and produce substantial papers based on key readings in the DMin program (Handley 2013).

WorldPartners (formerly Leadership Resources International)

A partnership began in Colombia when Roman Carmana and Pedro Hernandez of Christ for the Cities launched INSEPA (Institute for Pastoral Training) in partnership with Jaime Ortiz of El Seminario Biblico de Medellin. The National Association of Evangelicals of Colombia then adopted this effort as their pastoral training commission, which gave it credibility and broad support among many denominations.

This church-based initiative began with just three or four host churches. These critical partnering churches hosted the pastors overnight for weekend trainings and provided much of the needed funding. In addition to these local churches, four additional organizations joined the team as partners—a missions agency, a seminary, the World Evangelical Alliance (WEA) country association, and TOPIC Global (a coalition of nonformal pastor trainers).

Since many Colombian pastors have limited financial means, a key priority was making the training financially accessible. Though pastors were asked to pay for the teaching materials, the team often worked with publishers to get the materials at cost or slightly above cost. Sometimes the team paid for some pastors' transportation. Financial support was decided on a case-by-case basis.

The team also invested in pastor-trainers. Some were recruited from the seminary, while others were established pastors. The partnership group brought pastor-trainers together for weekend retreats to build relationships, vision cast, troubleshoot, and develop their training skills. On a couple of occasions, TOPIC leaders from the Philippines provided training from a cross-cultural perspective.

The INSEPA curriculum was a work in progress developed by Christ for the Cities leadership and the seminary. Eventually, the seminary recognized the value of the training and began offering a year of seminary credit for a two-year INSEPA training program. As a result, many INSEPA pastors ended up attending seminary.

Over time, INSEPA grew to include seven or eight host churches in multiple cities. Similar efforts began to emerge in neighboring Venezuela and Ecuador. The number of pastors being trained grew from sixty to three hundred. One pastor with virtually no ministry training was serving in a rural area. After completing the INSEPA training and graduating, he became recognized for his ministry gifts and wound up leading a large church in the capital, Bogota.

Not all partnerships between nonformal and formal theological training entities have been as successful as INSEPA. WordPartners once approached a well-established Majority World seminary about a partnership to train pastors. Since the seminary was eager to partner, a number of pastors were invited to an initial training on their campus. WordPartners provided the funding, the seminary set the schedule (a three-day training from 9 a.m. to 9 p.m.), and the training was done jointly by WordPartners staff and the seminary faculty.

This nonformal and formal training partnership failed for two reasons. First, the seminary did not share WordPartners's philosophy of teaching and ministry. Though WordPartners has a curriculum, they are not curriculum driven. Instead, they are process driven. The key to our teaching philosophy is practice. For example, instead of merely lecturing on hermeneutics, WordPartners staff briefly present hermeneutical principles and quickly move into exercises to practice these principles, followed by a period of reflection and discussion. This approach is learner centered and highly relational, illustrated by the maxim, "What is learned is more important than what is taught."

Second, the seminary seemed driven by its own institutional needs. The school was facing huge financial challenges and had not paid their professors in more than two months. This budding partnership was an answer to their financial needs. Since WordPartners was covering the expenses, the seminary structured the teaching schedule so that they could maximize the stipends paid to their professors. Though WordPartners felt the pain of these underresourced brothers, the pressing financial needs of this school took precedence over a healthy, mutual partnership to train pastors.

Advanced Leadership Training (LAC)

Advanced Leadership Training was birthed within Cru (Campus Crusade for Christ) and now partners with Kairos University. They focus on competency-based theological education (CBTE), pursuing outcomes impacting the leader's head, heart, and hands. They desire that their leaders would grow in Christ and be more Christlike. They want them to (1) love God and people more; (2) love God's word more; (3) be confident and competent in going to the word to deal with issues of life and society; (4) be confident and competent in developing leaders who develop leaders; and (5) promote holistic development through mentor teams. They desire that their leaders would be able to lead themselves, their teams, other leaders, and organizations.

Beginning with the end in mind frequently requires a dramatic rethinking of any institutional structure. Competency-based programs are no exception. In order to work directly toward developing the student for ministry, CBTE programs contain seven core commitments.

Contextual learning. Developing students for ministry requires that students are involved in ministry. Beyond an internship that constitutes part of a degree program, most CBTE students are already immersed full-time in a ministry environment. Assignments and learning opportunities are outcomes based and can be adapted to fit and contribute to the student's ministry context.

Partnered investment. Having students immersed in a ministry environment transforms the program from being primarily a service contract between students and a seminary to being a partnership in developing leaders between the seminary, church, and network. CBTE programs are increasingly developed in full partnership with students' future employers.

Team-based mentoring. Diverse mentor teams are engaged to develop students holistically. Working as a team to develop students in all areas of their lives, mentor teams often include (1) an academic mentor—a seminary faculty member; (2) a network leadership mentor—an experienced individual representing the denomination or host network; and (3) a practitioner mentor—an on-the-ground advisor from the student's ministry context.

Integrated outcomes. To ensure holistic development, the program is designed with integrated outcomes that aim to develop students in all areas of their lives. They integrate what they do, where they do it, and how they do it.

Timely instruction. By the end of a CBTE program, all graduates demonstrate achievement of the same set of standardized outcomes. However, the order in which those outcomes are achieved is highly individualized. Under the direction of their mentor teams, students can tailor their learning pathway to the specific needs they face in ministry at a given time. This promotes "just-in-time" learning, immediate application, and the opportunity to deepen learning through reflection.

Recognition of prior learning. Many students seeking theological education come to schools with prior education and experience. Traditional programs will usually grant advanced placement to students who have completed accredited courses similar to those in the program—credits given for prior credits earned. However, in a competency-based program, credits are awarded for demonstrated competency, not completed courses. An individual's prior formal learning will likely reduce the length of time it takes to demonstrate competency, thereby reducing the overall length of the program. In effect, advanced standing for prior credits is granted.

CBTE programs also recognize informal learning and experience. Since the goal is competency, not credits, students who bring extensive life experience, personal study, or ministry service to a program also have the opportunity for advanced placement. They may start the program already able to demonstrate several of its outcomes.

Rigorous and adaptive assessment. The rigor of a CBTE program rests on its ability to effectively assess students. Standardized outcomes and indicators are clearly defined and provided to mentors and students. Mentor teams use these rubrics to evaluate a student's strengths and prior learning on program entry so they can focus energy on maximizing strengths and shoring up weaknesses. Continual assessment throughout the program ensures that students graduate only when they have demonstrated mastery in each competency and are fully equipped to serve their ministry context (Tan 2022).

Summary

In general, the participants in this track expressed appreciation for the quality and design of the formal training and the practicality of the nonformal training. Formal education was highlighted as more comprehensive but also overly structured. Some felt that it was outdated. Nonformal training was more contextual and based on felt needs emerging from the current situations. But it can also lack quality control. One group summarized their assessment as follows: "Non-formal [training] appreciates the depth and breadth of the formal training, whereas the formal [training] appreciates the church-centered character of non-formal training."

When assessing the case studies, some key observations were made. First, relationships and connections were important. A3 had a relationship with Fuller Seminary. New India Bible Seminary forged a relationship with LeaderSource. LAC built on its connections with Cru and later with Kairos University. Second, sharing a common vision or seeking a mutual philosophy of ministry was also important. The groups and ministries present already shared some common approaches, and they developed them by building on one another's strengths.

Dialoguing further, the group envisioned what the future of collaboration would look like. First, they desired to accelerate global pastoral training and to see these initiatives grow. Second, everyone agreed that increasing the number of trainers and mentors was important. Third, in addition to formal and nonformal organizations partnering, they felt it was important to include churches in this process.

The participants then reflected on what it would take to increase collaboration and accelerate pastoral leadership development. First, they affirmed that connecting pastors with leadership trainers to encourage synergy would be important. Second, leadership training ought to be done using indigenous approaches (e.g., drama, music, sport) instead of Western ones (e.g., reading and lectures). Third, through partnerships between formal and nonformal organizations as well as churches, they could streamline and simplify curriculum, building in feedback and accountability measures. Fourth, they agreed that investing in the training of more trainers and mentors was also important. Finally, they affirmed leveraging technology for more digital approaches to training, including building shared wiki spaces.

Regarding priorities and next steps, the group affirmed the need for a shared vision and buy-in from churches as well as formal and non-formal institutions. They affirmed that building more relational bridges was paramount. A summit on partnership was suggested to take these ideas forward and also allow formal and nonformal training groups to validate and encourage one another. In addition to a partnership summit, the group also mentioned the possibility of micro-gatherings, hubs, and networks of formal, nonformal, and church leaders meeting regularly. Finally, the group called for prayer that collaboration toward accelerating training leaders would be realized.

Summarizing the track at the ICETE 2022 consultation, Craig Parro concluded:

> The Formal Theological Education (FTE)-Non-Formal Theological Education (NFTE) dialogue over the years has been unidirectional in the sense that FTE is the older and wiser brother. Questions usually centered around what NFTE folks can learn from the FTE, especially regarding standards and assessment. ICETE 2022 shifted the conversation into bidirectional benefits, by also asking the question: What can FTE folks learn from NFTE? This new question challenged the older and wiser brother notion, and I believe, was well-received by FTE folks. (Parro, email, February 28, 2023)

Conclusion

As we strive to strengthen education for mission today, this multiyear communication process between formal and nonformal advocates proves instructive. The process began with a series of conversations between parties that were not on the same page. Yet over time, as they got to know each other and allowed their perspectives to be shared, progress was made. Collaboration requires time and relationship building. It also takes initiative and work toward common goals. As we collaborate and learn from one another, we can become stronger in the work of global theological education and pastoral training. Continual collaboration is essential for those involved in form and nonformal training.

Appendix: Objectives, Guiding Questions, Activities

I. Create a deeper understanding and appreciation for what each sector provides

   A. Take an appreciative inquiry approach, asking each sector: What do you especially appreciate about the strengths that the other sector brings to pastor training?

   B. Ask each sector: What would you add to what you just heard in terms of the strengths that your sector contributes to pastor training?

   C. Ask: Many in the nonformal sector have studied at formal theological institutions. What did you value about your formal training? Why are you now advocating for nonformal pastor training?

II. Demonstrate both the feasibility and the synergistic power of collaboration

   A. Present three models/stories of formal/nonformal collaborations, varying in terms of development and geography: Jaison Thomas for Seminary, Joe Handley for Asian Access, and Craig Parro for TOPIC.

   B. Ask: What distinctive features or principles contributed to the success of each of these collaborations?

   C. Ask in a small group setting: Describe effective collaborative models that you have seen.

D. Ask in a small group setting: What were distinctive features/ principles that contributed to the success of each of these collaborations?

E. Each group reports out the best model from their group.

F. Ask: What are the barriers or hindrances to effective collaboration between the two sectors?

III. Develop an initial plan to collaborate across sectors

A. Ask: What are the gaps or unmet needs that your organization has in your pastor training efforts that another organization might be able to fill?

B. Ask: What potential partner might be able to help you accelerate your pastor training capacity?

C. Ask: What next steps might you take?

References

Handley, Joseph. 2022. ICETE Presentation. November 16, 2022.

ICETE. 2022. "ICETE Manifesto II." Accessed November 29, 2022. https://icete.info/resources/manifesto/.

ICETE Academy. n.d. Formal and Non-Formal Theological Education in Dialogue. Accessed January 10, 2024. https://icete.academy/course/view.php?id=172.

Knowles, M. 2002. "Malcom Knowles, Informal Adult Education, Self-Direction and Andragogy." *The Encylopedia of Pedagogy and Informal Education.* http://infed.org/mobi/malcolm-knowles-informal-adult-education-self-direction-and-andragogy.

Parro, Craig. 2022. ICETE Presentation. November 2022.

Tan, Henry. 2022. ICETE Presentation. November 2022.

Tendero, Efraim, Craig Parro, Jaison Thomas, and Joseph Handley. 2023. "Welcome Letter ICETE Collaboration Workshop Track."

Chapter 15

The Intersection of Two Missiological Voices

A Contemporary Education Model for Chinese Missionaries

Daniel Low

With an estimated 10 million young believers joining the Chinese church each year, the church in China is projected to be numerically Christianity's largest church by 2050 (Young 2021; Nation and Liu 2022). This phenomenal revival and growth since the 1980s and 1990s has resulted in increased mission work, and some Chinese Christian leaders have courageously embraced the "Back to Jerusalem" vision to complete the Great Commission (Hattaway et al. 2014; Young 2021). Yao (2014) likens this fervor to a rekindling and recapturing of the missionary vision of the previous generations of Chinese Christians. As a result, numerous formal or informal organizations have emerged to participate in this vision, with a focus on preaching the gospel (Mok-Chan 2022).

In 2022, one of these organizations (hereafter G) approached Christian Witness Theological Seminary (hereafter CWTS—a Chinese seminary accredited by The Association of Theological Schools and located in San Jose, California) to request training for its missionaries who are serving among various unreached people groups (UPGs) in more than twenty-two locations within the 10/40 window. Based on conversations with G's key representative (hereafter J) in the United States, CWTS learned that the missionaries left for their respective fields having only acquired about a year of theological training and subsequently have no further access to further training. This information concurs with Yao's (2014) observation that a significant number of missionaries are sent out without adequate training, spiritual care, and mission study.

Due to these gaps, J expressed to CWTS the goals G has for the training of its missionaries. These include the hope that missionaries would

(1) gain both theological and missiological frameworks and practical skills that will enhance their effectiveness and well-being on the field; (2) complete a graduate degree program at the conclusion of the training; (3) complete part of the training during their furlough, hopefully in the United States; and (4) interact with both CWTS faculty members and network of churches during their furlough.

CWTS is excited to partner with G to provide the training and the seminary's leadership has approved the program with a targeted launch in the spring or fall of 2025. Amid the hope that such a program will address the needs of G's and other Chinese mission organizations' missionaries, CWTS is also cognizant of several immediate challenges. First, the missionaries have limited financial resources to pay for training developed by a United States–based seminary. CWTS currently charges $347 (RMB 2400) per credit hour. Unless CWTS provides financial aid, the amount needed to complete the training is beyond the reach of many of the missionaries. Furthermore, even if they secure the needed finances, the current political tensions between the United States and China have resulted in the consistent denial of visas for Chinese students entering the United States. For example, in 2022, 83 percent of applicants from China who were approved for admission to CWTS were denied student visas. CWTS will need to explore with G other legal and viable avenues for its missionaries to be on campus during their furlough.

Second, what are the courses that will meet the needs of a graduate degree program and the missionaries while also extending their prior training as well as enhancing their effectiveness and well-being on the field? Third, what will be the teaching and learning methods that will best facilitate the training, considering that the missionaries will attend part of the training while on the field and the other part of the training during furlough in the United States? Finally, what form of delivery will ensure sustainability for CWTS?

At the same time, CWTS is also mindful of Lin's (2023) compelling research concerning the limited effectiveness of theological institutions or seminaries in training missionaries for cross-cultural missions. While Lin's study is based on the responses provided by North American missionaries, what lessons might CWTS learn from this study as it develops the training for Chinese missionaries? How will CWTS's training tap into the positives highlighted by Lin (2023), for example, the provision of quality theological courses and contextualization courses? At the same time, what measures can CWTS adopt to minimize the negatives, for example, the gaps in preparation of specific skill sets for cross-cultural ministries (e.g., communication, leadership, family, and personal resilience)?

The rest of this chapter presents a model of mission education that addresses the goals identified by the organization while keeping in mind the strengths and limitations of seminaries to provide effective missionary training as identified by Lin (2023). The model contains three main characteristics. First, the training is practical. Practicality means that the missionaries, who are adult learners, can apply the acquired skills and knowledge to strengthen their ministries, complete the training, and receive the graduate degree. Second, the training is feasible. This includes accessible teaching and learning resources that motivate learners to persist in the training while on the field and on furlough, as well as local resources and expertise from their respective locations incorporated into the teaching and learning so that learning is contextual (Merriam and Bierema 2014). Third, the training is sustainable. Sustainability is evidenced by CWTS's program being well-received by G's missionaries and hopefully by other Chinese mission organizations and churches, resulting in the willingness of networks of churches and donors to collaborate with CWTS to provide needed funding for training.

Practicality of Training: Applicable and Stackable

There are two key strands related to the practicality of the training. First, the training is applicable. According to Merriam and Bierema (2014, 55), adult learners "want to know … how what they learn will apply to their immediate situation." Thus, the ability to apply the learning, immediate or future, serves as a key motivation for learners to be engaged and motivated in the learning process.

Second, the program is stackable, modeled after the "stackable credentials" offered by various community and/or technical colleges in the United States. With the onset of the pandemic in 2020, higher education for adult learners has witnessed increased volatility due to the shifting market conditions and job instability. Adult learners, who are at various places in their life journey and laden with many pressures, look for one or more of these facets in their ongoing learning: (1) flexibility to honor their many commitments while being able to enhance their knowledge and skills; (2) preference for skills training and nondegree programs; and (3) use of distance online learning (Southern Nazarene University Professional and Graduate Studies 2021; Strada Center for Education Consumer Insights 2020).

Taking these recent developments in adult education and the missionaries' needs into account, a stackable program for G will provide a practical way of helping the missionaries "progress along the education continuum while earning credentials … [via] organizing programs into a series of certificates that build on each other" (Center for Occupational Research and Development 2018, 1). The missionaries, during various pockets of availability—extended or limited—can take incremental milestones to engage with continuous learning and work toward degree completion.

Approaching Applicable

How then does CWTS provide a program that is applicable for the missionaries? What relevant courses will be offered? What does recent missiological research inform us about the types of courses that will help a missionary with limited training become adequately or well-prepared for the field? Are these reflective of the courses that J highlighted as areas of need (missiological and theological frameworks, cross-cultural strategies to share the gospel, leadership skills to lead local believers, training of local leaders to mobilize local believers, cross-cultural teamwork strategies, and church-planting and growth strategies)?

Lin (2023) points to key areas (e.g., fundraising, managing, leading teams and believers in cross-cultural contexts, language skills) that need to be included in preparing missionaries in cross-cultural contexts. These areas also concur with the eleven critical competencies identified by Boan, Aten, Greener, and Gailey (2016, 430) for faith-based development work, which the authors note "parallels missions" and research on the Chinese mission movement by Yao. Yao (2014) focuses on four key challenges facing the Chinese missionary movement today: (1) the need for systematic training in the areas of "Bible, missiology, languages, cultures, cross-cultural communications"; (2) the need for improved mechanisms or structures for better training, evaluation, and missionary care; (3) the need for adequate training in theology of mission and religions; and (4) the need to address the "signs of theological disorientation and … questionable mission approaches and rhetoric" that have led to a dangerously triumphalist Christendom mentality.

While CWTS will not be able to comprehensively address these competencies and challenges due to their extensive scope, the courses proposed in ongoing conversations with G and J will include the following key categories.

- Cross-cultural competencies—leadership and communication skills, self and community care, interactions with other religions, and cultural research skills.

- Mobilizing movements across cultures—strategies to plant churches, evangelize, and disciple, and habits for resilient personal and family formation.

- Resource development—social entrepreneurship, networking, and personal and community fundraising.

What teaching and learning models or strategies for adults may be adopted to deliver these courses?

Merriam and Bierema's (2014) broad overview of the major theories and research in adult learning, regardless of traditional learning theories (e.g., behaviorism, humanism, social cognitivism, and constructivism) or more recent ones (e.g., andragogy, self-directed learning, transformative learning, and experiential learning), presents a critique of these theories. Specifically, they criticize (1) the limits of the theories (e.g., focused either on changing behavior or attending to needs); (2) the assumptions about adult learners (e.g., they are insulated from their immediate contexts— culture or otherwise—and fully in control of their learning, they desire self-direction in their learning); and (3) the impact of learning (e.g., the areas transformation remain unclear, the assessment of societal individuals impacted by the learning remains difficult). Thus, the adoption of a teaching and learning model that will bring about a transference of learning—from the classroom to the field—will necessarily entail a hybridity of approaches to minimize inherent gaps within Western models of teaching and learning as identified in the previous paragraph.

Merriam and Bierema's (2014) expansion of Merriam, Cafarella, and Baumgartner's (2007) framework for adult learning provides a compelling way forward. The expanded framework is characterized by faculty being continuous learners and reflective practitioners, learners being engaged with their heads, hearts, and bodies throughout the courses, and a program that is keenly aware of the learners' contexts and intentionally incorporates local resources into the courses. The intentional integration of learning being cultural and communal is critical for three reasons. The first is the purpose of the training, which needs to be focused on adequate preparation of the primary learners (i.e., the missionaries) for fruitful ministries with the secondary learners (i.e., the people groups served by the missionaries).

Second, the design of the training needs to accommodate the learning tendencies of the Chinese missionaries. Due to the limitations of ascribing learning patterns to ethnicities (Ott 2021), the design process will initially need to be intuitive, combining both awareness and adaption during the early phases of the program.

Third, CWTS's program needs to strengthen the cross-cultural teaching skills of Chinese missionaries by helping them understand the learning patterns of various people groups. By strengthening this skill, the missionaries will hopefully recognize the importance of learning with and from local communities (Elmer 2006), thus moving away from a sense of cultural or spiritual superiority.

Another useful resource that CWTS will use to guide the development of the teaching and learning model for applicability is Ott's (2021) *Teaching across Cultures*. While CWTS has been primarily teaching Chinese students from China, Taiwan, and Hong Kong, Ott's five dimensions of how culture influences teaching and learning will help as we navigate a new terrain of teaching Chinese missionaries in different locations. The dimensions of cognition, worldview, social relations, media, and environment are also compelling for the following reasons.

First, the characteristics within each dimension can serve as the foundation for questions that CWTS can ask G as the school uses design thinking to develop the training program. For example, under the cognitive dimension, we can ask, What are the ways you as a learner receive and process information? What are your preferred ways of presenting information?

Second, these dimensions force CWTS to reckon with the fundamental nature of cultural differences in terms of teaching (faculty) and learning (missionaries). The faculty will most likely come from North America, and CWTS must provide principles and tools to help them to understand their learning audience.

Third, the media dimension discusses the use of visuals, art forms (e.g., songs, drama), and cross-cultural online learning. These facets are critical for the development of the training given the platform for learning and the locations of ministry.

Approaching Stackable

As pointed out earlier, a stackable approach from CWTS allows the missionaries to accumulate various certificates over time. Each certificate will focus on a particular set of skills, and the successful completion of all certificates will lead to a master's degree. The proposed program currently consists of twelve courses. With each course being three credit hours, the total degree program is thirty-six hours long. Since courses will be eight weeks long, within a traditional semester, a missionary can complete two courses. The courses are grouped into six certificates or stacks, with each certificate constituting two courses. CWTS's rationale for a stackable approach (agreed upon by G and J) is multilayered.

First, the approach provides flexibility in terms of the sequence of each certificate. The sequence is not fixed so that missionaries do not need to complete any certificate before moving on to another certificate. Each certificate and the two courses within each certificate are targeted toward a different set of skills and knowledge.

Second, this approach also provides flexibility for how the missionaries choose to complete each certificate and the program. For example, if a missionary can only complete one of the two courses in a certificate, she/he may complete the missed course the next time it is offered.

Third, flexibility is provided in terms of the entry requirements to join the various certificates and also exemptions from various courses in each certificate. For those who are exempt from some courses, the time to complete all the certificates is shortened. The entry requirements are based on the competencies and needs of the missionaries instead of all missionaries needing to meet a standardized set of entry requirements (e.g., an undergraduate degree) as required by a regular master's program. This is an important difference, particularly for missionaries who only desire to complete certain certificates to meet their existing needs or challenges. If missionaries without an undergraduate degree desire to earn a master's degree after completing the certificates, they can make plans to complete an undergraduate degree while completing the certificates.

Assessments for entry can include evidence of prior learning in areas related to certificate courses, ability to engage with English resources, and each missionary's portfolio consisting of samples of reflection on their ministries, personal and institutional assessments of their strengths and weaknesses, suitability to undergo the training, completed or ongoing field projects with a clear description of the planning and evaluation process, and institutional evaluation of the missionaries' ministries and recommendations. The various modes of assessing suitability are an adaptation of the best practices recommended by the Council for Adult and Experiential Learning (CAEL, 2017), an organization that advocates for nontraditional students.

According to CAEL, nontraditional students reflect one or more of these characteristics: having a spouse or other dependents, working a full-time job, taking classes part-time, and having parental responsibilities for at least one child as a single parent. CAEL notes that increased flexibility provided for nontraditional students by assessing and crediting their prior learning has led to greater continuity in enrollment and greater persistence toward graduation. These benefits are surely worth CWTS's consideration as the missionaries are in multiple ways nontraditional students.

Feasibility of Training: Accessible and Contextual

A training that is perceived as doable by students has two facets. First, it is accessible. G's missionaries are located in more than twenty-two locations within the 10/40 window, so training accessibility is easily achieved via online learning. CWTS believes that students' motivation to access teaching and learning resources and completion of the training program is far more important. With the virtual classroom offering both synchronous and asynchronous class sessions, what are the strategies that CWTS should adopt to encourage students to stay connected?

The second facet points to the "importance of where learning occurs, that is, the context itself shapes the learning" (Merriam and Bierema 2014, 118). Beyond the online resources provided in the courses, learning is also situated in the missionaries' respective locations using the tools at hand.

The tools include symbols (e.g., writings, artwork, artifacts), oral traditions (e.g., stories, poems, songs), and people (e.g., leaders, neighbors). The strength of contextual learning is that it removes "learning from that which only occurs within the person's mind and highlights the importance of context and social determinants of the learning that takes place" (118). The learning outcomes are authentic and lend themselves to being applicable.

Approaching Accessible

Online teaching and learning for G's missionaries, which primarily focuses on skills to understand and work across cultures, challenges CWTS to think deeply about the ways to enable students to be motivated to access teaching and learning resources and complete the training. While an intuitive, affordable learning management system (e.g., Populi, Thinkific) is a nonnegotiable, three other critical requirements must be met—(1) the quality of instruction; (2) the quality of the design of the online training; and (3) the quality of the courses, assignments, and feedback.

Danielson (2015) states that good online instruction begins with faculty moving away from the traditional role of lecturer—one that simply dispenses content or knowledge (see Freire 2000). Instead, they become content facilitators or co-investigators in dialogue with their students through the embodiment of strong andragogical skills (81). These skills include effective lesson planning and organization, use of relevant technology, up-to-date content knowledge, and personal attributes (e.g., clear and engaging communication style, empathy toward adult learners, and approachability). Sogunro (2014) states that these skills naturally lead to increased motivation among adult learners.

Good quality design for online learning is possible with the use of design thinking. Design thinking or user experience (UX) design is defined as a "non-linear, iterative process ... to understand users, challenge assumptions, redefine problems, and create innovative solutions" (Interactive Design Foundation 2022). There are five stages in design thinking—empathize (research users' needs), define (state users' needs and problems), ideate (create ideas and challenge assumptions), prototype (create solutions), and test (try out solutions). CWTW plans to adopt this design process so the training will fulfill the critical requirements of quality instruction, quality design and quality courses, assignments and feedback.

The above two requirements will impact the third requirement. According to Sogunro (2015), quality courses, assignments, and assessments along with timely and constructive feedback go hand in hand to strengthen the motivation of the students to complete a program as these naturally meet their needs. Quality courses, assignments, and assessments provide clear objectives, rubrics, topics to be covered, as well as a schedule. Adult learners are motivated by timely and precise feedback giving them an indication of "their own academic progress" (30). Since G's missionaries are burdened with a variety of responsibilities, the onus is on CWTS to ensure that courses provide clarity and precise, timely feedback so that the missionaries find the training motivating and feasible.

Approaching Contextual

Danielson (2015, 213) states that in mission studies or any similar field, "the issue of context becomes vital." While the application of the training to the missionaries' contexts is critical, the connection to the local teaching and learning resources or tools is equally important to ensure that the training is not limited to the abstract so that the students do not disengage. Thus, spaces are created within each course to incorporate local resources or tools, which include symbols, oral traditions, and people. Ways of incorporating these resources include assignments that require references to local print forms, a cloud-based sharable storage that invites students to contribute relevant resources, and contextualized approaches that make sure that these resources are used.

Based on J's emphasis that the missionaries acquire skills, the incorporation of these resources will enable students to see the immediate relevance of their courses (see Danielson 2015). Connectivity between online resources and contextual resources will aid the applicability of each course and the missionaries' relationship building and cross-cultural communication with the local communities. The latter is significant as G's missionaries are committed to long-term ministry in their respective locations.

Sustainability of Training: Communal and Collaborative

Beyond the practicality and accessibility of this training, an inevitable and often challenging issue within Christian institutions is the sustainability of the training. Due to the pandemic, Christian institutions of higher education have not been spared from having to downsize campuses, discontinue programs, and reduce full-time faculty members. These difficult moments were widely reported by *Christianity Today* in 2021 and 2022. While CWTS has been able to continue to operate with minimal disruption during these difficult moments, it is fully cognizant of the funding required to launch and sustain this training, considering the limitations of G's missionaries to pay for the courses.

The initial strategies that CWTS proposes are twofold. The first addresses the online environment to support the students—creating virtual spaces that lead to sustained participation by G's missionaries throughout the program to build community and maintain an optimal number of participants for learning dynamics and the continuation of courses. The second addresses the external environment to support the students with CWTS reaching out to both G's networks of supporters and churches to seek sufficient funding for the training.

Approaching Communal

According to Danielson (2015), the learning community—albeit a virtual one—remains an extremely important part of the educational process. While forming strong online communities has its complexities, today's plethora of online tools and learning management systems (e.g., Slack and Thinkific) can help to manage these due to their user-friendly features. CWTS will need to use one or more of these to offer constant feedback and maintain a high level of personal interactions.

The organization of the online communities for the missionaries can be further enhanced by tapping into communities of practice (CoP), an idea developed by Lave and Wenger to provide a framework to understand "learning … within a social context" (Seaman 2008, 269). Wenger's (2009, 98) definition of CoP is "groups of people [in this context students in the program] who share a … passion for something they do and learn to do it better as they interact regularly" through sharing expertise, competence, stories, and experiences. CoP also naturally lends itself to contextual learning as missionaries are expected to draw on local expertise, stories, and experiences as they complete their assignments.

Approaching Collaborative

Since 2012, CWTS has consistently operated with a modest annual surplus. The support of donors has been vital to the financial health of the seminary. With the launch of this new training program and the financial constraints of G's missionaries to pay for their training, CWTS will need to tap into its existing base of donors and also expand this base by promoting the launch of this new program through various face-to-face events, word of mouth, and relationship-building meal gatherings. Based on CWTS's previous experiences in advertising the seminary, sensitivity and tact are needed to avoid being mistaken for being brazen in our approach to source funding for the training, regardless of the reasons for the funding (e.g., student scholarships, hiring personnel, IT infrastructure).

Another potential source of funding for the training is G's donors. CWTS could collaborate with G to reach out to them and promote this new partnership. Again, this promotion will need to be skillfully and sensitively carried out since CWTS does not know G's donors. Prudent and creative planning to offer training that will both meet the needs of G's missionaries and hopefully the other similar Chinese mission organizations will be a critical step in inviting donors to share in this journey with CWTS.

Conclusion

CWTS's development of a training model that will be practical, accessible, and feasible for G's missionaries needs to be nuanced—a careful listening to two voices within the shared task of missiology. First, the voice of on-the-field Chinese missionaries needs to be on the table if the training program is to bring about their effectiveness and flourishing. Thus, the adoption of strategies (e.g., design thinking, ongoing conversations with G and J) to discern the key facets for the design of the training is critical. These facets also need to be triangulated with current best practices in adult education and teaching adults in cross-cultural settings (e.g., CAEL's prior learning assessment, Merriam and Bierema's adult learning framework, and Ott's cross-cultural teaching dimensions).

Second, the voice of Western missiological research and insights is equally important if CWTS is to be an effective co-laborer who walks alongside the Chinese missionaries to address the key challenges and gaps that they and the Chinese missionary movement encounter. As pointed out by Lin (2023), there are existing positives within missions training provided by seminaries. Tapping into these strengths will produce a well-rounded and rigorous training program for the Chinese missionaries. Yao's (2014) observation and exhortation are timely and astute as CWTS takes its next steps with G: "The Chinese churches [including mission organizations] are at a critical point in their mission outreach. ... Let us [i.e., training agencies, seminaries, churches] pray for them, engage them, and assist them. Together, we can make a significant difference around the world."

References

Boan, David Michael, Jamie Aten, Susan Greener, and Robert Gailey. 2016. "The Well-Prepared International Development Worker." *Missiology* 44, no. 4: 430–47.

Center for Occupational Research and Development. 2018. "Stackable Credentials Tool Kit." Perkins Collaborative Resource Network. Accessed January 28, 2023. https://cte.ed.gov/initiatives/community-college-stackable-credentials.

Council for Adult Experiential Learning (CAEL). 2017. "Chart the Path to Adult Student Success." Accessed January 28, 2023. https://www.cael.org.

Dam, R. F. 2024. "The 5 Stages in the Design Thinking Process. Interaction Design Foundation - IxDF." https://www.interaction-design.org/literature/article/5-stages-in-the-design-thinking-process.

Danielson, Robert A. 2015. "Navigating the Online Missiology Classroom: Class Design and Resources for Teaching Missiology Online." *Missiology* 43, no. 2: 208–20.

Elmer, Duane. 2006. *Cross-Cultural Servanthood: Serving the World in Christlike Humility*. Downers Grove, IL: InterVarsity Press.

Freire, Paulo. 2000. *Pedagogy of the Oppressed*. New York: Continuum.

Hattaway, Paul, Brother Yun, Peter Xu Yongze, and Enoch Wang. 2014. *Back to Jerusalem: Called to Complete the Great Commission*. 2nd ed. Carlisle: Piquant.

Lin, Arthur. 2023. "The Role of Theological Institutions in Missionary Training." *Journal of the Evangelical Missiological Society* 3, no. 1: 128–43. https://journal-ems.org/index.php/home/article/view/59.

Merriam, Sharan B., and Laura L. Bierema. 2014. *Adult Learning: Linking Theory and Practice*. San Francisco: Jossey-Bass.

Merriam, S. B., R. S. Cafarella, and L. M. Baumgartner. 2007. *Learning in Adulthood: A Comprehensive Guide*. 3rd ed. San Francisco: Wiley.

Mok-Chan, Wing Yan. 2022. *Huo chu he ping—zheng quan shi ming de shi xian* [Shalom, the Practice of Integral Mission]. New Territories, HK: Christian Communications Ltd.

Nation, Hannah, and Simon Liu, eds. 2022. *Faith in the Wilderness: Words of Exhortation from the Chinese Church*. Bellingham, WA: Lexham.

Ott, Craig. 2021. *Teaching and Learning across Cultures: A Guide to Theory and Practice*. Grand Rapids: Baker Academic.

Seaman, Mark. 2008. "Birds of a Feather? Communities of Practice and Knowledge Communities." *Curriculum and Teaching Dialogue* 10, no. 1/2: 269–79.

Sogunro, Olusegun Agboola. 2015. "Motivating Factors for Adult Learners in Higher Education." *International Journal of Higher Education* 4, no. 1: 22–37. https://doi.org/10.5430/ijhe.v4n1p22.

Southern Nazarene University Professional and Graduate Studies. 2021. "What Will Adult Education Look Like Post-Pandemic?" *Southern Nazarene University* (blog). April 13, 2021. https://degrees.snu.edu/blog/what-will-adult-education-look-like-post-pandemic.

Strada Center for Education Consumer Insights. 2020. "Public Viewpoint: The Value of Online Education." July 29. https://cci.stradaeducation.org/pv-release-july-29-2020/.

Wenger, Etienne. 2009. "Communities of Practice: A Brief Introduction." Accessed January 31, 2009. http://www.ewenger.com/theory/.

Yao, Kevin Xiyi. 2014. "The Chinese Church: The Next Superpower in World Mission?" Missio Nexus. July 1, 2014. https://missionexus.org/the-chinese-church-the-next-superpower-in-world-mission/.

Young, Lionel F., III. 2021. *World Christianity and the Unfinished Task: A Very Short Introduction*. Eugene, OR: Wipf & Stock.

Chapter 16

Leadership Development of Indian Missionaries in Today's Context

John Amalraj Karunakaran

The Context of Missionary Training in India

In the last five decades of exponential growth, the indigenous missionary enterprise in India has focused on training cross-cultural missionaries and local evangelists to plant churches in places and among peoples with little Christian presence. As new indigenous missionary-sending agencies were founded, formal missionary training institutes also emerged. Over time, leadership development became one of the major concerns for the Indian churches and missions as the issue of leadership succession into the next generation surfaced. How has this concern been addressed by the indigenous mission movement?

In the context of the cross-cultural missionary training in India, the focus has largely been on church-planting skills rather than comprehending the holistic nature of God's mission. In today's missiological understanding, the church's participation in the mission of God is not necessarily dependent on church-planting skills, which are assumed to be critical. God's mission is focused on developing leadership that grows vision, increases abilities, and extends relational influence through the time-tested process of disciple-making or mentoring. Some popular literature tends to suggest that leadership is a gift. In his collection of essays on leadership, Thomas Wren (1995, ix–xii), writing from a historical perspective, set out three premises in his preface presenting a holistic understanding of leadership. The first is that leadership is central to the experience of human beings. Second, leadership is for all and not for the privileged few. Third, understanding leadership helps to achieve the common goals of a group of people (x–xi). If leadership is for everyone, then every missionary trainee must be discipled to become a leader in their context.

What is Leadership and Leadership Development?

Academic leadership study is less than a hundred years old, and yet there is no scholarly consensus on defining leadership (Ledbetter, Banks, and Greenhalgh 2016, xvii). Among many scholars who have attempted a definition, Douglas McConnell's (2018, xiii) definition makes a lot of sense in the context of cross-cultural mission. He defines leadership as a "sacred duty" that requires those who accept a leadership role or responsibility to be a "learner" learning to lead. McConnell explores cultural learning in the context of its application to Christian leaders serving in mission organizations. If leadership must be learned, then there must be intentional efforts to integrate the missionary training curricula with leadership theories and practices that enhance leadership development. We all recognize whether a person has the appropriate leadership skills for a given task or when they fail to perform according to expectations. However, what we do not admit is the fact that leadership skills can be developed through intentional learning.

There have been academic discussions on leadership development and how cost-effective these interventions are for the outcomes of both profit-making and nonprofit organizations (Murphy 2011, 5–6). However, there seems to be a lack of understanding about the development processes across an individual's lifespan and what we mean by leadership development. The Center for Creative Leadership is made up of American consultants who are recognized for their research and practices through which they have studied both the process of leadership development and its intervention for both profit-making and nonprofit organizations. They define leadership development as follows: "The expansion of a person's capacity to be effective in leadership roles and processes. Leadership roles and processes are those that enable groups of people to work together in productive and meaningful ways" (McCauley, Velsor, and Ruderman 2010, 4). This definition is comprehensive and founded on the philosophy that people can learn, grow, and change. Several complex factors contribute to gaining the ability to learn among which motivation, personality, and learning tactics are foundational. Research into leadership development also affirms that leadership abilities may have some roots in genetics, the environment of early childhood development, and adulthood experiences. Robert Clinton (1988, 4, 245) understood leadership development by focusing on the efforts to change the capacity to influence across time and life span. He further contends that training and development of leadership is part of the church's "mission mandate," making it a priority function.

The context of leadership development within the Indian missions and churches needs serious attention. In his critique of twenty-five years of the Indian mission movement (1972–1997), Rajendran (1998, 187–88) comments that there has not been any intentionality to train and develop future leadership within the Indian missions and churches. Theologian Ivan Satyavrata (2004) points out that in the context of glocalization, integrating local and global resources for contextual continuity, contemporary relevance, and faithfulness to Christian tradition is needed in training leaders. It is in this context that this chapter attempts to explore leadership development and training of Indian missionaries in today's context.

After more than two decades since these insights, we need to identify the focus being given to leadership development and whether it meets the changing context of India within the context of missionary training in India. Missiologist Atul Y. Aghamkar focuses on the globalized Hindu context, showing how the Indian diaspora has spread across the world and taken their religious and cultural beliefs to their adopted lands (Aghamkar 2017, 131–54). Describing the globalization of Hinduism and the globalized Hindu Indians, he points out the need for global Christian leaders to be informed, equipped, and mobilized to serve them. In another essay, mission leader Theodore Srinivasagam underscores the need for developing leadership training resources in understanding Hinduism, using appropriate language, and applying relevant methods to engage them by overcoming cultural hindrances (Srinivasagam 2017, 155–75). He focuses on the context of the growing church-planting movements where the need of the hour is developing small group leaders, area leaders, pastors, and regional and national leaders to understand Hinduism. These insights for the need to develop global leadership with interfaith engagement further provide the impetus to explore the status of leadership development for the Indian missionaries.

This article argues that an effective missionary training curriculum, along with imparting knowledge and skills in church planting (disciple-making), needs to explicitly focus on leadership development in today's context. First, I will describe the present status of missionary training in

India and the role of leadership development to fill in the gaps. Second, I will discuss how the curricula can be enhanced through the integration of leadership theories and missiological reflection. Third, I will show how *cultural intelligence* is a key to effective leadership within multicultural contexts. In conclusion, I present recommendations for the task of making *disciplers* or, in other words, *disciple-leaders* so that they can fulfill the mission mandate to wider multicultural communities.

Present Status of Leadership Development

There are more than three hundred mission agencies affiliated with the India Missions Association, the national federation of missionary sending agencies. Half of the organizations claim that they have some level of training for their workers. It is fair to assume that all of the others have short-term orientation programs on church planting and evangelism or recruit those who have already undergone training from other institutes. Occasionally they send their workers for training at other institutions. There are a few who undergo nonformal training before they are sent to fulfill their mission call.

The Indian Institute for Intercultural Studies (formerly the Indian Institute of Missiology), which was founded by the India Missions Association in 1994, came into existence when there were around eighty missionary training institutes that needed to streamline their training to become more effective (Barnabas 2004, 60–61). After ten years, the Indian Institute of Missiology was able to formally grant affiliation and accreditation to twenty-seven institutes. The focus of the curriculum development involved discussions on how to integrate academics with practical skills, spiritual formation, and character formation and offer different levels of training that would cater to the needs of the grassroots as well as higher levels of training (Amalraj 2004, 50). As of today, after a process of periodical quality assessment, only forty-five institutions maintain affiliation, and fifteen offer accredited training programs (Jayakumar Ramachandran, email, March 14, 2023).

In the wider Indian context of theological education and missionary training, there are around 250 Bible colleges and seminaries affiliated with the two major accrediting bodies for theological education, while a few Christian universities and autonomous colleges offer training with an academic focus and have some components of leadership development.

Many offer Western-imported and contextualized leadership training programs with a focus on equipping lay leaders and training pastors and mission workers within the churches. Jayakumar Ramachandran (2018, 24–26) observes that several small-scale training institutions have mushroomed and only a few among them attain institutional membership in an accreditation body. He expresses concerns about the purpose of theological education for the needs of mission, the quality of the education, the modus operandi of theological education being irrelevant to the trainee's context, the lack of interdisciplinary approach, the dichotomized understanding of theology and missiology, the lack of focus on character formation, and the lack of awareness on contemporary socio-science issues. Ramachandran concludes by observing that theological education in the West itself is not missiologically focused and this blind spot has been replicated in the Western theological education paradigm in the Majority World (30). He calls for contextualized training that is shaped to resolve contemporary multidimensional missional challenges through prophetic and productive partnerships.

Since this article is limited to training programs for cross-cultural missionaries in India, I will focus on the case of a pioneering missionary training institution now known as the Outreach Training Institute of the Indian Evangelical Mission.

The first indigenous mission agency founded in India was the Marthoma Evangelistic Association in 1888, establishing Christian ashrams and sending out workers across cultures (Rajendran 1998, 55). Later, the Indian Missionary Society and an interdenominational mission agency, the National Missionary Society, were established under the leadership of V. S. Azariah in 1903 and 1905, respectively. At the end of the colonial era, there was a season when many foreign missionaries had to leave the country as new restrictions emerged. The following decades, especially the 1970s and 1980s, saw an explosion of indigenous mission agencies founded with a renewed passion to plant churches across the country.

In his presentation during the World Evangelical Fellowship Missions Commission Conference in 1982, Theodore Williams (1983, 33–34) listed three pioneering missionary training institutes. The first was the Indian Missionary Training Institute, providing cross-cultural training; the second was the Bethel Bible Institute, where a six-month church-planting training was offered for missionaries recruited by the Friends Missionary Prayer

Band; and the third was the ACTS (Agriculture, Crafts, and Trade Studies) Institute, which trained Christian young people to acquire a skill or trade as they served as Christ's witnesses through their vocation.

While many indigenous missionary sending agencies were being founded, there were not many formal training programs for Indian cross-cultural missionaries being sent into the mission fields (Williams 1983, 33). Williams wrote that the first formal missionary training was founded in 1976 by the Indian Evangelical Mission in partnership with the Bible and Medical Missionary Fellowship (now Interserve India) to give "special missionary training" for those working in pioneer situations. The Indian Missionary Training Institute was a joint effort, and other mission agencies also used it to train their missionaries. He added that they expected the trainees to come with a year of Bible training, and the short three-month training focused on elementary linguistics, primary health care, church growth, personal evangelism, Hinduism, cultural anthropology, survey of the tribes in India, practical talks on family life, financial management, and writing missionary letters. There was no mention of leadership aspects covered in this training. The Indian Missionary Training Institute, now called the Outreach Training Institute (OTI), has a unique cross-cultural missiological training program that runs for six months (Dinakaran 2022, 23). The curriculum has been revised extensively to incorporate new topics with around fifty modules along with a holistic approach to training. Ajaykumar, an OTI staff member, describes their training as follows:

> OTI is not a regular Bible Theological Seminary or College. The Missiological Course in OTI is a Cross-Cultural Training extended to all those who have a calling towards cross-cultural ministry. Each curriculum module has been carefully created to promote the growth of the trainees' character, knowledge, and skill. The six-month classroom learning includes non-academic activities that will hone teamwork/building, discipling, developing leadership, and other abilities. It comprises about fifty modules. It opens many people's eyes to cross-cultural ministry. Most of the teachers are our missionaries but we also are blessed from people of different other organizations! Apart from modules like Foundations for Maturing Church, Sharpening Interpersonal Skills, Discipleship modules, Applied Anthropology and Cross-Cultural Communication, Language Learning Skills, the Missiological course also looks to the entire formation of the missionary, their family life, health, preaching, and teaching, encountering

other faiths, ministering to children, strong Biblical doctrines and many other. On the whole, the trainees' commitment is stirred, revived, and molded. (Dinakaran 2022, 23)

Their philosophy of missional training included the components of discipleship, leadership, scholarship, relationship, and stewardship (Elias 2022, 3–4). The description shows how leadership development has been included in the training program of one of the oldest missionary training institutes in the country. A closer observation of the curriculum reveals that leadership topics are built around biblical studies, making an application to the mission field context. It included topics like lay leadership, local leadership, biblical leadership principles, different leadership styles, developing leaders, management in leadership, and team leadership in mission. The curriculum in general has an emphasis on cross-cultural communication, while leadership development is part of the experiential learning through activities outside the classroom along with a few lectures on leadership examples from the Bible. The need for learning leadership theories, especially on how culture affects the exercise of leadership in cross-cultural contexts, has yet to be grasped in the present curriculum.

The Bethel Bible Institute, which offered training for missionaries recruited by the Friends Missionary Prayer Band, is no longer receiving trainees since the mission agency has changed its policy due to low recruitment of new missionaries and has opted for distance learning and on-the-field training. The ACTS (Agriculture, Crafts, and Trade Studies) Institute continues its training of Christian young people mostly from rural areas, providing them with vocational skills.

In a consultation on Two-Thirds World missionary training at Manila in 1989, Ebenezer Sunder Raj mentioned three pioneering training institutions in India that existed during that decade that were a partnership initiative: the Institute for Cross-Cultural Communication (Bible translation and literacy), Yavatmal College for Leadership Training (YCLT), and Outreach Training Institute (Sunder Raj 1991, 61–63). The Institute for Cross-Cultural Communication no longer exists, having been replaced by other training institutes. The YCLT continues its missionary training program with formal accredited courses in leadership development and management, which reveals efforts to integrate leadership theories with missiological reflections. This leads us to discuss the need for the integration of leadership theories in cross-cultural missionary training.

Integration of Leadership Theories and Missiological Reflection

Within theological and missiological education, academic scholarship in leadership development has been neglected in favor of biblical studies and owes its root to the changing theological climate during the third decade of the eighteenth century (Bosch 2011, 260). David Bosch explains that Pietism led to the significant development of Protestant missionary ideas, which shifted with the influence of the Enlightenment era that emerged in Europe. This led to the "construction of an absolute dualism between the sacred and the profane," which continues to have a profound influence on the missionary movement in India (260). The popular focus on using biblical heroes and biblical teachings on leadership over and above any references to the academic scholarship on theories and practices may be traced to this dualism of sacred and profane. This is then transferred to biblical teaching versus academic knowledge instead of integrating "the human spirit, fully engaged" in their calling (Ledbetter, Banks, and Greenhalgh 2016, 20). In their review of Christian leadership literature in the American context, Ledbetter, Banks, and Greenhalgh critique the most common way of drawing out leadership principles from the life and ministry of Jesus, cautioning that the context of Jesus's leadership is strikingly different from today's leadership context, with the commercialization of economic life and institutional architecture. This makes it difficult to simply use our hermeneutical interpretations without running into difficulties (74–75). The biblical scholar Henry Cadbury (1937, 4), who is also cited in the review, put it succinctly, "We fall into anachronism in thinking of Jesus' thoughts" in reading a history of the past centuries, assuming it was like today when we now live in a different environment.

On the other hand, Ken Blanchard, whose situational leadership theory gained academic recognition and his *Lead Like Jesus* training programs have become popular in India, defends his interpretation by pointing out that the skepticism about the relevance of Jesus as a role model and his teaching to specific twenty-first-century leadership situations are not necessarily valid. He argues that there are universal leadership principles that can be drawn from the life and ministry of Jesus and his apostles. The root of these debates is probably the dualistic nature of thinking where we make a distinction between sacred and profane, stemming from part of our Pietistic theological formation.

Evelyn and Richard Hibbert point out the assumption of many Christians that there are biblical values that are supracultural—such as loving our neighbors and forgiving one another. What we fail to understand is that Christians from different cultures express these values in different ways shaped by their culture (Hibbert and Hibbert 2014, 21). Leadership is also exercised differently in diverse cultures.

In his work on leadership development within the context of mission organizations, Pluddemann (2009, 168) holds to the perspective that "nothing is as practical as a good theory," and he integrates theory with the theology and practice of leadership and the methodological implications of biblical principles to understand cultural challenges. Similarly, McConnell's (2019) efforts in unpacking organizational theory within a complex mission environment for organizational leaders, which are based on the missiological understanding of how culture functions in shaping, catalyzing, and driving organizational leadership, are useful as a missiological framework for studying cross-cultural leadership.

In his reflection on the leadership crisis in today's church and missions, Samuel Mathew (2013, 2), bishop of the Believers Eastern Church in India, calls for a revitalized and reemphasized leadership from a biblical perspective. In his quest for evolving an adequate model and pattern for leadership effectiveness, Mathew attempts to integrate culturally defined leadership concepts and biblically based teachings to formulate a pattern of leadership for the church and public services. However, in his writings, he makes scant references to cultural understandings or academic research on the influence of culture on leadership behavior, resulting in reiterating theological and biblical reflections of the past. The inadequate integration of academic research and missiological reflection raises the question of how important cultural intelligence is for the practice of leadership.

Importance of Cultural Intelligence in Leadership Development

In the context of geographical, linguistic, social, and religious diversity in India, it is difficult to describe the local Indian culture in which the framework for leadership development can be constructed. Religion and culture are integrated into how people interact, so it is a challenge to make a distinction or any generalizations. S. M. Michael (2015, 29) describes the Indian culture as "multicultural for ages, multilinguistic, multireligious, and multiracial." Among the Christians in India, their cultures have been influenced in multiple ways by Western denominational traditions, the Pentecostal movement, colonialism, and regional ethnic and linguistic traditions. The sociopolitical changes and the subaltern theologizing have made their mark on the emerging Indian Christian cultures. Above all, they reveal how the Western missiological emphases, missional approaches, and cultures have also contributed to shaping them. If culture can be learned, adapted, shared, and integrated, then the Indian Christian culture can be transformed (Howell and Paris 2011, 36).

Rajiv Kumar and Jagdeep S. Chhokar (2013, 225–26) offer a summary of varied conceptions of culture by highlighting the dynamic nature of culture. They review recently published empirical work after making brief references to previous reviews of cross-cultural leadership research. Their reviews point to the fact that directive leadership is more problematic in individualistic cultures and that culture plays a role in the differences seen between self and others' ratings in 360-degree feedback. They further identify concepts of ethics, ethical leadership, and reactions to unethical practices that vary across cultures (225). They add that some studies point out that other factors may be at play beyond cross-national cultural differences. They identify issues that need further research including the multidimensional nature of culture and the universal nature of leadership across cultures. Discussing concepts of culture, they state that there is no universally accepted definition of culture (226). It can exist in any "human collectivity … an organization, profession, age group, or a family" (Hofstede, 2010, 10). They cite other researchers who observed that for proper interpretations of behavior, contextual information is important, arguing that effective leadership in a multicultural environment needs contextual information.

Leadership development within a multicultural context is critical as assumptions about effective leadership vary (Plueddemann 2009). This is relevant to the Indian missionary training context. Unpacking leadership development across cultures, Plueddemann asserts that whether it is an individual effort, loyalty to a patron, or royal lineage, cultural assumptions often determine any model of leadership development. Reflecting on his foundational proposition that leadership is the gift of the Holy Spirit, it is important to clarify in a missional context that there are different levels of leadership within an organization or church, and "leadership as a gift" may become a limitation in developing leaders (55).

Plueddemann further suggests that based on biblical insights and examples, a broader perspective must be developed as it is life's challenges and problems, such as living outside one's comfort zone, that primarily help expand our horizons and create an opportunity for leadership growth. He underscores the fact that even the best education only plays a secondary role in developing leaders and that leadership development is a lifelong mentoring process. He adds that even egocentric individualistic leaders, family-centric leaders, and ethnocentric leaders can be mentored to understand the needs of a group and mature toward a broader and global perspective.

Plueddemann proposes four steps that may be effective across cultures in developing leaders: (1) identifying people with leadership potential; (2) assessing their strengths and weaknesses; (3) challenging them with tasks beyond their comfort zone; and (4) supporting them in fulfilling the tasks (208). This is in line with the research on the process of leadership development where it is affirmed that leaders not only learn through their experience but also develop the ability to learn—a complex combination of motivational factors, personality factors, and learning tactics (McCauley, Moxley, and Velsor 1998, 5–7).

Cross-cultural leadership demands intercultural competency—the ability to adapt and persevere in diverse contexts. Pioneering Indian mission leaders have often displayed the characteristics of adaptation and integration in building a mission movement. Arguing that learning to lead with cultural intelligence (CQ) is an ability to be effective across national, ethnic, and organizational cultures, David Livermore (2010, 3) writes, "Leadership today is a multicultural challenge." Providing a research-based framework for cultural intelligence, Livermore presents a four-step cycle (CQ drive, CQ knowledge, CQ strategy, and CQ action) that is relevant for business, government, and nonprofit settings (4). Michael Moodian (2009), editor of *Contemporary Leadership and Intercultural Competence*, has brought together academicians to summarize their understanding of the evolving role of cultural diversity in the workplace, focusing on how to apply cultural comprehension to organizations and discussing the available tools to measure intercultural competence. Even though these tools seem to be primarily for an American audience, they can be adapted to develop the intercultural competence of the Indian mission leaders.

One of the foundational pieces of literature dealing with leadership and cultures in organizations is the discussion on intercultural dynamics within organizations and nations (Hofstede et al. 2010). Geert Hofstede, Gert Jan Hofstede, and Michael Minkov argue that there is a diversity of culture that influences the interactions between people, resulting in differences in the way people think, feel, and act around the world, and that intentional education and training can help foster better intercultural encounters. Hofstede uses the metaphor of computer software and subtitles it "software of the mind," exploring the differences in the national cultures and their distinction from organizational cultures (Hofstede 2010, 5). He analyzes stereotyping, differences in language, cultural roots and intercultural dynamics and explores the unwritten rules of the social game or the values of people in more than fifty countries around the world. This study is limited in its scope as it does not involve not-for-profit organizations. Despite various critiques of Hofstede's study, it provides insights into the dimensions of culture that may be useful for the study in the Indian mission context.

Societal cultures primarily influence "who is seen as a leader and which leaders are effective" (Hanges et al. 2016, 64–65). This influence on leadership effectiveness has been explored in the last few decades. The Global Leadership and Organizational Behavioral Effectiveness (GLOBE) project that was initiated during the 1990s attempted to discover "universal leadership attributes as well as to determine if organizational/ societal culture predicts culturally contingent leadership attributes" (64). In summarizing the GLOBE leadership study, we can conclude that there are only a few leadership attributes or behaviors that are universal, and the remaining are all contingent on the local culture. For example, the authors illustrate that more people in performance-oriented societies expect an autonomous leadership style, and in collectivist societies, more people expect charismatic leadership. The vast survey of global leadership literature confirms that there are significant differences in people's expectations based on their cultures, which determine leadership styles. Interestingly, a 2014 study on CEOs by GLOBE shows that culture did not influence the behavior of the leader or the effectiveness of leadership. On the contrary, it influenced the leadership style and, through that, the leadership behavior (66). This study on leadership and culture has provided empirical data on the role of culture in the study of leadership behavior, resulting in evolving evidence-based leadership theories (House et al. 2014). The study demonstrated that leadership expectations are predicted and endorsed by cultural values. Although the study is on the leadership of profit-making multinational companies, there are several lessons we can apply in the practice of leadership in the church and mission context.

By drawing principles from the above studies, Pluddemann (2009) shows the challenges of communication, understanding time, and the understanding of leadership and power distance in cross-cultural contexts. He reflects on the relevance of contemporary leadership theory for effective cross-cultural Christian ministry and mission in the global church and argues that the practice of leadership in a cross-cultural setting can be enhanced by integrating biblical principles and research experience in social science.

There are several critiques of the GLOBE research design, methodology, and assumptions of describing national cultures. In his critique, George B. Graen proposes the Third Culture Bonding (TCB) model for understanding cross-cultural leadership. TCB uses procedures to resolve cultural differences and practices through creativity by discovering new organizational practices and management techniques that are acceptable to people from different cultures (Graen 2006, 100). It helps in understanding differences, reconciling, and transcending cultures through rigorous research with a focus on building mutual trust, respect, and commitment to interpersonal relationships.

Sherwood Lingenfelter (2008, 83–89) focuses on issues of cultural diversity and ministry partnerships that arise when leading multicultural teams. He argues that many kinds of cultural biases create obstacles to effective leadership and ministry partnerships. Proposing the covenant community as an alternative, Lingenfelter examines the biblical roots of the idea of "covenant relationships" and then describes what a covenant community may look like from a theological perspective.

McConnell (2018) explores cultural learning in the context of its application to Christian leaders serving in mission organizations. He focuses on leadership issues that intersect culture, human nature, individuals, and groups in God's mission. He draws out insights through case studies and illustrations from various intercultural contexts to emphasize the need for leaders to develop cultural intelligence as a valuable skill to lead followers

McConnell's interdisciplinary perspective on the world is practical. Based on studies in mission and culture, he encourages Christian organization leaders to think missiologically to shape and catalyze organizations missionally. McConnell poses three questions on "culture and human nature" to understand what is human and what is cultural, how culture is stored and transmitted by individuals, and what difference this makes to organizational leaders. In answering these questions, he discusses where answers are found in cultural and cognitive anthropology. Finally, McConnell analyzes the self, family, and others in order to care for the people the organization is serving.

Presenting their vision for multicultural teams in the mission context, the Hibberts propose that the formation of a multicultural team is complex and takes time as team leaders facilitate the processes of mutual negotiation and compromise to create shared team values, which helps to manage conflicts within the community (Hibbert and Hibbert 2014, 17).

Missiologists like Pluddemann, Lingenfelter, McConnell, and the Hibberts have suggested different approaches to developing intercultural competencies for leaders, while Livermore argues for cultural intelligence in exercising leadership in the missional context. There are gaps in research on the cross-cultural Indian mission context, and further study on these gaps may provide a wealth of cultural insights for developing future leaders. This is only the beginning of opening the scope for a focused study on Indian mission leadership and their intercultural competencies based on the premise that culture affects leadership behavior.

Conclusion and Recommendations

This article explored the importance of leadership development for cross-cultural Indian missionaries. This leadership development should introduce them to leadership theories and cultural intelligence along with present learning from biblical and theological insights. I argued that along with giving knowledge and skills in church planting (disciple-making), an effective missionary training curriculum needs to explicitly focus on leadership development. In describing the context of missionary training in India, we reviewed the case of a missionary training institute where leadership development is a philosophy for learning, but the training institute focuses more on biblical insights. Second, we discussed how leadership development needs the academic integration of leadership theories and biblical-theological insights. Third, we recognized the importance of intercultural competencies as a key to effective leadership within multicultural contexts.

Monodeep Daniel (2007, 82) showcases models of leadership for the Indian church, discussing how the societal culture of the caste system has affected the church leadership to the extent that they have become irrelevant to the Indian context. This justifies what Plueddemann (2009) states, that the crisis of leadership within the church and mission organizations may not be the shortage of personnel but rather a lack of discipleship and mentoring for character formation in leadership development for cross-cultural engagement.

The first recommendation for the training of cross-cultural missionaries is that it needs the academic integration of leadership theories and biblical-theological insights. Second, we need to integrate *cultural intelligence* into leadership practices. Third, more research into the diverse societal culture of the Indian mission leadership is needed for more relevant leadership development. Leadership development is the task of making *disciplers* or *disciple-leaders* who will fulfill the mission mandate to wider multicultural communities within a holistic paradigm.

References

Aghamkar, Atul Y. 2017. "Christian Leadership for the Globalized Hindu Context." In *Leadership Development for the 21st Century Asian Mission*, edited by Hoyt Lovelace. 131–54. Seoul: East-West Center for Missions Research & Development.

Amalraj, John. 2004. "Role of IIM in Enhancing Training Programmes of Missions." *Indian Journal of Missiology* 6, no 1.

Barnabas, C. 2004. "The Missionary Training in India: The Present Status and Projection for Future." *Indian Journal of Missiology* 6, no. 1.

Bosch, David J. 2011. *Transforming Mission: Paradigm Shifts in Theology of Mission*. 20th-anniversary ed. American Society of Missiology Series 16. Maryknoll, NY: Orbis Books.

Cadbury, Henry J. 1937. *The Peril of Modernizing Jesus*. Lowell Institute Lectures 1935. New York: Macmillan.

Clinton, J. Robert. 1988. *The Making of a Leader: Recognizing the Lessons and Stages of Leadership Development.* Colorado Springs: NavPress.

Daniel, Monodeep. 2007. "Models of Leadership in the Indian Church: An Evaluation." *Studies in World Christianity* 13, no. 1: 67–90. https://doi.org/10.3366/swc.2007.13.1.67.

Dinakaran, Nelson. 2022. "Outreach Training Institute, The OTI @ a Glance." *Outreach.* November 2022.

Elias, Raja Singh. 2022. "Formal and Informal Missionary Training." *Outreach.* November 2022.

Graen, George B. 2006. "In the Eye of the Beholder: Cross-Cultural Lesson in Leadership from Project GLOBE: A Response Viewed from the Third Culture Bonding (TCB) Model of Cross-Cultural Leadership." *Academy of Management Perspectives* 20, no. 4: 95–101.

Hanges, Paul J., Juliet R. Aiken, Joo Park, and Junjie Su. 2016. "Cross-Cultural Leadership: Leading around the World." *Current Opinion in Psychology* 8 (April): 64–69. https://doi.org/10.1016/j.copsyc.2015.10.013.

Hibbert, Evelyn, and Richard Hibbert. 2014. *Leading Multicultural Teams.* Pasadena, CA: William Carey Library.

Hofstede, Geert H. 2010. *Cultures and Organizations: Software of the Mind.* 3rd ed. New York: McGraw-Hill.

House, Robert J., Peter W. Dorfman, Mansour Javidan, Paul J. Hanges, and Mary Sully de Luque. 2014. *Strategic Leadership across Cultures: The GLOBE Study of CEO Leadership Behavior and Effectiveness in 24 Countries.* Thousand Oaks, CA: SAGE.

Howell, Brian M., and Jenell Williams Paris. 2011. *Introducing Cultural Anthropology: A Christian Perspective.* Grand Rapids: Baker Academic.

Kumar, Rajiv, and Jagdeep Singh Chhokar. 2013. "Cross-Cultural Leadership." In *The Oxford Handbook of Leadership*, edited by Michael G. Rumsey, 225–42. New York: Oxford University Press.

Ledbetter, Bernice M., Robert J. Banks, and David C. Greenhalgh. 2016. *Reviewing Leadership: A Christian Evaluation of Current Approaches.* 2nd ed. Engaging Culture. Grand Rapids: Baker Academic.

Lingenfelter, Sherwood G. 2008. *Leading Cross-Culturally: Covenant Relationships for Effective Christian Leadership.* Grand Rapids: Baker Academic.

Livermore, David A. 2010. *Leading with Cultural Intelligence: The New Secret to Success.* New York: American Management Association.

Mathew, Samuel. 2013. *Leadership Development and Practice: A Biblical Perspective.* Delhi: Indian Society for Promoting Christian Knowledge.

McCauley, Cynthia D., Russ S. Moxley, and Ellen Van Velsor, eds. 1998. *The Center for Creative Leadership Handbook of Leadership Development*. San Francisco: Jossey-Bass.

McConnell, Douglas. 2018. *Cultural Insights for Christian Leaders: New Directions for Organizations Serving God's Mission*. Mission in Global Community. Grand Rapids: Baker Academic.

Michael, S. M. 2015. *Christianity and Cultures: Anthropological Insights for Christian Mission in India*. Pune: Ishvani Kendra.

Moodian, Michael A. 2009. *Contemporary Leadership and Intercultural Competence: Exploring the Cross-Cultural Dynamics within Organizations*. Los Angeles: SAGE.

Murphy, Susan Elaine. 2011. "Providing a Foundation for Leadership Development." In *Early Development and Leadership: Building the Next Generation of Leaders*, edited by Susan Elaine Murphy and Rebecca J. Reichard, 5–6. London: Routledge.

Plueddemann, James E 2009. *Leading across Cultures: Effective Ministry and Mission in the Global Church*. Downers Grove, IL: IVP Academic.

Rajendran, K. 1998. *Which Way Forward Indian Missions? A Critique of Twenty-Five Years, 1972–1997*. Bangalore, India: SAIACS Press.

Ramachandran, Jayakumar. 2018. "Theological Education in Reference to Mission Challenges in the Majority World." *Occasional Bulletin of EMS* 31, no. 2. (Spring): 18–48.

Satyavrata, Ivan. 2004. "'Glocalization' and Leadership Development for Transforming Mission in India." *Transformation* 21, no. 4: 211–17.

Srinivasagam, Theodore R. 2017. "Leadership Development in the Hindu Context." In *Leadership Development for the 21st Century Asian Mission*, edited by Hoyt Lovelace, 155–75. Seoul: East-West Center for Missions Research & Development.

Sunder Raj, Ebenezer. 1991. In *Internationalizing Missionary Training: A Global Perspective*, edited by William David Taylor, 61–63. Grand Rapids: Baker Books.

Williams, Theodore, ed. 1983. *Together in Missions*. Bangalore, India: World Evangelical Fellowship Missions Commission.

Wren, J. Thomas, ed. 1995. *The Leader's Companion: Insights on Leadership through the Ages*. New York: Free Press.

Contributors

WILL BROOKS (PhD, Southern Baptist Theological Seminary) is the acting provost and director of the DMiss and MAIS programs at a seminary in Asia. He is the author of *Love Lost for the Cause of Christ* (2018) and *Interpreting Scripture across Cultures* (2022) and co-editor of *World Mission* (2019). He is also the lead editor for the *MBTS 神学文集 Theological Journal*.

LARRY W. CALDWELL (PhD, Fuller Theological Seminary) is chief academic officer and dean, and professor of intercultural studies and Bible interpretation, at Kairos University (formerly Sioux Falls Seminary). He is also senior missiologist for Converge International Ministries (formerly Baptist General Conference).

MATT COOK (PhD, Southern Baptist Theological Seminary) serves as assistant professor of global missions and world religions at Freed-Hardeman University. His research interests are in diaspora missiology.

PAUL CORNELIUS (PhD, Fuller Theological Seminary) is president of William Carey International University. He previously served as the regional secretary of the Asia Theological Association (ATA) and principal of the Hindustan Bible Institute and College from 2006–2009.

DAVID R. DUNAETZ (PhD, Claremont Graduate University) is chair of the Department of Leadership, Organizational Psychology, and Public Administration at Azusa Pacific University. He was a church-planting missionary in France for seventeen years with WorldVenture and currently serves as editor of the *Great Commission Research Journal*.

RICHARD EVANS (PhD cand., Fuller Theological Seminary) served for ten years as a lecturer at All Nations Christian College, UK.

ANDREW FENG (ThM, Dallas Theological Seminary) helps mobilize young leaders to use their giftedness beyond the four church walls. He served abroad for five years and has worked for Yahoo and consulted for KPMG.

JOSEPH HANDLEY (PhD, Fuller Theological Seminary) is devoted to accelerating leaders for mission movements. He is the president/CEO of A3, a global network equipping leaders who accelerate mission. He is a global catalyst for leadership with the Lausanne Movement and affiliate faculty at Fuller Theological Seminary.

MINWOO HEO (PhD cand., Trinity Evangelical Divinity School) conducts research on the Lausanne Movement and serves as a local church pastor in Chicagoland.

EVELYN HIBBERT (EdD) is a founding leader of the Angelina Noble Centre, an international research center for women in cross-cultural ministry. She has extensive education experience in Christian and secular contexts, including both face-to-face and online learning. She has worked with a full range of adult learners in different intercultural settings, from those without schooling to postdoctoral researchers.

JOYCE JOW (PhD, Biola University) makes disciples of Jesus among university students and focuses on leadership development throughout Asia.

JOHN AMALRAJ KARUNAKARAN (PhD cand., Asbury Theological Seminary) has served for three decades in various Indian mission organizations. Presently, he works with Interserve India.

DANIEL LOW (PhD, Biola University) currently serves as associate professor of practical theology at Christian Witness Theological Seminary, designing and teaching missions and education courses. Previously he taught at William Carey International University, Raffles Christian School Jakarta, and Concordia University Chicago.

SARAH LUNSFORD (PhD, Columbia International University) serves as adjunct instructor of global studies at Liberty University. She served as an international church planter in Asia and is the author of *Missiological Triage*.

GREGORY MATHIAS (PhD, Southeastern Baptist Theological Seminary) is associate professor of global missions and director of the Global Mission Center at New Orleans Baptist Theological Seminary. Previously, he served in cross-cultural ministry in the Middle East.

KENNETH NEHRBASS (PhD, Biola University) is an assistant professor in the College of Behavioral and Social Sciences at California Baptist University, where he is also the director of assessment. He is the author of *Advanced Missiology* and *God's Image and Global Cultures.*

CRAIG OTT (PhD, Trinity Evangelical Divinity School) is professor of mission and intercultural studies at Trinity Evangelical Divinity School and is author of numerous books and publications including most recently *Teaching and Learning across Cultures.*

MIMSIE ROBINSON (DAIS, Assemblies of God Theological Seminary) is missions pastor of Bethel Gospel Assembly in New York. He has been involved in discipleship in India, Nigeria, Equatorial Guinea, South Africa, and Venezuela.

LINDA P. SAUNDERS (PhD, Columbia International University) serves as adjunct professor of intercultural communication and cultural anthropology at Liberty University. Previously, she spent fifteen years in cross-cultural ministry in Venezuela. Her published works include *Reading Hebrews Missiologically.*

EDWARD L. SMITHER (PhD, University of Wales; PhD, University of Pretoria) is professor of intercultural studies and history of global Christianity and dean of the College of Intercultural Studies at Columbia International University. His recent works include *Mission as Hospitality: Imitating the Hospitable God in Mission* and *Christian Mission: A Concise Global History.*

MATTHEW SOKOLOSKI (PhD, University of Arkansas) serves as associate professor of Bible and philosophy at Freed-Hardeman University. He is the author of *Developing a Defense: Christian Apologetics and the Existence of God.*

JESSICA A. UDALL (PhD, Columbia International University) is professor of intercultural studies at Evangelical Theological College in Addis Ababa, Ethiopia, and adjunct professor of intercultural studies at Columbia International University. She has served cross-culturally in Ethiopia and among immigrants and international students in the United States. She is the author of *Loving the Stranger: Welcoming Immigrants in the Name of Jesus.*

PHIL WAGLER (MA, Tyndale Seminary) serves as global director of the World Evangelical Alliance's Peace and Reconciliation Network and as global liaison with the Evangelical Fellowship of Canada. Phil has served God's mission in pastoral, educational, denominational, and mission agency roles for thirty years.

NICK WU (MA student, Dallas Theological Seminary) serves as content manager with Indigitous US. He helps lead young adults in digital missions projects and creative media. He is a professional videographer and has produced short documentaries for missions.

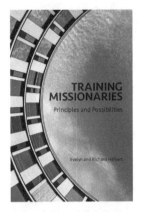

Training Missionaries: Principles and Possibilities

Evelyn and Richard Hibbert

Missionaries must know God, be able to relate well to other people, and understand and engage with another culture. Effective training has been shown to prevent people from prematurely leaving the field. This book details four key areas that every missionary training program must focus on developing. It shows how these can be holistically addressed in a learning community where trainers and trainees engage in cross-cultural ministry together.

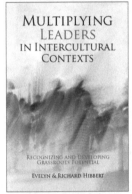

Multiplying Leaders in Intercultural Contexts: Recognizing and Developing Grassroots Potential

Evelyn and Richard Hibbert

This book focuses on how to develop grassroots Christian leaders across cultures. Another focus of the book is shaping the character of developers as they humbly walk beside leaders in the leaders' community. The authors use the four C's of Christian leadership—Community, Character, Clarity, and Care—to weave together research, experience, and practical application to show how these characteristics are expressed across different cultures.

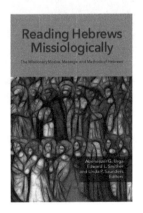

Reading Hebrews Missiologically: The Missionary Motive, Message, and Methods of Hebrews

Abeneazer G. Urga, Edward L. Smither, and Linda P. Saunders, Editors

The discussion on the theology of mission in the New Testament usually focuses on Jesus and Paul, with minimal attention given to the General Epistles. However, *Reading Hebrews Missiologically* tries to fill that gap and focuses on the theology of mission in the book of Hebrews. The twelve contributors—from various theological, geographical, and missiological contexts—explore the missionary motive, the missionary message, and the missionary method of the Epistle to the Hebrews.